DATE DUE

What They Did Right

Reflections on Parents by Their Children

Edited by Virginia Hearn

Tyndale House Publishers, Inc.
Wheaton, Illinois

Coverdale House Publishers Ltd.
London, England

All Bible quotations in this book are taken from the
Revised Standard Version, unless otherwise stated.

Library of Congress Catalog Card Number 74-23717.
ISBN 8423-7920-7. Copyright © 1974 Tyndale House
Publishers, Inc., Wheaton, Illinois 60187. All rights
reserved. First printing, December 1974. Printed in the
United States of America.

For Russ and Chris, who made me wonder—
and for Walt, who tries.

Contents

Preface

This book had its origins in personal anguish. When (along with a husband) a six- and a seven-year-old entered my life, I frequently found myself without imagination or grace to cope with the problems that arose.

Although not believing that children are "programmed" into Christian faith, I began asking friends who had grown up in Christian homes "what their parents did right." The enthusiastic answers of some, especially David Gill and Sandi Hedlund, the catalytic presence of Victor Oliver (managing editor of Tyndale House Publishers) in a Vietnamese restaurant in San Francisco, and the spark of the Spirit of God, it seems, gave birth to the idea for this book.

I am touched by the response of the thirty-six individuals, almost all known personally to me or my husband, who agreed to write a chapter. For many it is their first appearance in print, though a few have written articles; a few, books. All sensed the personal exposure entailed by an autobiography with such a slant, and wondered if they were up to it. Some wondered if the product of their recollections would be recognizable to any other member of their family. In the early months of this project my enthusiasm was bolstered by that of participants in our Crucible writers' workshop (part of a local Christian "free university"). My husband, Walter Hearn, painstakingly worked through the manuscript and as usual proved a fine editor.

"How many books have even one good idea in them?" Eric Hofer said in response to a criticism that his latest brainchild had been rather short; "Mine has six."

The authors of *What They Did Right* may surpass even that. Readers who would be interested in contributing to a second similar volume are encouraged to contact the editor through the publisher.

Virginia Hearn
Berkeley, California
November 1974

1

David Gill

David Gill is husband to Lucia Gill, father to Jodie and Jonathan Gill, instructor in church history and ethics at the California Center for Biblical Studies, and student in the doctoral program at the University of Southern California.

If a videotape existed of my first twenty years, I'm sure that any editor would pick out two particular scenes to represent my relationship to my parents.

The first scene would have my father, dark circles beginning to appear under his eyes, unable to stifle an occasional yawn, patiently giving an explanation for the existence of suffering in the world. The clock shows 1:16 A.M. in the study, but the indefatigable questioner, a twelve-year-old adolescent, shows little sign of weakening. The conversation will have to end soon, then four hours of sleep for the father, five or six for me. Within two to four weeks another marathon discussion will take place, maybe on a single topic, more likely ranging from the fortunes of the San Francisco 49ers to the nature of women.

The second scene would show my mother at a frosh-soph football game, one of only two or three people in the grandstand (which would be packed with 2,000 for the varsity game the next day). Oh, she was also there when I played varsity; but what really symbolizes my mother are those times when she was there and almost no one else was.

At times of course we had disagreements, at times harmony escaped us—but those were the exceptions. My father was my counselor, pastor, teacher, and friend. My mother was my number one fan, comforter, and friend. Both of them were always available to me. They thought I was important. Their authority and leadership weren't something that was beaten into me; they won my respect and loyalty with their actions.

The early years: a Christian foundation

I was the second of four children. Three sisters, one older by a year, the others two and four years younger, aided my parents in my upbringing. While I have no doubt that my relationships were special as the only son, my parents never tired of reminding us that we were all of equal value in their sight. My father would comment, shaking his head in mild disbelief, on the fact that each of us was so different and yet came from the same womb. But although, for tactical reasons, I argued that I was getting the worst of it, I secretly knew then (and openly admit now) that both my parents studiously avoided favoritism.

My church attendance began before I was conscious of much more than the existence of a warm thing called Mother. Church attendance was simply a fact of life for us, and while we belonged to a small, theologically exclusive and ingrown fellowship, it was something holy. It was a time to meet God, to worship at the Lord's Table. My father was a quiet but steady and encouraging part of the leadership. Sundays were referred to as "the Lord's Day" and you could just as well have called Wednesday evening "the Lord's Evening," for my attendance then was almost as regular as on Sunday from my earliest recollection.

Church was important to my parents for one reason: Jesus Christ was the focal point of life. My father's devotion to Christ was transparent. I think I grew to love the Lord because I loved my father, and you just couldn't separate the two. My mother entered the picture here as everywhere, though, and it was at her side that I knelt in the living room at age six wanting to "be saved." The conversion experience "took" and I have never doubted that that was the night of my "second birth."

Our family devotions were neither perfect nor cast in an

inviolable pattern. But during the streaks which were frequently begun, sustained for a period, then interrupted, I learned much of what I first knew about the faith. Of even greater significance for the long run, I believe, was the reading practice (out loud), as each of us read two verses in going through a passage. We kids began participating in the reading when we knew little more than *and, the,* and *thee* (King James has always ruled at my father's house). There was always encouragement, never ridicule. I have no doubt that those experiences were responsible for my prematurely developed vocabulary and my love for reading during grammar school and following.

We never went in for camping trips or vacations in the usual sense. Occasionally there was an exception, but normally my father's two weeks off was carefully planned for migrations to Los Angeles or the Pacific Northwest for Bible conferences twice a year. We went on picnics or rides in the car, and my father was often interested in playing catch or wrestling in my earliest years. But recreation together as a family was infrequent, certainly not central to our family unity, and not really missed. My father was my friend and teacher, never my coach or teammate.

When I was about eleven I asked to be baptized and soon after that began taking communion. About then, too, I began to read and underline my personal Bible and my interest in the Christian faith began to intensify, a process that has never stopped. Even during the rugged years of adolescence my basic commitment to Christ was there. I faltered badly in practice but seldom or never in basic commitment. I attribute that to my parents' example and to their encouragement. As with other things, they didn't attempt to force me into the Kingdom; they preferred to lead and love me toward the goal.

Building responsibility: mainly my father

My parents aren't a lot alike, but they are a complementary team. Although they overlapped and supported each other's involvement in my life, it isn't hard for me to identify fairly precisely the kind of role each played in my life. I turned to my mother for pep talks, enthusiastic support, and instant help in activities. But it was always to my father that I turned for those long discussions (short ones as well), for counsel, for the same sort of discussion I now enjoy in graduate seminars.

The most important lesson my father taught me was responsibility. He had two constant reminders for me, going back as far as I can remember. First was: "Remember, Dave, you're a young man now." Implication: be responsible, be mature, don't trade on your youth for irresponsibility. Second was: "Never forget that you belong to the Lord." Implication: live for Jesus Christ, think and act as though He is constantly present.

Some bounds were well defined for me: movies (except an occasional Disney flick like *The Living Desert*), dances, and parties were out. Even in those areas, though, it wasn't by way of legalism. Rather, my father took time to explain in as much detail as I desired what was implied in being a man of God. Result: I was almost invariably won over to his position and rarely felt deprived. In other areas I was given an open field, such as student government activities, athletics, drama, and music. Participation was encouraged with the ever-present reminder: "Remember who you are (a man, not an infant) and who you belong to (the Lord)."

With few exceptions the strategy worked without a hitch. I got involved in student government in seventh grade and only lost the taste for it after high school. I managed to get excused from any of the infrequent Sunday practices and got heavily involved in sports, especially football and track, all the way through high school. I picked up a guitar and, while in high school, organized a folk/comedy group called the "Snurd Brothers," which performed at school assemblies, talent shows, and the county fair. I seldom regretted missing the parties and social life of my pagan high school friends. My identity wasn't wrapped up in those things but rather in the mix of Christian commitment, athletics, student politics, and music. When dating assumed importance it took place with church activities or folk concerts in Berkeley and, when I could afford it, dinner in San Francisco.

The times I let my parents down were learning experiences for me. My outgoing and outspoken ways could become obnoxious to my teachers from about the third through the ninth grades. Seventh and eighth grades were the worst. Physically and even spiritually I was growing, but socially I suffered the ills of adolescence. Several times my parents were called in by teachers or even the principal to discuss my case—often with me present. My mother could get weepy, and my father's disappointment, even shame, hung over me like a cloud as I shriveled into a repentant and embarrassed boy, thinking about my failure to monitor my joking mouth in some class. But my father never beat me or called me a creep in those situations. He did something more effective: he let me see in a few quiet words how I had dishonored the Lord and my family. I had betrayed his trust and misused my freedom.

The worst episode was in a school play during ninth grade. Through a drama class I won the part of a thug who had about four lines, late in the play. Without thinking through the consequences, I delivered my lines flawlessly at the evening performance. My whole family plus a cousin sat in the crowded auditorium, proud when they arrived. Although I confess to much worse in private a few times, my threat on stage, "By God, I'll leave you here to starve to death," stunned my father. When I had dressed and gone to the waiting car for the ride home, you could almost cut the gloom with a knife.

"To think . . . my son . . . using the Lord's name in vain."

I knew the commandment of course. I wouldn't argue in favor of the justice of my father's judgment. What did come through loud and clear was this: my parents had a stake in me. I carried the family name and honor. More, I carried the Lord's honor with me.

As soon as I was ten years old I got a morning paper route. Financial responsibility was a big thing with my father. He got out of high school in the depths of the Great Depression and worked for thirty cents an hour. As I was growing up, he was working his way up to a middle-echelon executive. From about age ten to fourteen I delivered newspapers. It wasn't worth it for the money (although it was nice to earn your own), but it got me started toward healthy appreciation of work and financial realities. And, predictably, my father would already be up folding papers (and reading one at the same time) when I rolled out of the sack each morning.

During high school days I worked many hours at gas stations, a donut shop, and a dairy products store. I experienced success and frustration, and I began to experience more freedom. In eleventh grade I bought a '54 Ford, but had to sell it two months later because it was too costly. In twelfth grade I bought a '56 Chevy, poured my money into fixing it up and customizing it, blew an engine or two, and learned some wonderful lessons: never own anything but the minimum means of transportation (Volkswagens have done me fine ever since); avoid monthly payments like the plague; avoid getting into "conspicuous consumption" and other ridiculous and enslaving aspects of the American automotive scene. My parents let me pay every cent of my car insurance, repairs, gas, as well as the initial cost.

Building enthusiasm: mainly my mother.

If my father and I had special closeness in our relationship, that was natural since I was his only son. My mother's attention was drawn to my three sisters pretty much, as least as far as the kind of counseling I have been describing. But my father had a weak spot, and it was here that my mother made her presence felt. He had a tendency to get discouraged and even brood over supposedly unsolvable problems. If my mother lacked the logical insight which my father so amply demonstrated, she more than compensated by her unbounded enthusiasm for life.

My mother is a doer, an activist. She's an enthusiast, a saleslady, a problem solver. If her solutions don't all work, never mind, she'll come up with five more to try in their place. Whenever I did anything—piano recitals, football games, folk music at county fairs—she was there. Before I had a car I often walked or rode a bike. But she was always ready to drive me and my friends anywhere, any time. She and Mrs. Vargas would show up at those frosh-soph football games providing an audience of two—even at most away games. She claimed to be a football fan (really, I don't know if she knows the difference between a draw play and a reverse). She was really a fan of her four kids and burst with pride and enthusiasm any time we did anything she could be proud of. She thought I was the handsomest and smartest kid in the world. She thought my sisters were (though a bit overweight) the prettiest of the world's women.

I learned not to take her judgments on our merits with total seriousness! But what I did take seriously were her positive thinking and enthusiasm. Why shouldn't I try to be the best? *I* knew I wasn't the smartest, handsomest, or best athlete, but due mainly to my mother's infectious spirit, I gave everything I had to my endeavors and had fun on the way.

After all, in her own specialties my mother approached life in the same way. I always knew our home was open. I could invite my friends over for dinner and with a moment's notice (or so it seemed) she would lay a feast before us, bouncing up and down from the table serving us, showing interest in whatever we were doing or talking about. She would take us to the park, swimming, skating. Anything for the kids.

I have no doubt that my mother gave me the power of positive thinking. She gave me that healthy restlessness in my innermost being that always drives me toward involvement and participation if not to leadership itself. The emotional won over the rational in my mother. I still have trouble carrying on a debate or argument with her. But I am profoundly thankful for that, and so is the rest of the family. She was the spark plug that got us going. While I have an increasingly sober estimate of my abilities and limitations, I owe it to my mother that in word and deed she gave me the mentality of a doer, achiever, competitor, and sometimes a leader.

Postscript: from child to parent

In the ten years since high school many things have intervened and substantially changed my relationship to my parents. My father seems weary of thinking at times. My mother seems to wane in enthusiasm a bit. They are thinking of retirement, visiting their grandchildren, and maybe traveling. I married the girl I began dating as a senior in high school and now have two preschool children of my own. Theological differences ended the long relationship I had with the little church my parents attend. My mother had trouble understanding why God had me work with "those people" in Berkeley and why I chose to wear long hair and a beard for a few years.

Even through my high school graduation I never failed to see the logic and sense of my father's position on various issues, theological and social. The topics that concern me now are more complex, the questions more difficult. Some topics we can't really discuss without unsettling him. Yet my admiration and appreciation of him and his mind continues.

This all reminds me of the privilege and responsibility of raising my three-year-old daughter and two-year-old son in the "nurture and admonition of the Lord." I pray that my wife and I can, by God's grace, teach and infect them with a sense of responsibility, a predisposition to be thoughtful, a supreme loyalty and love for the Lord, and a boundless enthusiasm to become—and then enjoy—whatever God has for them.

2
Deborah Bayly

For the past five years, Deborah Bayly has taught people, and seventh and eighth grade social studies, at an all-black school in Chicago. A creative teacher, she does a lot with her children outside of class, and recently spearheaded a medieval fair at the school.

"Train up a child in the way he should go: and when he is old, he will not depart from it." That's a verse I've often heard my parents quote. They have always believed that it's important to begin this training early: better make an occasional mistake than exert no definite influence whatsoever.

Recently I was visiting with a friend while her eight-month-old son crawled around the room. A large floor vase of dried flowers attracted his attention, and he reached up to pull them down. But before he touched them, he turned around and looked at his mother to see what her reaction would be. She admitted to me that these flowers presented a problem, because she could never decide which was more important: preserving their beauty or encouraging her son to develop a healthy sense of curiosity. Thus she sometimes allowed him to play with them, and other times told him not to touch them or removed them from his reach.

I understood the philosophical quandary, and knew it would extend far beyond the simple problem of whether or not to allow a baby to play with some flowers. And I knew that the baby sensed that his mother was unhappy when he played with them, even though she didn't forbid him to do so.

I mentioned this incident to my mother, and asked for her opinion. She observed that my friend should have made up her mind and stuck to her decision, regardless of what she decided. The important thing was for the child to recognize that his mother meant what she said. My mother also pointed out that children who sense indecisiveness in their parents get into the habit of constantly doing things just to see if they can get away with them. This kind of "testing" becomes increasingly annoying as a child grows older.

Dad and Mother didn't wait to start reading the Bible to us until we were old enough to understand everything we heard. We were sitting quietly for family devotions by the time we were two. If we were old enough to enjoy picture books, we were old enough to understand that we were listening to God's Word. Besides, our parents believed that children needed to learn how to sit still and be quiet—and family Bible reading was a good time for us to start learning.

I think that this daily Bible reading was an important part of our training. Dad usually chose the book we would read, generally reading a chapter a day. In this way we heard the entire Bible every few years. I cannot honestly say we always enjoyed this routine. But when we begrudged the time it was usually because some adult (or adults) prayed for too long, or because we were already late for something and getting later with every minute that Dad continued to read. The moral? When children are involved, choose an appropriate time and keep it reasonably short.

I'm not advocating that a parent stop and consider what the effects of his every action will be on his child in ten or twenty years. (As a child I knew a few adults like that, and pitied their children.) But I do think that one of the important things Dad and Mother did was to start training us in matters they considered important when we were quite young, taking into consideration the fact that we would be very much the same people at ten that we were at two. Thus we weren't encouraged to do things the adults thought were cute if they were the kinds of things that would become offensive when we were a few years older. For example, the first time a two-year-old talks back to a parent he may be doing it quite innocently, and it is often amusing. But if he is given the impression that this is entertaining, he can hardly be blamed for continuing to do it. Nor can he be blamed for being terribly confused if sometime later—maybe not until he gets to school—he gets into trouble for this same behavior.

Growing up is never easy. But it can be made more difficult by parents who change their minds and require their children to meet different expectations as they get older.

Regardless of how consistent the powers-that-be are, however, children will persist in breaking the rules. We were ultimately held accountable to our parents for any misbehavior reported to them. (We were also praised upon the rare occasions that meritorious behavior was reported.) I think it redounds to the credit of the adults who knew us as children that they took the interest and made the effort to report on our conduct to our parents. When our parents punished or reprimanded us, it was on the basis that we had done something we knew was wrong: we had been disobedient, unkind, impolite, or whatever. They avoided that horrible temptation to play on our guilt feelings by dragging their disappointment in us into the picture. (Some other adults I knew weren't so scrupulous.) They also avoided what may be the worst pitfall of all, dragging God onto the scene.

As a child in Pennsylvania, I had a good friend who had an exceptionally wonderful mother. But I think I would have wasted away had I grown up in that home, because every time my friend did something wrong, her mother would say something like, "Do you think God was happy to see you do that?" I remember humorously calling this friend a "bubblebrain" when we were both about ten years old. Her mother, alas, overheard, and asked me if I thought that Jesus would have called someone a name like that. I thought He might have, but was too intimidated to say so.

This approach to child discipline leads to a lot of problems: I would have been willing to retract my name-calling if that was what my friend's mother wished, even though I didn't mean to be malicious. But the only things I felt God disapproved of were the things specifically spoken of in the Bible. We were forbidden to do a great many things when we were young, not on the grounds that they were wrong, but on the grounds that our parents didn't want us to do them. Playing baseball in the flower beds and arguing with each other in the hearing of our parents were two such things. We knew children, however, who were allowed to do both of those things. Had we been taught that God was somehow involved in not wanting us to do them, it would have left us confused. Did God change His mind, or were these friends of ours in danger of damnation because they were disobeying Him?

In our family, God was definitely recognized as the Head of the house, the supreme Authority. But our parents were the immediate authority over us. We knew what the Bible taught about right and wrong. But we weren't expected to recognize an authority whom we couldn't see, touch, or hear, until we had learned to recognize the authority of our much more tangible parents.

We had a lot of guests in our home. Some came to spend the evening, some came and stayed for months. Of course they all had influence on us. A few were boring, and once in a while there was one whom we children couldn't stand. (How I hated giving up my bedroom for one of them!) But usually we enjoyed the excitement of having different types of people around. Mother and Dad were always trying to make us sensitive to the needs and feelings of other people, and with so many visitors they had plenty of opportunities to provide us with "in-service training." If the guests provided fascinating conversation at the dinner table—which they often did—my older brother and I scarcely noticed the extra work of cleaning up more dishes afterward. We also got ample opportunities to practice hospitality on our own friends, because they were always welcome in our home.

Washing the dinner dishes is one of the jobs that has traditionally been the responsibility of whatever children were old enough to do them. There was no attitude in our family that housework was for women only, so my brother and I had similar chores. But there was one notable exception: in the spring and summer he always got to cut the lawn, while I was stuck with the same old loathsome task of scrubbing the bathroom.

I'm sure there were many times when, by the time Mother had checked and rechecked the job one of us had done and made that child come back several times until it was done right, it would have been easier for her to have done it herself. However, the training not only taught us how to do a variety of things around the house; it taught us the necessity of doing any job we did properly, and helped instill a sense of responsibility in each of us.

In general, our parents made little fuss over the fact that I was the only girl in the family. The same rules applied to all of us, the distinguishing factor being age rather than sex. Of course as individuals with unique personalities we all received slightly different treatment, but this again wasn't a difference based primarily on sex. I think that this was a wise policy, since I would have fiercely resented any restrictions on my freedom had they been based on my being a girl. Generally speaking, if a parent honestly feels he has a valid reason for not allowing his daughter to do a certain thing, if he thinks it through a bit longer, he may realize it wouldn't be wise to allow his son to do it either. For example, in many Chicago neighborhoods concerned parents hardly allow their daughters to leave the house alone after they turn eleven or twelve. But their sons continue to roam the streets at will. If the girls are in danger of being molested, the boys are equally in danger of being molested, beaten up, or pressured into joining a street gang.

One of the ways our parents helped us to develop strong self-images was by creating a strong family unit. Of course family ties are formed by a lot of intangibles conveyed by the parents in a variety of ways. I've seen solid loyalties in many missionary families even though the children had to spend extended time separated from their parents. But concrete ways exist to help build a feeling of family unity. One good way is to have an agreed-upon time everyday that the whole family will be together. In our house, this was dinner time. Whether or not we had guests, we all sat down and ate a usually unhurried meal, which was followed by family devotions.

This was almost always an enjoyable time, but there were occasional exceptions. Dad and Mother would bring up the subject of any trouble that one of us might have gotten into recently, which of course ruined dinner for every one. We often tried to agree that unpleasant subjects wouldn't be discussed at the table, but sometimes it was diffficult to abide by this decision.

Dad was out of town a lot, but we followed the same dinner routine whether or not he was home. Sometimes when he was gone and we had been reading aloud an especially good book, Mother would read to us while we ate. If we were lucky, she would get hooked, and read chapter after chapter—always saying the next one would be the last—until it was way past our bedtime, and far too late to read the Bible. If this happened often enough during one of Dad's absences, he returned to find the marker in the Bible in the same place that he had left it a week before. That mildly exasperated him, and privately amused us children.

Some parents feel they must be "pals" to their children. They make great effort to do something they think the children will enjoy but which is a dreadful bore to the adults themselves. Our parents never had time for such nonsense, and we were happy to be left to ourselves most of the time.

This made the occasions when the whole family was able to do something together all the more enjoyable—whether it was playing a game of Clue on Friday night, roasting hot dogs and marshmallows over an autumn bonfire, or visiting friends of our parents who had children who were friends of ours. A large part of the reason such occasions were so enjoyable was that Mother and Dad enjoyed the activities as much as we did. They weren't condescendingly amusing us, nor were they impatient to finish because they were bored. (Few things were worse than being dragged on a "family outing" to the home of friends of theirs, and being expected to enjoy ourselves playing with children whom we either didn't know or didn't like.)

In addition to all the usual ways of helping children develop positive self-images (such as respecting their feelings and encouraging them to express their opinions), our parents had a few extras of their own. One was their birthday extra. Most families celebrate birthdays, I suppose, in one way or another. But in our family, birthdays were a Big Thing. As much as Dad traveled, he usually managed to be at home for those special days. If he absolutely had to be out of town, we postponed the celebration until his return.

The person whose birthday it was was an honored personage from the time he woke up until the time he fell asleep at the end of the day. He was treated with special favor by all members of the family: he didn't have to do any work, others waited on him if he so desired, he chose the dinner menu—including, of course, the kind of cake and ice cream we would have for dessert. We always used our "Sunday" china and silver on birthdays, and every birthday cake was a personalized creation made by Mother. We never knew what form it would take until it was placed on the table. I remember helping her one year, laboring for hours making a cake train with an engine, a coal car, two other cars, and a caboose, each iced a different color. Naturally there were also presents—not just money with instructions to go and buy whatever we wanted, but real presents lovingly chosen and beautifully wrapped.

Every family needs to have its own traditions. Many people celebrate Memorial Day, Fourth of July, or Labor Day in a special way. We have our annual Winter Picnic. Every year on a bitterly cold Friday night (usually sometime in January), two members of the family put their heads together and decide that the time for the annual Winter Picnic has arrived. The next morning they arise early to make the necessary preparations for an outdoor breakfast. When everything is almost ready, they awaken the household with the glad tidings that the Winter Picnic is awaiting them. Everyone puts on his warmest clothes and piles into the car. We go to some nearby uncrowded park, build a roaring fire, and have a picnic—refreshingly free of flies and mosquitoes.

Another family tradition is this: each spring the first person to find a wild violet and bring it home has a cake baked for him. (Last spring Dad beat us all. In the middle of February he found one and requested an angel food cake. His right to the cake might have been contested, since he was in southern California at the time!) These private traditions seem to help unite the family by giving them certain experiences a bit different from others they have in common with the rest of society.

Our parents and most of their close friends never told us to do one thing while doing the opposite themselves. They lived the Christianity they taught. As I am constantly discovering, this seems to be a rare quality among adults. But without it, all the well-planned training in the world is wasted.

3

Jonathan Baylis

Jonathan Baylis, twenty-three years old, is a recent graduate of California State College, Sonoma, where he majored in Community Work (part of an experimental Liberal Studies program). A proponent of the biblical balance between redemptive concern and social passion, he is presently seeking to integrate his background in community work with formal theological training at Regent College (British Columbia).

As I try to organize my thoughts about my family and Christian upbringing, it is clearer than ever that the personal character of my parents was the prevalent influence on my life.

My parents sought to obey God day by day. They introduced me to Jesus and gave me an example of what it is to serve Him. I chose to follow Jesus too. It was my own decision. My family provided me with important evidence on which to base my choice. I decided. No set of practices or formulas could have "canned" my decision.

I am thankful to my parents for their openness about their struggles, especially during my early childhood. If they had tried to impress upon me that their life was so "together" that there was no tension, I would have been confused indeed. From even my earliest memories I can recall tension, struggle, and crisis. Most of the crises that we faced were unintelligible to me when I was small, except that there was trauma and strain. The action was not always whispered behind closed doors.

Living in the open awareness of crisis, it wasn't long before I accepted it as normal. Being aware that my parents had to fight battles didn't cause me anxiety or insecurity. My own needs were always met. My only fear was of separation from my parents. Actually, I think my feeling of security was strengthened by the fact that I was provided for in the face of crisis. Had my mother and father attempted to hide their difficulties from me, I would have seen inconsistency in the tension that I felt. My exposure to these intense struggles built up my parents' credibility in my eyes and helped me to be a realist myself.

Sometime during my earliest years I remember noticing the difference between believers and pagans. My parents knew people in both situations and had them in our home. There were people my parents liked and disliked in both categories. The mixture was helpful in that it gave me perspective with which to differentiate between human and spiritual qualities in people at an early age. Having both Christians and non-Christians share our life has also helped me feel at ease in destroying the barriers of "sacred and secular" in my own friendships.

As I grew a little older and started school, my own circle of acquaintances grew, throwing new light on my family life. I could see by observing the lives of my contemporaries that our family was radically different from the norm: a certain sense of direction set us apart. My parents' active ministering life-style was affecting my outlook. More than just church attendance and the various cultural abstinences that were required of evangelical Christians in the '50s, our family seemed to have a force within them that caused them to place high priority on visiting lonely people, preparing Bible studies for groups of people, organizing things, praying with people, and reading books and articles with a special sort of urgency. I didn't really understand what was going on and I often resisted it. It wasn't until years later that I realized what great wealth I had gained through experiencing the radical nature of Christianity as a child.

It's interesting to me how much I seem to have benefited from a special balance in my parents' treatment of me in my child-hood. In some important ways they refused to take me seri-ously. Many things I said and did just to get a rise out of them failed miserably. My father particularly had a sense of what was and was not important about what I said. Often my urgent demands went unmet, with no explanation.

Yet in other ways I was taken very seriously. I was always held to my promises and commitments, even when I was very young. My mother and father made sure that I was aware of the gravity of my disobedience and the importance of my obedi-ence. I never doubted that they cared for me, but they ignored my demands and responded to my real needs. They weren't interested in my notions, but they showed great concern for *me,* keeping me healthfully aware that I didn't always know what was best and that I had to trust.

When I was nine years old and still had five years of grade school ahead of me, we made our last move as a family, a move that had great influence on my growing up. My father bought a house in the suburbs, where with a few other families we began the "grass roots" ministry of building a church.

In the beginning years of the work, there were so few of us that everyone, including children, had their share of responsibil-ity. Taking my pint-sized portions of responsibility re-volutionized my Christian experience. I was official loader and unloader of our portable Sunday school and church facilities. I was the plastic model specialist for our children's craft club. And at times I was upwards of 50 percent of my Sunday school class. As I grew, my participation grew. I had a lot of attention from adults younger than my parents, and developed meaning-ful and creative relationships with them. I could never feel alienated from the church because I *was* the church, or a small part of it anyway.

My dad has always been big on work. One thing I associate with our home is my work responsibilities. My father felt that as long as I was reaping the benefits of our household, I should be contributing what I could toward its proper maintenance and development. This meant that a significant portion of my free time was required of me to do yardwork and other household tasks. A portion of nearly every Saturday and often weekday afternoons I spent gardening, digging, cleaning, sweeping, and washing.

So in a definite sense I experienced part of the responsibility for the things I enjoyed. There was never room for me to expect things to be given to me, free from any output on my part. I was given all I needed and much of what I wanted, and I was expected to carry what part of the load I could.

It was a good thing, but at the time I hated it. Many of my friends in suburbia could expect great privileges from their parents without ever having to lift a finger. I sometimes picked up on their thinking and really resisted the responsibilities that were mine. I had to be dragged to my chores. I complained a great deal. My father wouldn't budge. Slowly and painfully I learned the discipline of taking responsibility for myself. I learned to work hard. Having learned these things as a child has saved me a great deal of trouble as an adult.

Not only did my imposed work responsibilities train me for adult life, but they served as a well-integrated means of directing my relationships and activities during my school years. Because I had work responsibilities, there was no need to impose artificial restrictions on what I did or whom I spent time with. Generally I was allowed to do most of what I liked in the time I had in between my obligations to the household. This way my time with my family was kept up to healthy level, balancing out the time I spent "at large" with my schoolmates. The pagan influences on my life were balanced with the Christian ones.

Most of what my parents communicated to me of their faith came about through personal example in the context of day-to-day situations. I learned to understand the nature of faith in God by observing their lives. I saw my father's active lay ministry and the diligence with which my mother supported him in it. I could see the proportions to which spiritual life made their lives different. I could see that it was real, and I knew that it could apply to me.

I had many discussions about Christian principles, particularly with my mother, but the examples were more important. We had a regular devotional time after dinner in the evening but that was only a tiny portion of the communication that went on.

When we talked about Jesus in the context of what was happening, it meant much more to me than just at an arbitrary discussion period.

The summer following my completion of grade school and just prior to my going to high school, my father took me traveling in Europe. We traveled with a group of college students and graduates for eight weeks, all over the Continent. Not only did I see areas of the world where things were done differently from what I was used to, but I had a prolonged opportunity to try out my developing adulthood on adults, with whom I traveled exclusively. By experiencing cross-cultural situations I gained a perspective that allowed me to see just what was unique about my own culture. It was a summer of quick maturing in several ways.

Following my European adventure, I entered high school. A major role my family played during my high school years was supporting me in the cultural activities I chose to become involved in. One of my main involvements was with the developing young church. Encouraged by my parents, I put a lot of time and energy into the high school fellowship of the new church. The high school fellowship not only provided a good outlet for my social energies, but it provided a context in which my father passed on to me some of his organizational know-how. Working with my high school peers facilitated a good deal of evangelism and provided a forum for my parents and me to discuss Christian work. Some of those discussions were quite profitable.

About the time I wanted to try out some of my own construction skills, the church purchased an old schoolhouse to remodel for their meeting place. My parents encouraged me to become involved in the remodeling. I worked for two years alongside the men in the congregation at the long reconstruction project. The riches of this experience far exceeded the many building skills I learned. I worked with some wonderful men, learning what it was like to be a working member of the body of Christ.

A particularly significant part of our family life-style was entertaining. Not only did we entertain friends, but we took in foreign students and visitors from out of town who were new to us in many ways. I learned about hospitality. The Christians who were in our home were often spiritual resources for me. To entertain people who were different from us was helpful as well. I gained perspective from them. So I cannot emphasize enough the significance of our open home on my growth.

My own friends were of interest to my family, and they welcomed them in our home. They encouraged me to emulate my friends' good qualities and to resist vices and faults. They encouraged me to build strong, helpful relationships in the light of sharing my commitment to God. Never did they set limits on who my friends could be.

Because our church was still small, I had virtually no peers there until I brought them myself. All my friends, including girl friends, were from outside the fellowship to start with. I dated freely (and much to my pleasure) girls from various walks of life during high school. Because my responsibilities were great enough to limit my social life a good bit anyway, few rules were necessary to restrain me. The only ones I can remember in regard to dating were that I be home with the car at a reasonable hour.

In my early high school years there was some controversy about the types of social events I was to attend. At first I was required to miss the high school dances, but it wasn't long before that became a matter of my own discretion. By my last years in high school, I had a fellowship of several peers who had become Christians during high school.

Both my parents were school teachers while I was growing up. Their realistic attitudes toward grade school helped me to cope with it as well as I did. Grades were never the be-all-and-end-all of our lives. I was never especially rewarded for good grades or punished for bad ones. The teacher wasn't always held up as the final judge; my parents knew teachers too well for that.

What was emphasized was my attitude. I was punished for disobedience, dishonesty, or rebellion, and rewarded for creativity, perseverance, and honesty. I was expected to try to do all my school work. If I had tried and failed, there were no threats. In short, my mother and father saw my school life as a means to an end. It was neither insignificant or all-important. I had a lot of problems in school that we were able to ride through with this realistic attitude. Consequently, I learned much from the experience of coping with grade school and it did not destroy me.

We approached high school with the same attitude, making the best of the situation and realizing its purpose without making it an all-important concern. I was optimistic in my first year but began to be more cynical as time went on. I saw most of my hours on the campus as an inefficient waste of time. I was aware of the teachers who hated teaching and the administrators whose thinking would have been more contemporary in a previous century. The built-in impotence of student government and the ever-present punitive approach to the classroom situation were demoralizing. The prison-like effect of a closed campus with patrolled hallways and infinite lists of regulations spewing forth ad nauseam over the campus-wide P.A. made me painfully aware that I was the recipient of a form of social injustice.

My protest was loud and my parents heard me out. They encouraged me to direct my energy in positive directions through those aspects of school that I could enjoy, urging me to deal responsibly with the problems I faced. They sympathized with some of my gripes about the school system and helped me to apply the biblical principles to which I was committed. I was aware that however corrupt the system to which I was subject, I was never justified in compromising my own personal standards of truth and integrity.

I also knew that if I was to be realistic about any aspirations I had toward higher education, I would have to keep my high school experience at least somewhat intact—despite its bountiful absurdities. By the grace of God and with my parents' encouragement and support, I completed high school. We didn't by any means cover up the problems of high school —much less solve them. We merely held them up to the light of authentic Christian responsibility and proceeded with an attempt to be uncompromising ourselves.

I mentioned earlier that my parents had a way of not taking me seriously that was helpful in my childhood. Yet they seemed to adjust to my growth. When I was of high school age, more of what I said was of importance. Some of my applications of Christian principles while I was in high school were quite differ-

ent from my parents'. It was then that I began to sort out my
responses to the social and political systems that I was becoming a part of. My decisions to resist military conscription, support "left of center" politics, and mingle with "street people"
may have surprised my family. But as I showed my own seriousness about what I was doing, they became quite realistic
about it too.

A certain amount of tension developed over the shaggy appearance I insisted on and over the way my activities looked to
the tidy little suburban community where we lived. I am sure,
however, that the tension I was aware of was only a small part of
the heat my parents felt from the church and community about
me. Looking back on this struggle, I see the strongest indication
of how seriously my parents did take me: they bore intensive
criticism without passing much of it on to me. There were a few
forced haircuts and some arguments, but most of the
community's condemnation of the family about me never got to
me. My parents trusted me completely. They knew where my
heart was, and they didn't resist my becoming who I was.

A certain element of risk was involved in trusting me. It
wasn't really a "safe" thing for my parents to let me discover
myself: at the time, my self-confidence probably outweighed
my wisdom by about double. I'm the first to admit that my
activities were not without compromise. I did get hurt sometimes and I did fall. There were times I could have destroyed
myself. But I thank the living God that He gave my parents the
good sense and self-discipline to realize that it would have been
better for me to destroy myself than to be restrained until I
either severed myself from them and their God, or until my
spirit was broken.

The beautiful thing about my parents' letting go of me was
that not only did I have room to go wrong but I also had room to
make my own decisions to obey and trust in God. Without the
risk of failure, there was no chance of success.

When I was sixteen and seventeen I needed a lot of space to
try out my developing manhood on the world. My need wasn't
necessarily to rebel, but to establish my own identity. I needed
to try out my own "wisdom," immature as it was, on decisions

that counted. To the degree that anything stood in my way, it became the object of rebellion.

Because my family didn't knock me down when I pranced about with all my adolescent wit and wisdom, they didn't become "the enemy." They tolerated most of my rhetoric, trying always to encourage me in positive directions. My enemies became suburbia, *Time* and *Life* magazines, the Oakland *Tribune* (I was into journalism), Ronald Reagan, and the "military-industrial complex," much healthier objects of rebellion than dear old Mom and Dad.

The growing-space trust I required increased with my age. I really wanted to live on my own when I was seventeen. Because of my commitment to finish high school I stayed around another year. And much to my amazement, I survived all the way through high school and the following summer in the suburbs.

One example of how much my father trusted me was his leaving me in charge of his household bills, payments, garden, and property when he took my mother and sister to Europe for the summer after my graduation. I was completely on my own and have been ever since then. When my family returned, I left for college in Sonoma County and established my own home, where I live now. My need for growing space was perhaps at its peak when I was eighteen. I think my family was aware of this. Although it must have been difficult for them to release me the way they did, it was the only realistic alternative.

During the last few years of my residence in my father's house, he helped me establish links with the Kingdom of God in other places besides the suburban community that I was in reaction against. Friendships with Christians outside it were my main source of spiritual stability during my move and once I was away from my home. They provided a continuity of fellowship that I might otherwise have lost. My father introduced me to Inter-Varsity and the Cal Christian Fellowship in nearby Berkeley. He had Inter-Varsity staff people in our home where I could get to know them. He sent me to Inter-Varsity conferences where I could see the reality of God's movement in a context quite separate from suburbia. As I spent time with people like Jim and Marge Berney, Walt and Ginny Hearn (all of whom you will hear from in this book), I was provided with examples of Christian life outside the place I was leaving and in the spaces where I was heading. As I rejected life at home in suburbia, I had the perspective to see that I wasn't leaving my Lord. I can't emphasize enough the importance of these friends and my parents' encouragement to get to know them.

During my first years on my own, it seemed necessary for me to have distance both geographically and psychologically from my family. I was (and still am to some degree) in the process of establishing my personal identity as separate from my family. I spent time with them periodically, but the greater majority of my time was on my own. My ties with Inter-Varsity were closer to me than my family for a while. I had to deal with life situations entirely apart from "home" input. My family loved me and supported me in any way they could, but they resisted every temptation to try to control or check up on me. I was trusted and I knew it. I was loved and I never doubted it. Our relationship had to be somewhat limited so I could work on my faith, capabilities, ideals, morals, and life-style.

It was a hard time for all of us. As much as I would have liked to open myself up to my family completely, I just couldn't—for fear I would lose ground in discovering myself. The fact that my family seemed to understand my needs and that they stood by with a continued vote of confidence gave me great strength in my own pursuits. My integrity grew because of my parents' trust. I claimed freedom at their risk as well as mine. Through their release of me I learned to make decisions that counted.

I have examined the evidence and I have decided to make their God mine.

4

Sharon Gallagher

Sharon Gallagher is editor of Right On
newspaper, published in Berkeley by the Christian World Liberation Front. She is also a contributing editor to the Post-American and has
done advanced study at L'Abri (Switzerland),
Regent College, and the Graduate Theological Union.

As an only child of a busy minister and his wife I was rarely left
at home with baby-sitters. Being carted around to the places my
parents' ministries took them gave me a view of a larger world
than the street and town I lived in. We were entertained by
millionaires, poor farmers, and a variety of people in between.

Most of the Plymouth Brethren assemblies my father
preached in were made up of first- or second-generation Scotch,
Irish, and English, who prided themselves on their knowledge
of the Word and their lack of "churchiness" (choirs, robes, a
pastor, etc.). On some Sundays we'd be at a Spanish-speaking
assembly, where I'd hear long, heartfelt prayers addressed to *el
Señor*. Other Sundays we'd be at the all-black chapel in Watts,
where people sang with some feeling for the music and occasionally allowed the Spirit to move them in a hearty "Amen."
The large older women would call us "honey" and envelop us in
warm hugs. They'd have services all day, with an afternoon
meal of chicken, sweet potatoes, and pies. Then there was the
assembly my father had grown up in. An old Irish crony of my

father's father would introduce him with: "Sammy is speakin' today."

At one time my father was training a team of young men to preach and give testimonies. Every Thursday night they'd go down to a skid row mission to "practice." My mother would sing. I'd be on the platform with my parents—scrubbed, starched, and pastel—looking out at thirty or so men who were waiting for the service to end so they could line up for beans and coffee. Some of them would fall asleep during the meeting, or begin talking back or mumbling to themselves. From my safe perch I enjoyed watching these people do all the things one "doesn't do" in church. Afterward there might be a man talking to my father, sometimes weeping. The man might have been a doctor or lawyer. Maybe he had a praying mother. It was a constant reminder to a preadolescent of the frailty of human flesh. Growing up in suburban America, where grown men don't cry, I got a glimpse of a larger reality.

Temperamentally, my parents were opposites. My father was logical, fair, even-tempered. From him I got the concept of a just, sometimes stern God who told you the difference between good and evil plainly, and punished you if you transgressed. I had a different experience from most kids I knew, in that my father worked at home. That is, he worked in his study in back of the house, and would come in for lunch and the mail. He wasn't the stranger that fathers are who disappear at eight and reappear at six. In that sense our home was more medieval. My father was available, but happy to spend hours alone with his books.

My mother thrived on people and excitement. She would tend to overlook my transgressions, and from this I learned the concepts of mercy and unconditional love. Occasionally, though, a straw would break the camel's back and I would be punished in an emotionally charged way, in contrast with my father's evenly measured-out style. What I remember most, though, isn't the punishment or my crime. What I remember are those times when my mother apologized to me because she felt that a situation had been unjust. For an adult sincerely to ask a child for forgiveness made a strong impression. For one thing it made bitterness impossible. It was an admission that my mother had no claim to perfection or exemption from anger, but was a person in whose life the Holy Spirit was working.

Because of an illness my father had developed in his late twenties, my mother was forced into a more active role in his ministry, assuming responsibilities usually designated as "male." She did all the driving and did things like painting rooms and laying linoleum. In fact, there was little my mother thought she couldn't do. Mother's ministry, even though women weren't allowed active roles in the church, wasn't solely one of "helpmeet." She had Good News clubs, women's classes, and speaking engagements. Several times she went to work for Christian organizations. These jobs underpaid, but that was part of the whole emphasis. My parents never attempted to keep up with the Joneses. We had a house large enough to accommodate our meetings and guests, and a reliable car for the traveling necessary for my father's ministry. But things served us; they had nothing to do with our identity.

Through these Christian organizations I became further aware of a wider world. When my mother worked for World Gospel Crusades we had a bank on the kitchen table called "Meals for Millions." Pennies we put in the bank would actually give a meal to a hungry boy or girl somewhere else in the world. The relationship of our pennies to their meals gave me some idea of where Christians in the U. S. were in comparison with the rest of the world. Later, when my mother worked for World Vision, I met little members of the Korean Orphan Choir, boys and girls so hungry for love and affection that they would hang hopefully to the hands of people who paid any attention to them.

Yet the people I grew up with had little or no political consciousness. They hadn't heard about the "third world." I have an aunt who has continued to defend Richard Nixon in spite of Watergate, yet she has lived for twenty-five years in a Chicano ghetto of East Los Angeles. She was there before brown power or Chicano consciousness, before the rest of L. A. was aware that *barrios* existed in their city. She had Bible classes and ministries in schools and hospitals. She was there because the gospel compelled her to be there, and as an adjunct she began distributing food and clothing to the people—because they needed it.

There was always a lot of communication in our house. I'm told that I learned to talk before I walked. My father was going to seminary and pastoring a small church. My mother, left alone in the house, talked to me on an adult level about ideas, personalities, etc. I remember being appalled by a neighbor woman who would answer her children's questions with "Because I said so." Of course, she had more than one child. But I can't remember ever being given arbitrarily laid-down rules. A reason was always given. All my parents' values were based on a biblical morality. Even when I disagreed with individual applications of their view of the world, I knew that they were based on the understanding that the universe had a real moral order.

We lived in the San Fernando Valley about twenty minutes from Hollywood. When I was seventeen I was bored with high school, won a beauty contest, and started modeling. At this point my parents intervened. Their puritan sensibilities were offended by the money I was making for not doing "real work." Consequently I got out of modeling, which was a good thing: I could see myself becoming more and more of an object, falling under the neon charm of Hollywood over the hill—which provided just about all the trend-setting in the cultural wasteland of L. A.

In a way my parents' reaction to culture was an anti-modernistic prejudice. When I was five and went to see Walt Disney's *Cinderella* with a little friend, my mother told my father it was an opera (I wasn't allowed to go to movies). And it would be typical of her to believe that it probably was an opera so I could go.

Later in high school I confronted my father with the fact that we saw the same movies on TV five years later. He acquiesced but said he didn't want me in a worldly environment, where people were smoking, etc., around me. So he didn't want me to go to walk-in theaters. I could, however, see other specially approved movies. And so as a senior in high school I was the only girl I knew who could go only to drive-in movies. I did know other girls, even from non-Christian homes, who weren't

allowed to go to drive-in theaters because of the sexual possibilities the darkened cars offered to adolescents.

It was typical of my parents that such a thing didn't occur to
them. They trusted me. They were never strict about hours to
be in. (My social life, primarily with church kids, tended to be
self-regulating.) They were flexible with the situations and were
never suspicious of me. Somehow that trust was conveyed to
me as something more valuable than most of the things I could
have done to shake it. Their trust in me, their taking my word as
a responsible person, made it very difficult for me to lie to them.
I guess I knew I could get by with it, and that put the full
responsibility for the act on me. My tactic was always to argue
and harangue rather than to sneak.

When I was sixteen I dated a non-Christian boy against my
parents' wishes. Besides being unsaved he had sideburns, wore
flared pants, and played in a band. For then, he was pretty far
out. Once we went to Disneyland on a Sunday. I explained to
my parents that I felt that that was a relaxing way to keep the
Sabbath, but they were incensed with my worldliness. Even
though I argued with them, my own sense of guilt in violating
parental standards worked on me. I turned every conversation
with him into a sermon and insisted that for every date we had,
we go to one Christian function too, I guess to balance things
off. I heard that later the poor guy did become a Christian, in
spite of my confused efforts.

Once as a freshman in college a mixed group of us were going
to Ensenada, Mexico, for the weekend. The unchaperoned
group probably wouldn't have been approved by the college, so
we signed out for separate destinations. But just before we left I
called home and told my mother what we were really doing. I
simply couldn't have enjoyed the trip otherwise.

The free church traditions of my Brethren father and Menno-
nite mother provided them with a strong sense of our separateness. To whatever extent they were right or wrong in limiting
certain types of interaction with the culture, they were clearly
saying, "We are different—a race set apart." There was never
any question of my doing what all the other kids did. We were
not part of the world system.

I fought certain issues. But I did have a sense that there was a

positive, pure aspect of being separate. I had heard testimonies
of people who had gone through different trips and found meaning only in Christ. But beyond that, the lives of non-Christians I
knew seemed hopelessly meaningless and empty. Because of
the counseling my father did, I had also seen plenty of evidence
of what happened in the lives of people who went their own
instead of God's way.

In order to help me maintain a healthy subgroup identity, my
parents went to great trouble to make sure I'd get to our youth
group activities, no matter how far away. And it was with
people my own age, away from my parents' watchful eyes, that
I made most of my spiritual decisions.

My father was second-generation Irish, my mother second-
generation German. The Mennonites my mother was raised
with had moved as a body halfway around the world several
times. They moved from Prussia to the Ukraine because they
were pacifists, and when the Bolsheviks took over Russia, to
the United States and Canada because they were Christians.
My father's people, too, had changed countries but hadn't given
up their small Brethren fellowships. From their histories I
picked up a feeling that we were pilgrims and transients, not
belonging to any nation or culture. Rather it was our Christian
community, worship, and above all, our relationship to the
Lord that determined who we were.

In the Christian college I went to, the standards were more
middle-class American than Christian. This wasn't something
imposed by the faculty but brought with the students from
home. As a female student I knew that how I looked was my
identity, that what I wore was more important than what I
thought. My value was determined by whom I dated. Many of
the women, I think, sensed that they had been sent to the school
to meet "nice Christian husbands." This was evidenced by
senior panic, the rush to get engaged before graduation. We
were miniskirted, sports-car conscious, not much different
from the secular campus near us—except it took longer for
things like the flower child movement to reach us.

Even though we'd signed a statement of faith to be admitted
to the college, most of us didn't talk much about Christianity. It
wouldn't have been cool. When I was a freshman the school

was divided into Rat Finks (fun people) and Spiritual Giants (quiet sober people who led Bible studies). Many of the Rat Finks have since gone into full-time Christian work or are leading committed Christian lives. It was just that we didn't know how to handle our Christianity outside of talking in pious clichés.

As a junior in college I visited the Christian World Liberation Front in Berkeley. I was impressed that the young couple I stayed with cared about the kids on the street as individuals. Instead of discussing what to do about "those people," they were sharing God's love with them, giving them food, shelter, and the gospel. They were both college graduates, but they were living simply. They hadn't gotten into buying a new washing machine or making house payments but were putting their time and energy into people.

This impressed me to the extent that a year later when I graduated I went back to Berkeley and CWLF, as an alternative to the jobs and schools I was considering. My parents' reaction to my move to Berkeley was mixed. I went there at a time when a lot of rioting was going and they were worried about my safety. Also, my parents—who had lived their lives on faith financially—were worried about my finances! Overriding these concerns, however, was the fact that they were glad I was serving the Lord, the thing they had taught me was the highest aim in life.

5

Michael L. Chambers

Michael L. Chambers, a twenty-four-year-old minister in the Christian Church, is now finishing his M.A. in philosophy and Christian doctrine at Lincoln Christian Seminary (Illinois). He lives with his wife Pam, a number of cats, and a beloved Old English sheepdog ("a total oaf, nuisance, and center of constant upheaval in the house"). A church growth and world missions major, he did an undergraduate internship among the Chiricahua Apaches in Arizona, studied commerical art, and earned a black belt in Gujuryu Karate.

My earliest memory is of a meadow beside our little house in Bondville, Illinois. More specifically, it is of a cow in that meadow trampling a kite, just fallen. The cow intended no injury; she was just curious. But my heart was broken, and the memory is vivid. Another feature is vivid, too: my grief was shared by my father, who quickly jumped the fence to retrieve the kite—the first of many times in my life he would reassemble "broken pieces." I was two or three at the time.

My father later became a preacher in a small country church, where he worked for thirteen years at a salary that finally peaked at forty-five dollars a week. Our experience in that setting shaped most of my attitudes toward life. We moved to a rented farmhouse—Mother, Daddy, my sister Linda, and I—at my folks' expense. The church offered no "parsonage" allowance, utilities, or car allowance. The house was equipped with neither running water (much less, hot) nor telephone nor central heating. The winters were bitter. But many fond memories have their source here. In fact, even those inconveniences were mainly a lark for Linda and me, with the definite exception of periodic treks to the "house behind the house."

I was here I tried to burn the barn. I'm still not sure why I did it, although fire has always fascinated me. I "discovered" the blaze, via smoke pouring from the barn loft, while playing one afternoon outside with my sister. We rushed, shouting, into the house. In God's providence, my father was home. He fairly flew over the fence and the short space of the barnyard to begin hauling water, one bucketful at a time, from the cow tank to the loft. We pitched in, and all was well until my father found an unburned portion of the match packet I had used to set fire to the hay. I was sent to the house, and confined to the bedroom I shared with my sister, waiting for the wrath to come.

An odd feeling now gripped me: I had seen panic on my father's face, watched his erratic movements to put out the fire, and suddenly knew that I had deeply hurt him and my mother. They were able to stop the blaze, but had the barn burned, they would financially have been ruined.

My father didn't come into the bedroom to spank me; in fact, he never even spoke to me about the matter until much later. Perhaps he felt the profuse list of punishments I had written down meanwhile was sufficient for the time. This was not typical. (Among the several penalties to be ruthlessly inflicted on me, I supposed, were staying in bed for one week, no television and no bike riding for one month. In retrospect, I can hardly believe that staying in bed, missing the latest adventure of "Walt Disney's Mickey Mouse Club," or being prevented from rattling down gravel country roads on a beat-up, thirdhand twenty-four-inch bicycle could be considered appropriate chastisement, but such is the world through eight-year-old eyes.)

My father was just, and he punished, as a rule. For my sister, it was always a spanking; for me, as I grew older, it was "the belt." There were other methods, too. Once when my father was gone and I had been mean to my sister, my mother chased me around the kitchen with a wooden spoon, while I shouted as I ran, "I'll be a good boy! I'll be a good boy!"

My father ran a tight ship, but his justice was tempered with compassion. I seriously doubt that he would commit himself to a rigidly literal understanding of Paul's "Let not the sun go down upon your wrath" in Ephesians 4, but he practiced it to the letter. Invariably, when Linda or I had been punished during the day or evening, he would come into the bedroom before he retired and sitting on the edge of the bed, would say something like, "Daddy's just a big ol' grumpy bear, isn't he?"

Paul wrote in 1 Timothy 3 that an overseer in the church must manage his own household well, keeping his children under control. The people at church knew that this was one preacher who would keep his kids in line. I was accustomed to sit at the back of the auditorium during worship with a friend of my age who shared my more undesirable tendencies. We would usually read our Sunday school papers, talk, and quietly scuffle. I'll never forget the Sunday morning my selective hearing suddenly zeroed-in on these startling words from the pulpit: "Mick, if you and Eddie don't settle down, I'm going to move you down front here." I felt the eyes of the world upon me. I didn't act up in church again for at least a week.

II

I haven't spoken much about my mother. Perhaps my father, as the primary disciplinarian, is more conspicuous in my childhood memories. I could tell much about Mother, too, but everything has already been said in Proverbs 31. She has always been a quiet, gracious spirit, often the more prominent stabilizing force in our home in times of stress, always the center of warmth. Working with that country church in the face of extreme spiritual and financial challenge, my father was often despondent. Over the years he held several other jobs to make ends meet. Mother also worked, as a college teacher of music. We all shared the financial difficulty many preachers' families have known, but through it we grew together as a family. My mother had much to do with keeping hope alive and preserving cheer in a sometimes cheerless situation. Her quick smile, offhand manner, and musical voice made our house seem empty and cold when she wasn't around.

I don't mean to speak too harshly of life with that congregation. But it took much from my father and offered little in return. It shaped my attitude toward "church work" sufficiently to discourage my ever desiring to find myself in similar circumstances. But it taught me a lesson I haven't forgotten: a powerful God can sustain people committed to Him, even through long years of discouragement and frustration. My parents' commitment during those years is unquestionable in my mind, and they set a remarkable example of faith, patience, hope, and love for my sister and me.

III

Later we moved into a nearby city and my father changed the focus of his work. He was now a rehabilitation counselor in the Department of Mental Health in our state. The pattern of family life remained much the same, however, as we continued family devotions whenever possible, and shared in all things as a family should. But some things changed. The barn and open fields were replaced by neighbors' houses. My sister and I now had separate bedrooms. I found new friends in the neighborhood and soon shared their habits, including "tough" language, reading matter that was a step or two removed from *My Friend Flicka,* and now and then, a smoke. I was eleven or twelve.

The alien language never surfaced at home, but I wasn't so successful hiding the other vices. But when they reared their heads, my father simply capitalized on the occasion by initiating a related discussion for the purpose of teaching. Often the "discussion" bore more resemblance to a monologue, due to my profound embarrassment. Take, for instance, the time he discovered, flipping through some old magazines, some obscene additional artwork penciled in over some illustrations of women's exercises. A few days later he stopped in the bathroom while I was bathing and came the closest he ever brought himself to divulging the secrets of human reproduction. It was several days before I could figure out what he meant.

Or consider a later time, when I had become more careless in my smoking habits. I was a sophomore in high school. I began taking "walks" at night "to get some fresh air." I would walk to the end of our street to the service road along Route 66, and there, a safe distance from our neighborhood, smoke two or three cigarettes. Upon returning home, I would innocently but quickly go to my room to resume study. I figured I had rid myself of all telltale fumes by breathing in through my nostrils and out through my mouth on the way home; this was believed by us fellows to be sufficient deodorizing. Of course it hardly required a canine's olfactory perception to know immediately when I had entered a room. My father quietly took me aside one day and explained, to my shock, that he and my mother had known for a long while of this practice. He then reminded me that he had been a heavy smoker as a young man and had given it up after many heartaches related to the habit. He ended by saying that it was my decision, but I had some grief in store if I wished to continue smoking in our family. I quit very shortly thereafter.

Almost everything we did as a family was built around consideration of our good as kids. My parents were firm, and we weren't spoiled, but we were seldom left out of the picture. For example, Mother and Daddy, to my recollection, never went anywhere without us. I have only the dimmest memory of a baby-sitter, when I was four or five, in the afternoon or evening. But if both parents had to be gone overnight or on a vacation, we went with them. Surely that detracted in some ways from their personal enjoyment.

When my sister and I were very young, and we lived on the farm, my mother used to tuck us in for the night, help us say our prayers, and then leave the door open a little so we could see her sewing in the next room with the light on. It made the strange country sounds seem less foreboding, and more than once she consoled Linda or me when we suddenly awoke from a nightmare.

Years later, my mother would weep whenever I left home, even for a day's visit to the Indianapolis Speedway, for example. If I left the house to go anywhere in the evenings, my father would always tell me to be careful and ask me if I needed any money. As I grew more considerate of his feelings, I learned to say no, knowing that he would give me all the thirty-five or forty cents he generally had with him.

To this day, whenever any of the family leaves the house, someone is at the front door or a window to wave goodbye—a small matter like the others I've just mentioned, but reinforcing the assurance that each member was loved.

IV

My first encounter with death came when I was in the third grade; Linda was in the first. One afternoon while we lived on the farm, Linda and I excitedly jumped off the school bus and ran to the shed where we knew we would find the newborn kittens we had petted every afternoon for the last several days. The scene that met us was apparently the result of the mother's eating a field mouse which had been caught in some farmer's chemical spray, and passing the poison in her milk. The mother and all kittens were dead, lying in various postures, all indicating a terrible death.

We sobbed until we were sick, and Mother came out to see what was wrong. I have always had a tender heart for animals, but there seems to me a sense in which a small child shares an animal's suffering by an identification that few adults feel. Perhaps a child unconsciously sees in a pet a fellow creature who depends on someone else for shelter, food, and love, just as he does. Perhaps, too, he is suddenly brought by such an event uncomfortably close to a reality he knows all creatures must come to grips with, including himself and his parents.

My mother and father never forbade tears, and Linda and I were never taught that weeping was immature. I have seen my mother cry many times, and I have seen my father cry once, when his father died. He once told me that the man who can't weep is a man to be pitied.

Death was a time of sadness at our house, but not of despair. My parents helped us to understand that God's love and provision extend beyond the limits we know in this life.

V

Today I cherish the notion that honesty is the fundamental virtue. I have come to that perspective after much speculation and conscious reasoning. But I can't help but wonder whether the example of my parents predetermined the conviction. My father and mother both are scrupulously honest with themselves and in their dealings with others, and I think that their commitment transcends the mere pragmatic interests of parents wishing to teach by example. Consider the case of the Scotch tape flying saucers.

When I was eight or nine, I was attracted one day while shopping with my mother to a special display in our local A & P. The product was a certain brand of cellophane tape, and the promotion involved a card, attached to the tape dispenser, that had molded, punch-out "flying saucer" designs on it. These were of several kinds and colors, and all were launched by rubber band from a special launcher, also provided. I wanted a set of these very badly. Of course, the hitch was that one must buy the dispenser of tape to enjoy the attendant delights of commanding a fleet of flying saucers.

Having carefully checked both ways down the store aisle, I removed two or three cards from their dispensers and carried them home unnoticed. They didn't remain unnoticed, however. That evening (a Friday), as I shamelessly launched my saucers all through the house, my father asked the crucial question: "Where did those come from?" The reply was deft and steady: "I don't know."

Shakespeare said that the truth "will out." I don't know if he meant that it does this on its own or with help, but on that night my father wasn't taking any chances waiting for it to "out" of its own accord. Next morning we drove into town to the A & P, and he left me in the car while he went inside, presumably to settle up with the manager. I have no idea what went on inside that store, but I've never forgotten the lesson and the fact that my dad took the rap for me.

VI

Honesty, as I have said, I take to be fundamental. It is honesty, after all, that enables a person to admit to himself and to God his weaknesses. It is honesty that enables a person to accept God's infinite ability as Master-designer and Master-lover, the One incomparably fit to plan a person's life.

But honesty of this kind is painful: it indicts a man or woman, scorning personal achievements and scanning the recesses of their hearts with realistic light. It was with such painful tears streaming down that I committed myself to specialized training for the ministry the summer following graduation from high school. It was a fresh beginning, one that the Lord has blessed and I've never regretted. It signaled a lurch forward after a pause of years.

I had begun my pilgrimage at the age of twelve, being immersed by my father in the icy waters of a country-church baptistery in February. It was a genuine expression of my repentance—but that repentance was short-lived. By junior high and high school, my only interests were cars and car racing. Concerned involvement with the things of Christ was steadily displaced, since the auto racing scene is generally not conducive to healthy development of Christian faith. Mine was whittled away, with little resistance from me. Soon my school grades dropped, my interest in the future waned, and my faith had been seriously undermined (though its forms remained).

In retrospect, the behavior of my parents through that stage amazes me. Never did they harangue and moan about why wasn't I a better person or what was happening to my grades or why didn't I take up some other interests, like maybe stamp collecting. There were strong suggestions in this vein, but not wearying pleading. They simply went about the business of ordering their lives and that of the family generally, and chose to avoid incessant confrontation. I have never been able to harbor hatred in my heart for them longer than an instant, and I believe this is largely a result of their patience and kindness through everything. Paul gave good advice: "Father, do no provoke your children to anger, but bring them up in the discipline and instruction of the Lord" (Ephesians 6:4).

Though we were "PKs," Linda and I were never expected by my folks to be super-kids. They seemed to be happy enough that we were healthy and having typical problems. If they were ever embarrassed by our behavior specifically as the preacher's kids (as surely they must have been), we never knew it.

With that summer's commitment to leadership ministry, real spiritual growth began. My life since has been the weaving of a rich fabric in which Christian writers (most notably C. S. Lewis), close friends in classmates, professors, and "people of the pew," grandparents, parents, and my wife have emerged as the dominant colors.

So it is, that after many years of secretly hating my father's calling as a preacher and the loneliness of that work, I find myself, having submitted an honestly repentant heart to the Lord, placed by Him as a leader of His people where my wife and I now live. I have a passion for my work and a love for my people—a kind of echo of my parents' commitment and a reflection, I hope, of Jesus' own involvement with others.

6

Sharon E. Bube

Sharon E. Bube, this book's youngest author,
is a freshman at a leading western university.
She plans to study psychology and eventually
be involved in a Christian counseling career.

As long as I can remember, I've known that God was a serious matter. It was always obvious to me that He was someone my parents took very seriously and for that reason He also received my respect. My parents never pointed to God as a higher authority who threatened *me*, without placing themselves under His authority as well. His Word was equally true for us all.

This God wasn't just an adult's intellectual pursuit; since I was six weeks old, I've attended the regular Sunday worship service. By the time I was four, my dad had taught me a Children's Catechism as well as the Ten Commandments, the Lord's Prayer, and numerous hymns. I was learning who God is, that He made me and loves me, and what He considers right and wrong. Although I memorized much that I couldn't yet understand, I was learning that God's approval for my actions was important, and was in fact what lay behind my parents' expectations of good behavior. I knew that pleasing my parents was a serious matter, for it also involved pleasing God.

I prayed with my parents at night as far back as I can remember. I realize now that it's important that I prayed with them—that is, that they prayed with me. It wasn't a matter of their listening and smiling while my two older brothers and I said our prayers like good children. They too humbled themselves before the God who was really listening.

What amazes me most is the deeply ingrained respect and love I've always felt for my parents. Somehow they had authority in love, and I've tried to find the secrets of how they established this. I suppose it began back with their own love and submission first to God and second to each other. Both commitments were lifetime, secure, and joyfully entered into. Here lay the security I took for granted as a child. With this strong foundation for a home, I knew I was important and loved. My parents set goals for my good behavior at a very early age. They knew that in the strength and wisdom of the Lord, they could lead their child to do what was right.

So to begin with, they expected good behavior. As soon as I knew that I was to be silent in church, I was silent. It wasn't that I feared I would be whipped, but because I knew that silence was what my parents expected of me. I knew they still loved me, but I also knew that they wanted to hear what the preacher was saying. I can remember many sermons when, less than seven years old, I sat next to my dad and played quietly with his key chain or fingers. I knew he was listening, I knew I was expected to be silent so he could, and yet I knew I was important to him.

Now of course I was no more angelic in nature than the next kid, yet I was well behaved. Apparently throughout my early childhood, anything I did wrong was immediately corrected and I was simply not permitted to do it again. There was no struggle over who had the stronger will, my parents or I. Nor was there any question in my mind about getting away with something later after my parents had made clear that it was wrong.

Back when I was four or so, I remember telling my mom I had neatly put my shoes at the bottom of the stairs, when quite obviously I had merely opened the door and thrown them down. She immediately told me sternly, "That is a lie!" I was stunned while she explained to me that saying something was so, which I knew wasn't, was a lie. It was wrong and was displeasing to God. In no time I was in repentant tears and she was assuring me of forgiveness and love. The amazing thing is, I don't remember lying straight out again, either to my parents or to anyone else. My parents tell me now that they never had to say "No" more than once. Even today, though I seldom hear their "No," I would obey it.

The results my parents obtained were closely tied, I think, to their consistency. I received very little physical punishment from them, and then in only the severest cases. After that I had learned, and there wasn't a second offense. Physical punishment was never to vent their wrath. It was rather to give me immediate and necessary discipline, telling me plainly that certain behavior was inappropriate. I learned in that moment that the offense was wrong, that it would always be wrong (since the discipline was never a result of my parents' frustration or anger), and that I was therefore expected not to do it again. All this was bound in our mutual love: I knew my parents hated to punish me and I knew I hated to displease them. I personally was always immediately reassured of their love.

When I was seven, we moved across the country. I was always one of the most knowledgeable kids in Sunday school, and I continued excelling in this head-knowledge. Deeply ingrained in me was the importance of "being good" and I knew that going to church was tied in with this. I was beginning to find in our new church that I could understand the minister's sermons. My parents gave me a Bible which I treasured. As a family we always read Scripture before dinner, gave thanks before each meal, and by then I prayed with my mom and little sister later each evening.

I remember making resolutions to be perfect from then on, and failing immediately again and again. I knew God's importance intellectually, but I'm not sure how much I felt His relevance in a real saving faith. I was still trying to do it myself.

When I was nine, we moved again and shortly thereafter changed churches. Our new minister thrilled me, as he did my parents. I remember a sermon on the importance of having Christ dwelling in our hearts, returning home, and inviting Him into my heart—just to "be sure" I had. One night I talked to my mom, as was our custom, and poured out to her my desire to "really believe" along with my fear that I wasn't believing enough. She asked me if I really wanted to believe that Jesus died for me. I told her I wanted to very much, and she told me that this was enough. This was what He wanted. At this time, if not before, I understood that Jesus' death was for me and bought my salvation. I remember another such night expressing in amazement to my mom that I couldn't understand how anyone could look at what Christ had done for him or her and just not care. I saw then that probably the only way someone could reject Christ was never to understand the love He had for them, never to look the dying Christ in the face.

My conversion must have been real, for I began sharing my Savior with a girl friend. I remember praying for her and really being concerned that her soul be saved. My dad was particularly struck by one sermon about the strength of a family that prays together. We began having a special Sunday afternoon family Bible study and conversational prayer time. I invited my best friend to church, and in time she apparently accepted Christ. We felt a bond together in the Lord. My mom was my Sunday school teacher and each class member was reading the entire New Testament at home, a chapter a night. I had learned how a personal conversion was necessary to be saved, and I was learning how God was relevant to my everyday life.

Shortly thereafter I began falling into doubts. I guess I went through what maybe every child raised in a Christian home must go through. I had to look at all I had learned and ask if it was really true. Internally I had to challenge my parents' reliability and question whether or not I was just being indoctrinated about this God. He seemed so far away that I finally dared to ask if He was there at all. I said nothing about this to my parents, thinking it would disappoint them. I knew I was expected to believe and I couldn't bear letting them down. I was just plain ashamed.

The thing is, my parents hadn't failed. I had lived fourteen years witnessing their faith, and that faith had become part of me. I remember lying in bed one night just supposing that maybe God wasn't there—and what swept over me was this amazing dependence I already had on Him. I saw that if He wasn't there, my life was utterly lost, hopeless, and meaningless. I knew He had to be there. And I realized what I had known all along: that He is.

So with this confidence to build on as I turned fifteen, and for the last four years, I've been learning what it means to have Jesus as Lord, what it means to grow in Him. It began with a couple of weeks at a Christian camp. I learned I had experience on which to ground my faith, for I was beginning to know God for myself. I learned about the wealth of personal relevance in Scripture and was glad I had all that head-knowledge from years of Sunday school to draw from. I learned that God hears and specifically answers prayer. I learned that sharing my Lord with others isn't a burden but an overflow of my own joy. And I learned the beautiful fellowship I could have with many other Christians.

As I shared each new struggle and victory with my parents, I found they knew exactly what I was discovering. This living Lord I was just finding had been theirs all along.

Maybe the greatest thing I discovered was that my parents are pretty neat people. They could have preached at me since the time I was two that I better personally invite Jesus into my heart and let Him completely run my life or else I would go to hell. But they didn't. I wouldn't have understood such talk and I couldn't have grown into such a faith so easily.

But neither did they let me receive religious and moral instruction from neighborhood kids. They lived their faith and brought me up as a child of God who wants to please Him, in expectation of the time when I would truly understand how to be—and that I actually was—God's child.

My parents also knew how to give me just enough freedom so that I would choose to do right. On the important issues our values are the same. I have seen their scriptural bases and they make good sense to me. Whatever the "new morality" says, I believe that premarital sex is wrong. It is misusing and spoiling a gift that God meant to be a blessing in the right context. Values my parents have held, which were a matter of their times rather than of scriptural injunction, I have the freedom to examine and accept or reject. Despite the fact that my mom doesn't drink alcoholic beverages, I find nothing evil about wine in moderation. Yet I have respect for her decision and it may become mine.

As I got older, more and more decisions became mine and I grew into my parents' expectations. My love and respect for

them prevents me from abusing this freedom. And more significant than that now is the fact that my life is in the hands of my
Lord. This gives my parents the confidence to trust me. They
know that pleasing Him is my top priority.

My parents didn't exclusively confine me to Christian contacts. Let's face it: the world is basically made up of people who
don't love our Lord and who will always refuse to. It was
important for me to learn that life for a Christian is life as a
minority in a pagan world. So, since my Christian training was
basic in home and church, my academic education has been in
public schools. I think that education for me in private Christian
schools could have shielded me from the real world at a time
when it was necessary for me to learn and struggle. I had to
grow into my place as a Christian, not in a utopia of heaven but
directly in the context of the basically non-Christian world.

It was hard not to have real fellowship with schoolmates until
tenth grade, but the struggles in those earlier years built in me a
realistic view of the world and prepared me for the refuge of
fellowship I finally found in the numerous Christian kids in high
school. Throughout elementary and junior high school, I clung
to one or two Christian friends. Around me, clothes fads grew
into the crazes of going steady and on into experimenting with
cigarettes and pot, but my parents' values of "decency" and
"only Christian boys" and "take good care of the body God
gave you" were obvious ways of pleasing God. Such standards
just naturally became mine too.

As I watched anger and grudges among my classmates, I
couldn't feel these same ways myself. I knew the love and
forgiveness of my family at home. In some ways I was a
peacemaker. In other ways I was just not "with it." But somehow those whose approval I didn't have were never the sort of
people whose approval I valued highly. I guess as I grew I was
learning how to seek God's approval before people's.

But I was no wild evangelizer in school either. For years I
was a timid, almost apologetic, Christian. Particularly in junior
high, my image in others' eyes was important to me and while I
never sought to be outwardly sinful to be accepted, I did try to
be a sweet, friendly girl whom everyone would like. My morals
were strong (cheating and lying were never acceptable) and set

me apart from many of my classmates, but I certainly was no angel. I had crushes on every cute guy and, though I knew ultimately that only a Christian man would do, I was good at neglecting that fact for the moment and indulging in some romantic fantasy. Apparently, while conforming in some ways, I still personally wanted to please my Lord.

In tenth grade, many of my classmates finally accepted the Lord and began living openly Christian lives. I was no longer just one Christian in a pagan high school, but one of a group of kids who loved the Lord and about whom people were hearing. Each new Christian meant so much to me, after I had felt so alone in the years before. These kids knew my Lord too, and the fellowship we had together was great. It added strength to resist the pressures to conform to wrong ways. I had the approval I really cared about from those who were serving the same Lord. Together we prayed for the others in our school.

The most fantastic fellowship of all has come this year at the university. Here, many non-Christians seem more violently pagan than ever. And here, the bonds between Christians are deeper than ever. Just this year the Lord has taught me so much about being a member of His Body, about the joy of sharing and ministering to brothers and sisters in Him. Again and again I feel the bond of the Lord between two Christians as we meet on a non-Christian campus—and I'm even thankful that having been without it so long, I'm not apt to take it for granted now.

My lack of rebellion during my adolescent years is perhaps a remarkable witness to my parents' success. Parents, I think, are responsible for much of their children's rebellion when the kids 1) recognize their parents' inconsistency between word and deed, 2) want freedom from outdated rules which make no sense to them, 3) are prevented from growing up and having their own identities, or finally 4) are utterly alienated because their parents try to discipline them too late.

To my parents, even as I'm almost nineteen years old, I take my struggles and triumphs, my theological questions and giddy joys. The Lord has used their faithfulness from the start to draw me personally into His arms.

7
Jim Wallis

Jim Wallis graduated from Michigan State University with a triple major in political science, history, and sociology, then spent two years in seminary. Now editor of the Post-American, *he and other P-A staff have formed a community to "serve the Lord, serve the people" in Chicago's "Uptown," an area largely populated by Appalachian whites, blacks, American Indians and other inner-city ethnic groups.*

I had come home for a short weekend visit. My university campus had just been the scene of another series of anti-war demonstrations, and I had been in the thick of it. My father had been reading newspaper accounts of "the trouble" on campus that upset him. He was especially upset by his son's role in the protests and disturbances.

My father had grown up to love and respect his country. He trusted the nation's leaders. He had fought for "freedom" in World War II and he remembered friends who didn't make it home. This country had been good to him and his family. Why would his son turn against all that and believe, just as strongly, that the same country was guilty of terrible crimes against the Vietnamese, the poor, the blacks?

My father's resentment of my protest had been growing. This time he was really angry. How had he failed in my upbringing?

Why did I act that way? Who was responsible for my radical thinking?

I sensed it wasn't a time to argue. I said I would give him the names of the two persons most responsible for my present feelings and disconcerting commitments. My father sat down. He expected the names of radical figures from the headlines, of left-leaning professors. He was astounded when I told him that the two were he and my mother.

"You two taught me to care about people and their hurts. You taught me the way people ought to relate to one another. You bred in me a special concern for those who suffer most. Where do you think I learned the value of honesty and integrity? Of facing up to hard problems and questions? Most of all, of standing up for what I believe to be right, no matter who disagrees?" In many ways, I said, I was trying to be consistent with their own values. I was trying to apply them to the world as I saw it, which was different from the world as they saw it. My father sat there, not saying a word.

That conversation was a turning point in my relationship with my parents. From that time on, continuity between their values and mine was acknowledged. Eventually I made a strong Christian commitment which brought us together in significant ways. They too have undergone important changes in the way they view the world and their nation, and in the way they understand the demands of their Christian discipleship.

Like most parents, mine made the mistake of trying to protect their children from the world's unpleasant realities. And their view of the world was narrow and restricted. Their lives revolved around the family, the church, and the work-place in a way that protected them from learning painful facts about America and isolated them from the victims of the system they still trusted. Even their sincerely held Christian commitments became conditioned by the church's "civil religion," which served to bless the political and economic status quo rather than questioning it.

I was "converted" as a six-year-old. I remember being scared to death by a Sunday night evangelist who told us kids that the Lord would come to take our parents to heaven, away from us, and that we would be sent to a terrible place, alone. That awful prospect caused me to repent of the degradation and sin of my first six years, and so I was "saved." The cost of discipleship wasn't mentioned that night, nor did I ever hear that issue raised in churches as I was growing up.

The simple, self-justifying world view of my childhood and the church, conflicting with my growing awareness of the world's atrocities, caused havoc through my teenage years. The cracks became cleavages when a high school teacher (a re-volutionary in her own way, as I look back) gave me a book to read, *Crisis in Black and White* by Charles Silberman. Never had I been so affected by a book. I was shocked, betrayed, and angry at the brutal facts of racism. Worse, I felt painfully implicated.

My first idealistic impulses drove me to take my concerns to the church, with the hope that they would respond. Their defen-sive reaction and opposition spawned only greater awareness and more action on my part, which spawned more reaction, and . . . it's a familiar story. As the church people sought to justify themselves and the country they loved, that country seemed uglier and uglier to me. My parents, who had always taken a firm stand against any personal expression of racist attitudes by their friends, supported my raising the issue in our church. But as time went on, they became afraid and confused by my growing alienation. And then I could no longer stomach the church's uncritical support of government and of our culture's materialistic values.

Feeling lost at that point, I left church, family, and friends to join "the other side." I found a new home among others who were alienated and seeking to bring about fundamental social change, while searching out counter-cultural alternatives for their own lives. Much study, experience with the unrespon-siveness of political, economic, and educational institutions, and lessons learned from police clubs and tear gas turned me from an idealistic social crusader into a more sober, more politi-cally wise activitist, organizer, and strike leader.

Through all these changes, I understood through my parents something of a love that is unconditional, that doesn't depend on approval. The people of the church and my parents' friends responded to me chiefly by continuing to justify themselves. By writing me off, I thought, they could ignore the injustice of the present system and enjoy the fruits of prosperity. My parents were uncomfortable with that stance but still resisted the implications of my convictions. Yet even during my most severe disagreements with them, I knew that they loved me and would sacrifice greatly on my behalf. Love had always been expressed in very practical ways in my family.

Respect was another thing I recognized in my home. I remember very little exercise of arbitrary authority by my parents, although they were strong on instruction and discipline. We knew what they believed but we were respected and ultimately given the responsibility to make our own decisions. That must have been painful when our decisions went counter to what they would have done, or wanted us to do. Now, though, I think they are glad they handled things that way. (My father has only recently begun to grapple with the issues raised by the feminist movement. But he always showed respect and admiration toward my mother. He was never patronizing.)

In the course of events, I was led by the weakness and frustrations of "the movement" to more study, more reflection, and finally back to the New Testament. I began to see the wholeness of the gospel for the first time. Its dynamic power was there even in the midst of a church whose witness and life-style served to hide and contradict that power. I made a commitment to the radical demands of Christ. I went to seminary, only to discover that the church still responded in the same way as before. But this time I was ready for them. I knew now that their own Christian faith proved them wrong and could transform their lives as it had mine. I felt it was time for the church to rediscover its true identity. Along with others, I began to talk about "radical discipleship."

My parents felt deep joy over my Christian commitment. They were moved by my concept of discipleship to examine their own lives and attitudes. Now reconciled, we found freedom to explore together the meaning and implications of our common Christian faith. I began to appreciate the integrity of their struggles, an integrity I had seen many times before.

My father gradually became convinced of the immorality of

the U. S. adventure in Southeast Asia. He started to question the legitimacy of war and violence. When he stood up in his church to speak out on this issue, lifelong friends reacted in ways that hurt him deeply. His response was to continue to speak out. He put his own credibility on the line, asking others to examine these current issues in light of their Christian commitment.

My mother and father now both support me in my own ministry with the *Post-American*. They feel part of the paper's effort to bring a prophetic biblical witness to this land. They have come to realize that the gospel is a message of change. At the heart of Christian faith is our continual need to be transformed. Our biblical faith can never be used to justify complacency in our own lives or in our relationship to society.

The Church of Jesus Christ is that collection of people who have come together around the common confession that we are broken people who need to have our lives changed. Of all people, Christians should be those who can admit that we have been wrong, who can scrap old ideas and attitudes when we see their inconsistency. We have all been wrong about so many things. When we see that, and when we depend on God's Spirit, we no longer have to justify ourselves. We can be freed from our fear of change. My parents and I are learning these lessons. Jesus Christ has brought us back together again.

I hope that some day I'll find the openness and humility to say as my father now says, "You know, we've learned more from our children than they've learned from us." In that statement is the integrity, love, and respect that my parents have taught their children, influencing our lives more profoundly than they will ever know.

8
Jan Comanda

*Jan Comanda and her husband Joe are pres-
ently working as house-parents in a home for
disturbed children in California. They read,
think, and write, and recently have been able to
start brushing up on Latin together after the
boys and their one-year-old Ruth go to bed.*

Over a cup of coffee one afternoon when we were both in
Trinity Christian College in Illinois, my sister Beth told me that
she'd just written to our parents thanking them for being such
good ones. I did that too, when I was first in college. We talked
about it for quite a while. She'd been prompted to write this
letter by listening to friends talk about their parents and how
glad they were to leave home.

We each realized that we'd never been in a hurry to leave
home. We had felt comfortable there, and still do. Our home
was always a place of safety, of acceptance because of who we
were rather than because of what we'd done. We were loved in
spite of being a little overweight or not quite so smart as others
at school.

We had a large family, eight kids in all, which was part of a
larger community of families like ours, all of Dutch descent.
Many of our grandparents still spoke with accents. These
people had migrated from the "old west side" of Chicago to the
western suburbs, bringing with them their Christian Reformed

churches and Christian schools. We attended the Christian
school from kindergarten through high school and had the same
teachers as our brothers and sisters before us (sometimes even
the same teachers as our parents). Classmates and teachers
often identified us by family. I was called "Little Pete" after my
brother. He and I walked home from the early grades together,
having snowball fights with other family "teams." Peter was
somewhat handicapped by my being a girl, but we did come out
ahead at times.

Our parents knew the parents of all our friends and from
which families they had come. Most of us were expected to
attend one of the denominational colleges if we went to college
and then to marry, if not someone from our community, at least
someone from one of the other Dutch communities, someone
probably related to people our parents knew. After my marriage
to an Italian, even my grandfather (whom we visited in Grand
Rapids, Michigan, twice a year at most) remarked that it was
"going to be hard to get used to having an Italian in the family."

The Christian Reformed community was close-knit and involved almost every type of activity. We banked at the same
bank, held funerals at one of two funeral parlors owned by
Christian Reformed people, and generally patronized people of
our community whenever possible. We didn't all live in the
same neighborhood though (and therefore had friends outside
the Christian Reformed community). There was, however, little movement in or out of our community. Few people joined,
feeling somewhat awkward when coming from a different ethnic
background into a community so ethnically closed. Most of
those raised in the community remained in it or joined one
similar to it.

Still a member of the Body of Christ, still on the fringes of a
Christian Reformed community, I no longer feel so closely a
part of it. Instead, my husband and I are now part of a group of
Christians who feel it necessary to voice their concern and act in
seeking the justice that Christ came to institute. This means
more than supporting inner-city missions or "third world" missionaries. It means that each must seek to end prejudices he

finds in his or her own life, and to alter attitudes as well as injustices of which our society as a whole is guilty.

We are also searching for a way to establish Christ's Lordship over our whole lives, not relegating Him to Sundays and Bible reading after meals. This doesn't mean that everyone need become a minister or church organist, but it may mean taking a lower-paying job if it enables one better to serve Christ than some higher-paying jobs. In our area, many of the better-paying jobs are found in what are known as war industries. As Christ-followers, we feel ourselves unable to work in such businesses, even as a secretary or clerk. "Living poor," as we do, means consciously lowering our standard of living by sharing appliances, cooperative food buying, and being sensitive to the principle of planned obsolescence in the purchasing that we allow ourselves. It can make possible the freedom of choice that many people miss because they are tied down by the desire for material wealth.

The group of people with whom we now identify ourselves is ethnically wide open and contains men and women from many walks of life, some of which I would never have dreamed possible for a Christian—such as being an artist or musician. In Calvinistic theology with its work ethic, such "frivolity" is usually frowned upon. Yet I know now that these careers too can be ways of serving God. In this diversity the unifying factor is the Lordship of Christ. It's been exciting to realize the diversity of the Body of Christ and surprising to realize that my sheltered upbringing had kept me from contact with so many fellow members in Him.

Yet I never felt sheltered while growing up. In fact, sheltering is probably the wrong word to use to describe how I was brought up, because the purpose in remaining so closely tied to the Christian Reformed community was not to shelter us from sin and the world. Each person faces sin individually at some point or other, so rather than postpone the time when we would face it on our own, we were being prepared to deal with it by exposure to it. In school we weren't kept from reading literature that contained profanity and vulgarity, but read it under the guidance of Christian teachers who could talk about why it was used and how we should react to it.*

At home, too, we were taught that sin is a part of life since the Fall and that no one should point a finger at someone else. As we got older, we were told about illegitimate births, forced marriages, and divorces, not as scandals whispered behind closed doors but as events that we might have to face in our own lives or in the lives of friends. My mother believed that to shield us from these kinds of things would prevent us from being able to deal with them and with other hardships that we would have to face as adults.

In the home we weren't presented with specific dos and don'ts, but with principles that could be used to decide the specific instances we might come across. This was done casually, mainly through everyday conversations. There were many occasions for talking together. As little kids we fought to sit on Dad's knee while he and Mom drank their coffee, talking about what had happened that day. Coffee-conversation was the first order of business when Dad came home from his work as a carpenter. This tradition was continued when, as grade school children, we spent our first moments at home talking with Mom. In high school that became for some of us a coffee time sometimes lasting almost until supper.

---

*Discussing education at Calvin College, Henry Zylstra wrote: "Our library, precisely because it is the Calvin Library, should be larger and ampler than college libraries generally . . . We must know all the books that matter, the makers and modifiers of the tradition in which we stand, and of the traditions over against which we stand . . . For there are Bible colleges in which The Book renders the books superfluous, as though Bible and reader existed in a vacuum devoid of historical orientation, rational context, or cultural relevancy . . . It is so easy in the name of Christianity to turn one's back to art, to science, to politics, to social problems, to historical tensions and pressures, in one word, to culture. But once the conviction seizes on you that these all, precisely because they are cultural realities, exhibit a religious allegiance and an ultimate loyalty, that none of them is neutral but rather that all of them are faith-founded, all laid on an altar, all dedicated to a god, then you realize that they are at the very least important. Then you realize, too, that the true discernment of the God behind the culture, the assumption underlying the thought, the dogma beneath the action, the soul in the body of the thing, are precisely what it is the business of our schools as schools to disclose and to judge. In that lies the strengthening of the moral sinews of our young Christians. It is so that their choice for Christ and God can become a meaningful human choice." From *Testament of Vision*, Grand Rapids: (Wm. B. Eerdmans Publishing Company, 1958), pp. 75, 77, 99.

Then too, we talked around the supper table. Supper took a long time, but by the end of the meal we had all learned a lot about what each person was thinking. It wasn't at all an intellectual dinner discussion (although there was room for that too), just an informal say-what's-on-your-mind time of day in which even the smallest child could participate. Noisy? Yes, but it was an important experience for us to have adults listen to us and to have adults to listen to.

Later, as we got older, we often had coffee together after the little ones had gone to bed. Here again we could test our opinions against our parents' and hear what they had to say about the world events on the ten o'clock news—and, more important, about the big events of "our world."

Nor were these the only times for talking. We talked while doing the dishes, cleaning the basement, or on the way to a picnic. When the time came that any of us really needed advice, we could bring up any subject casually, and Dad and Mom might not even notice that it was of particular interest to us.

Through talking, we gained understanding of what was important to our parents. We could learn the principles that governed their lives without ever sitting down to a lecture called "What's Important in Life." In this way, too, we learned how decisions were made, how punishments were determined. Because the principles were given in a context of usefulness, we remember them better than if they had been memorized without our being able to see how they worked out concretely.

I once came to my mother after hearing a neighbor threatening her son with no TV for a week. My mother's immediate reaction was that it was no wonder the boy never obeyed. The threatened punishments were never carried out, because they were either out of proportion with his offense or because they were unenforceable. In this way, I learned that fairness and enforceability were principles behind the punishments we received.

Whenever possible the punishment was also meant to teach us to be responsible. If, for instance, we came in late one night, the punishment was to make us come in fifteen minutes earlier the next time, until we proved that we would be back at the agreed-upon time. Anyone with simple mathematical skills could see that consistent lateness would result in not being able to go out at all, while simply being on time for a while would result in returning to the original curfew. This always seemed more reasonable than the practice of being temporarily "grounded" for lateness and then being allowed out until the original curfew, with no proof of trustworthiness.

We were rarely allowed to sulk in the corner when we were being punished. Often our punishments involved participation in household chores. When my brother Pete was suspended from school for a week for ditching classes, my parents felt that they should punish him as well. His punishment was to spend his week at home, helping Mom with the spring cleaning. The work wasn't too hard, the company was good, and mother and son got reacquainted through a week of work and talk.

Both parents were also human enough to tell us that they too had done the same or similar things when they were young. Mom had been quite a class cutter herself, a good trick when you consider that her father was her school bus driver and taught at the school she attended. That had a lot to do with their understanding the situations we got ourselves into, but it didn't excuse us.

We learned that their faith was all-encompassing, taking in every activity from work to play to worship. Being Calvinists, they held to a "covenant theology." They believed that we were "children of the promise." This didn't mean that we were saved by virtue of having Christian parents, but that God's love extended to us and that He would call us to Himself in His own time. Believing this, they never felt it necessary to pressure us to "take Jesus into our hearts." *God* chose *us,* not we Him.

Recently my parents came to California to visit us, about the same time as a friend's parents came to visit her. Her parents, like mine, are middle-class people and the life-style of our friend is similar in many ways to ours. After both sets of parents had returned home, I asked her how their visit had been. "Terrible." Her parents hadn't approved of any of her friends ("If I see one more beard . . ."). They hadn't been able to reach any understanding of why their daughter chose to live as she did.

My parents, too, had misgivings about our way of life. It was hard for them to understand that we could be happy with very little furniture, and secondhand at that. Having chosen to buy our clothes on the basis of utility and long life, we're often limited to things that aren't in style. Even our choice of foods differs from theirs, since we rarely buy prepared foods or mixes (which are often costly in terms of nutrition supplied per penny). Even harder to understand is the fact that neither of us has settled into a "career" and that our future remains uncertain.

But we were able to discuss such matters within the context of our close family ties and common faith, and we'd had an enjoyable visit. The difference? My friend's parents, not being Christian, interpreted their daughter's life-style as a rejection of all that had meaning in their life. Although our life-style is different, both we and my parents still hold God to be the source of all meaning. They understand that we are trying to serve God in our life-style as well as in all other things. That, for them, is reason enough.

9
J. E. Runions

J. E. Runions, M.D., is associate professor of psychiatry at the University of Alberta and pastor of a Baptist church. He is married and the father of three young children.

The scenario is tedious: A pair of "Bible-belt" fundamentalists marry in the mid-1930s (dry, dusty, impoverished years on the Canadian prairies). In mild to severe poverty they produce four reasonably bright children.

As years pass, the family's economic status slowly rises to a comfortable but hardly luxurious level. The family's life-style is frugal, restrictive, and pietistic. They are intolerant of dissenting ideas. They rigorously press discipline, insistently demand precocity and excellence, relentlessly pursue "separation from the world." They interpret the Bible both literally and dispensationally. They believe fervently in the efficacy of prayer, and they engage endlessly in religious activities. They are suspicious of "higher" education, of "historic" churches, of "liberal" thought, of "professional" entertainment, of "religious" sects, and of "learned" professions.

Obviously a colossal family tragedy is brewing. The eldest—devout and obedient in childhood—will likely go to the university and become a militant Marxist. The next two (girls) should make early, ill-advised, unhappy, and brief marriages. The youngest will probably become pregnant at a tender age in order to escape from the toils of the family.

72

Yet none of that happened. I did indeed go to the local university, but I remain an orthodox Christian. My three sisters have had good educations, have made happy and enduring marriages, and are rearing their children devoutly. Instead of abysmal tragedy, the story is high comedy.

"What they did right" is as elusive as quicksilver. How did my parents raise a family successfully, at a time when many of their Christian peers were having a dreary succession of heartbreaks?

Four features of their parental leadership stand out: acceptance of biblical authority; capacity to give emotional nurture; unrelenting demand for excellence; and resilient, trusting faith in God. Both precept and model were congruent: they lived as they taught; they taught as they lived.

I think neither of my parents has an explicit world view. Yet they operate from an implicitly gnostic world view, like most Christians in the pietistic tradition. This tradition is characterized by (a) strong insistence upon an experiential, spiritual conversion and (b) a clearly defined code of conduct marked largely by prohibitions. To the gnostic, the *material* is strongly suspect and detracts from the *spiritual*, which alone is abiding and worthwhile. My parents' resolute insistence upon the inerrant, inspired authority of Scripture, however, preserved them from the fatal splitting of concept and conduct engendered by all forms of practical gnosticism.

Once when I was about seventeen, I asked if we could omit a genealogy from Chronicles at our evening Bible reading, on the grounds that it was "unprofitable." Mother promptly and peremptorily reminded me that "all Scripture is profitable. . . ." I expect that neither she nor I have changed our views on the family reading of a genealogy.

My parents were willing to be bound by the Bible. So before marriage my father had given up sports because he had only the Lord's Day for leisure time. My mother is a housewife because she believes that the Bible teaches that the wife should be in the home. Commitment to the authority of Scripture conferred upon them an authority and unity in living that allowed them to transmit to us the virtues of discipline, commitment, and response to divine authority.

Our family life was, as far as consciously possible, grounded in the Bible. From it our codes of conduct were derived (with a lot of unrecognized cultural tags). The Bible defined family roles ("children, obey your parents"), decision-making ("the husband is the head of the wife"), and social involvement ("come ye out and be ye separate"). Within their literal and dispensational system of biblical interpretation they laboured for great consistency of conduct in all the affairs of life. And that was an effective counterpoise to a gnostic pietism. "The hardest thing in life," Father often said, "is to be consistent."

We read the Bible, each family member participating as soon as he or she could read: a chapter of Proverbs after breakfast; and other books, sequentially, after the other meals. We believed the Bible. We memorised the Bible. (I still regard Bible memorisation with horror; I have always had a poor textual memory—which became the point of unpleasant conflicts when word-perfection to the King James Version was required.) On Sunday afternoons the Bible was our entertainment, through a variety of Bible games. Father was a superb raconteur, and so we learned the stories of the Bible well and early. We discussed the Bible. Its cadences and commands, its doctrines and narratives became a thousand hidden threads in the fabric of our personalities.

If now I have articulated a more explicit and coherent world view than my parents did, it is on the basis of the Bible. If I have accepted a broader (and nondispensational) basis of interpretation, it is because I have come to believe that the Bible demands it. If I have fewer prohibitions in conduct, it is because I believe I have been taught by the Bible. And where I have erred in thought, word, deed, life-style, child-rearing, and husbanding, I have not been sufficiently responsive to that Book which my parents love and taught us to love.

This over-arching authority of the Bible carries with it some dangers for me as I raise my family. Because I was so steeped in the Bible in early life I tend to take its authority for granted, and assume that my children will acquire the same responsiveness to it that I learned. I am sure that they will not, unless my wife and I are as explicit and consistent in teaching it to them as my parents were.

Mother and Father were preserved from a narrow hardness in living by their great capacity to provide emotional nurture. Mother was not a sentimentalist: she has some of her mother's Scots grittiness. But her warmth was undisguised and joyful. When we splashed gloriously in mud (cheered on by Dad), she was furious with the results (four mud-babies, and the girls with hair tied in ringlet rags for the day). She scrubbed us for dear life until we yowled. But she also laughed at the comedy of the situation. Later.

One of my earliest memories is of running into a barbed-wire fence when I was about three. Father gathered me into his arms and tenderly thanked God that I hadn't been injured. He is a tender man, and it is a tenderness not from his upbringing but from his constant converse with God. From the depths of God's sustenance both he and Mother nurtured us. Their expressions of feeling were spontaneous: anger sometimes, joy often, pleasure amply, tenderness usually.

As an adolescent I didn't always feel understood by my parents. Their pietistic approach to life didn't enable them to cope very well with "negative" feelings or ideas. But even when I let unacceptable feelings or ideas surface, I hadn't even a rind of doubt: they cared and they loved.

Part of growing up is struggling against limits, and learning to be thankful that boundaries are there to struggle against. From my parents I have learned the necessity of "setting limits" for children. Although strict, theirs were in retrospect not unrealistic. Even irksome limits were a sign that they cared. A lot. And because the limits were based on caring, they weren't inflexible hard rules. They were general rules which could be applied pliantly to special cases.

I've often wondered at the warmth they were able to share with us. Father's upbringing had been harsh, at the hands of an aging, opinionated, ambitious, middle-class father with merciless rules of conduct and no sense of humor. Mother had grown up in a poor, industrious laborer's home, full of emotional warmth and economic privation. I suspect that the emotional nurture my parents gave us derived from the marital love that bound them, and which they weren't ashamed to display. Despite hardship and poverty and little children and few amenities for years on end, the bloom on their marriage didn't wither. They were sometimes angry with each other, and sometimes hurt—but they knew the grace of reconciliation in large measure.

Perhaps the least fortunate aspect of my upbringing was the keen parental insistence upon excellence. Both parents were perfectionists, but Father was especially rigorous. In matters of accomplishment he would abide no nonsense. If we could play the piano, we were to play for Sunday dinner guests. If we could tell a story, we were expected to do so at Sunday school or church. Stage fright was not allowed. And we were to *achieve*. Good report cards from grades one to twelve, and then good transcripts in college, were almost our *sine qua non* of family living. Badges of excellence, such as a music recital or a school prize, became the occasion of family celebration.

As I reflect upon my adolescent years, I wish there had been the same stress upon excellence, but without the implication of wrong if the accomplishment or performance was short of perfection. Somehow my parents' dissatisfaction or disappointment carried an intense moral weight. (One of the more painful discoveries I have made about myself is that a lot of my drive is motivated by competition to exceed my Father's performance, demands, standards, and expectations so consummately well that I will always be beyond his perceptive and devastating criticisms.) And a continual obligation to perform superbly robs simple pleasures, especially rather passive ones, of their enjoyment. I would like my own children to acquire a passion for excellence, without also learning self-doubt, guilt over trivial errors, or fear of disapproval.

Beyond everything else my parents did right, they did this: they trusted God. Their lives had been made over to Jesus Christ. They were committed to Him. For Him they would risk everything without regard to expediency. Father left one job with large career possibilities because the route to success lay through wining, dining, and wenching the head-office executives. He had been called to live a life of separation. When wartime conscription was announced in Canada, he declared himself to be a conscientious objector, although he could have used medical loopholes for exemption. The massive financial and social hardships involved may have made him wince but he didn't shrink. When God called my parents to a social ministry, an abortive postwar attempt to provide a Canadian home for European war orphans, they sold out and moved to an obscure windswept prairie town whose only virtue lay in some adequate buildings for a children's home.

They were willing to entrust themselves, their fortunes, and their children to God, whom they knew as a loving Father. If doing God's will was their chief quest, they believed that His will included raising children to His glory. Hence they invoked the "effectual, fervent prayer of the righteous man." The few times that I awoke in childhood as they were going to bed, and often in my teen years when I was studying in the late evening, I could hear them praying together. And those prayers were ardent for the spiritual welfare of their children. They may have been strict and regimenting in many areas of life; they may have been conscientiously providing a certain Christian model; they may have been devoted to the Bible—but they trusted to none of that. Their trust was in God. They claimed His promises unto children's children.

Perhaps it was that vital faith that also enabled them to allow us to become adults, to separate from them, to do our own thinking, to adopt ideas and practices they wouldn't share. Perhaps that faith is the reason that our home was usually happy and was always warm, despite the scenario. Their God was big enough to keep their children, so they need not run our lives. They didn't always let go easily. The sky nearly fell in when I announced that neither dancing nor cosmetics seemed to me to be the marks of reprobation. And they earnestly urged and prayed that I should attend one of the larger Canadian Bible schools after high school rather than going to the university.

Yet in the long run, their commitment to Scriptures and their Christian faith let them free us. For we too were encouraged to study the Bible, to pray, to make our own act of commitment, to find the will of God. If we made our decisions on that basis, my parents accepted the decisions. So conflicts, sometimes intense, were rarely prolonged and did not become divisive.

For all my "liberation" and "sophistication," I'm not sure I have their venturesomeness of faith. But the model they provided is in some ways inescapable. I hope that my wife and I will be able to present our children with a model of Christian living as challenging and convincing, and with as many human features, as my parents presented to theirs.

10
Joan Terpstra

After teaching in secondary schools in Africa, Michigan, and California, Joan Terpstra left teaching in 1971 to become manager of a Logos Bookstore. She received both a B.A. (education) and an M.A. (French) from the University of Michigan.

Perhaps it all began when I asked Mom a question. My mind had wandered off into space and nothingness, and I began to wonder what it would be like if there were nothing—that is, if nothing existed. Then I began to wonder why there was anything. Why were we here?

"Mom, why do we live?"

Undoubtedly startled by such a query from a four- or five-year-old, my mother gave a brief but direct answer. "For God," she replied. That satisfied my childish mind, and soon the question and the answer were forgotten.

But the concept that life was integrally related to God was daily reinforced. We began our day at breakfast by thanking God for the night's rest, for health, for food. And in good Dutch Reformed tradition we closed most meals with the reading of a portion from the Bible—for, as Dad often said in his prayers, "We know that man shall not live by bread alone, but by every word that proceeds out of Thy mouth." Though Mom and Dad were brought up in the Christian (Dutch) Reformed Church, they both left it and became part of an independent fellowship that took very literally the Scripture, "Study to show thyself approved unto God, a workman that needeth not to be ashamed, rightly dividing the word of truth" (2 Timothy 2:15, KJV). Much that governed our upbringing, however, came from the Christian Reformed tradition of which they had been a part, and which surrounded us in Grand Rapids, Michigan.

I can't say that I always appreciated this Bible reading. Sometimes I found it boring or beyond my comprehension (it was always the King James Version). But I always listened sufficiently so as to be able to repeat the last phrase when Dad stopped reading, as he *always* asked one of us to do. I am convinced that this regular hearing of the Scriptures had its effect: I have a certain scriptural awareness attributable to these daily readings.

Another practice faithfully observed was our kneeling beside the bed at night and praying. We children began by reciting memorized prayers. As I reflect on them I realize that even this taught us something. I remember that the phrase "If I should die before I wake, I pray Thee, Lord, my soul to take" impressed upon me the fact of death, but also the fact of life with God after death. And this habit, for so it became, of kneeling and praying before going to bed was not something only for the children. I saw Mom and Dad do it too. One occasion made a distinct impression on me. I had been very ill with strep throat, but the day came when I was well enough to be out of bed. Before retiring that night I said my usual prayer, probably rather perfunctorily. Then my mother, also on her knees, prayed, thanking God for making me well again. I was embarrassed. Was God really that personal?

Dad's faith was so much a part of his life. He was a barber, and the highlight of his day was a good biblical discussion with a customer. We always heard about it at the dinner table, often to our dismay. "Can't Dad talk about anything else?" After having exhausted the newspaper in the evening, Dad studied his Bible. (He had worn out many.) Sometimes a question so intrigued him that he stayed up into the night to find answers. Reading fiction, he believed, was a waste of time. (Such an opinion was also held, even in the mid-twentieth century, by so admirable a Christian leader as A. W. Tozer.)

As an extension of the emphasis and teaching that took place at home, the church played a significant role in our family's life. It was church on Sunday for everyone, twice. When we were too young to understand the sermon, our allotment of peppermints (another Dutch Reformed tradition, I'm convinced) and the Sunday school paper kept us occupied. Later, we were expected to listen to the sermon. I don't remember any inspiring sermons, but I do recall that the Bible was treated as a textbook that everyone was encouraged to study for himself, to determine "whether those things [that the preacher said] were so" (Acts 17:11). Dad was a champion at this. If he didn't agree with the pastor, we heard about it.

Mom and Dad lived what they believed. Each in his and her own way was an example to me of what it meant to care for people. Dad was an elder in the church, and one of his responsibilities was to visit the sick. He took this responsibility seriously, and I know of no one who brought more comfort to these people than he. Mom had a heart for the friendless, and many times our home was opened to those whom others had passed by. I remember Eddie, who was nothing to look at and who had a speech impediment that made it difficult to understand him. Most people avoided him, but he was a guest in our home on a number of occasions.

There were times, too, when my parents were especially in touch with us. I remember vividly one occasion when Dad's strictness was softened as I was caught in the act of doing something that displeased him. I was about nine or ten, and I had gotten permission from my mother to buy a bottle of pale pink nail polish. (Mom was more approachable than Dad.) Dad discovered the polish on my nails, but instead of the spanking I expected, his voice was loving and gentle as he said, "Daddy doesn't want you to wear that." I have since felt sorry that we didn't see more of that side of him as we were growing up.

My memories of high school years reveal that the nurture given me during the early years was taking root. Youth meetings at church during the week were times of serious Bible study, and it was at that time that I got involved in studying the Bible for myself. In school we joined the Youth for Christ club, not because we were told to do so but because by that time we knew "in what direction we were going."

When I reached my senior year in high school, I was concerned with the question of how I was going to spend the rest of my life. I didn't have strong vocational inclinations, and my parents gave no guidance. But the verse on the plaque that I earned at Vacation Bible School was basic in my consciousness (I can't remember how long it hung on my bedroom wall):

> Only one life, 'twill soon be past;
> Only what's done for Christ will last.

And there was the Bible verse I'd memorized years before: "Now then we are ambassadors for Christ, as though God did beseech you by us: we pray you in Christ's stead, be ye reconciled to God" (2 Corinthians 5:20, KJV). It seemed a natural step, then, when a missionary from the Belgian Congo (now Zaire) spoke in our church and said that teachers were needed there, that I should respond to that call and say, "Here am I, send me." And so did an older brother. Both of us made the decision independently, though he preceded me to the Congo because he had completed his master's degree, whereas I hadn't yet started university.

The center of Mom's values was revealed in a statement she later made when I was doing deputation work in preparation for leaving for Africa. "Don't worry about your support," she said. "If it doesn't come from anywhere else, I'll take it on." And I know she would have, just as she had taken on the support of others along the way.

I sometimes wonder where I'd be now if the Congolese hadn't risen in revolt. As it happened, ten months after I set foot on Congo soil, the colony was granted independence by the Belgian government. Soon after, all foreigners were fleeing to the borders in an attempt to escape the undisciplined Congolese army which had revolted against the Belgian officers left in charge. And so we left.

Home again. After nineteen months in Africa, I was back in the States. What did it mean? Didn't God want me to be a missionary? I had looked forward to this as being a lifetime involvement, and abruptly it was over. My world began to crumble, the world I had built while being cradled in the acceptance of home. I knew that being a missionary was acceptable, and that I was accepted in that role. After all, wasn't Mom first to open our home to missionaries on furlough? And wasn't seeing our missionary budget climb one of the highlights in our experience of giving to the church?

I knew also that to have ended my relationship with my fiance (before going to the Congo) "for the sake of truth" was acceptable to my parents, that it was "noble" to choose "truth" over marriage. He was a Christian but belonged to a different church. I was so convinced that our, i.e., my parents', church was right that to marry him would have meant to compromise. I remember how uncomfortable I felt when I went with him to his church. (I realize now that my allegiance to the family tradition was stronger than that to my fiance, and I understand why that relationship didn't work out.)

The years that followed were difficult ones of working through my confused feelings. They were also years during which I first seriously allowed myself to question the "parental infallibility" that had somewhere along the line become established in my mind. This may be common among children, particularly daughters, from homes similar to mine, but I often felt desolate and alone as I tried to sort things out. Was our church's interpretation of Scripture the "absolute" truth? Was my parents' definition of right and wrong unquestionable? Was it wrong to take issue with some things, to seek answers for myself? It may seem strange that someone past adolescence was thinking in these terms, but as I reflected on my upbringing, I was able to see how such attitudes had developed.

Dad was a strong authority figure in the home. Spankings with his belt weren't merely token taps; we hurt afterward. I can remember Dad saying, "As long as you live in this house, you will do as I say." Nor did Mom leave all the punishment to him. And if we dared to venture a "Why?" with her, the response was often "Because I said so." So the five of us grew up with strong respect for authority, coupled with fear of disobeying or even questioning it (especially with Dad). To me as a child, parental authority came across as God's authority: my parents were speaking in God's stead. To question them, therefore, was to question God. To disobey them was to disobey God.

In one sense, of course, this is true: children are told to "obey your parents in the Lord." Yet the extent to which I accepted parental authority, and by extension all adult authority, was I think an unhealthy thing—for I eventually developed a sub-missive, nonquestioning personality. For one of my tempera-ment, to grow beyond that was not easy.

The parental commandments had held: "Thou shalt not go to movies." (They are an instrument of the devil.) "Thou shalt not dance." (Dancing is immoral.) "Thou shalt not wear makeup." (Jezebel "painted her face" and she was destroyed by God for her wickedness.) "Thou shalt not wear slacks." (Slacks are men's clothing, and it is an abomination for a woman to wear them.) So my sister and I had been the only ones who went to church youth outings in skirts. We were the only girls in church who didn't wear makeup.

Today I understand my parents' thinking. Many movies are destructive in their message or at best empty entertainment. Dancing can be immoral, or can lead to immorality. Wearing makeup is probably most often for the purpose of self-glorification. I don't object to the principles upon which Mom and Dad were basing their rules. But what I did come to resent was the fact that such standards were imposed on me. I seemed to have no right to question or decide such things for myself. I was being asked to give unquestioning obedience to unquestionable authority—the implication apparently being that my opinions were worth little, that I wasn't qualified to make decisions for myself. I personally would have appreciated some open, give-and-take discussions on these questions as they arose. It would have helped me if I had been encouraged to share with my parents what I was thinking and feeling.

Wrestling as an adult with this question of authority, it be-came clear to me that whereas a strong authority structure was effective in bringing about certain behavior patterns, it could in no way account for my steadfast faith in Jesus Christ. For I discovered that although the grip of parental authority loosened, the hold that He had on my life held firm. God was real to me. I had experienced His presence in my life. And I was receptive to His presence because I had seen reality in the relationship Mom and Dad had with Him—the way they spoke to Him in prayer; the way He spoke to them through the Bible. (Men far more educated than my father came to him to seek his wisdom in the Scriptures.)

As parents look ahead, I think they sometimes only half believe the wisdom of Proverbs: "Train up a child in the way he should go: and when he is old, he will not depart from it." But I think it's true. To be sure, not all of us children now observe all the rules of conduct set forth by our parents as we were growing up, nor do we all share their views about politics or hair styles. But one thing common to all five of us is a firm faith in Jesus Christ as Savior. And the "schoolmaster" that brought us to him was not a set of house rules nor a doctrinal statement learned in our youth. It was their example of living in relationship with a heavenly Father.

11

Peter Yuen

*A native Californian, Peter Yuen was a profes-
sional engineer for eight years before earning
his B.D. at Fuller Theological Seminary. The
Yuens spent seven years in Hong Kong and
Singapore training Christian workers, and are
presently ministering to international students
at the University of California.*

Like arrows in the hand of a warrior are the sons of
one's youth. Happy is the man who has his quiver
full of them (Psalm 127:4, 5).

In a sleepy little village near the city of Canton, the great
metropolis of South China, a young man was going through the
wedding reception line waiting his turn to confer some extraordinary blessing on the newlyweds. What memorable and truly
meaningful thing could he say besides "Congratulations, Chuk
Son, and I wish you all the best, Bo Hon"? (A kiss for the bride
would be unthinkable in that culture.) When he finally came up
to the bride and groom, he warmly greeted them and thoughtfully pronounced: "May you bring forth twelve children, Chuk
Son and Bo Hon!"

I'm glad my parents did. It is the "mean" one, mathemati-
cally speaking, who writes. Being number six of twelve, I
always felt pivotal, striving to relate to the older siblings and at
the same time pressing for a leadership role among the younger
set.

Ma was the disciplinarian. Pop was easygoing, but he made the big decisions. And some he made were major in their effect on my life.

With one son my parents left that sleepy Canton village and ventured to America, settling in tenant farming in the Sacramento valley near the little town of Courtland. It was there that numbers two through seven were born. Then the Depression struck and wiped out the farm. We moved into Courtland and struggled through seven years, hand-to-many mouths, retailing fish to other farmers.

Ma and Pop had such dignity about them, and ingrained such personal pride in us, that we never thought we were poor. We were never hungry. In retrospect, I can see many signs of poverty in our earlier life: the man from the power company coming to turn off our electricity, and Pop and a neighbor persuading him not to do it; one bottle of soda pop for the whole troupe on a very hot day; mayonnaise and that on only one side of a mayonnaise-only sandwich. But somehow we always had the necessities. Although family friends and social workers indicated our qualification for welfare aid, Ma and Pop always took personal responsibility for all our needs and declined aid from poverty programs.

Before the 1950s Chinese were discriminated against and not permitted naturalization. For good reason, the goal of everyone who came to "Gold Mountain" (early Chinese slang for the United States) was to earn his fortune, return to China, and live high on the dragon. Some made it, others didn't. As the rumblings from the '29 crash continued into the mid-thirties, some Chinese around us succeeded in making their fortune. Others found increasing difficulty in making ends meet. Such was the case with our growing family.

One particular man living in the neighboring Chinese community of Locke just seven miles down the Sacramento River had earned enough in his clothing shop to pack up and return to China with his family. He made a generous offer to my parents to take over his business: no money down, pay as you earn. On the surface it looked like a one-option decision. But my parents, who always prided themselves on the conduct of their growing number of children, recognized the increasing incidence of misconduct and juvenile delinquency among the Chinese children in Locke. They felt that even if only one of us came under the bad influence of those kids, that would be too great a price to pay for the fortune they were so certain they could earn.

Yet financially, things were getting increasingly difficult in Courtland. My father had heard about Nevada City, a little town in the foothills of the Sierra Nevada mountains where there were only two or three Chinese families. They were all in the neighborhood grocery business, struggling to eke out a living by their willingness to provide personal service.

So at age forty-eight, knowing little English and having a brood of ten children ages one to nineteen, my father decided to turn down sure fortune in Locke and the familiar Chinese community and venture out to a grass-roots American community and raise these children.

This was the most sacrificial decision my parents made. It was in Nevada City that my attitudes in life were formed. I learned to think American. I learned loyalty to a community. I learned sacrifice for others, seeing some eighteen heroic fathers and older brothers of my school friends give their lives in World War II to preserve the kind of life we loved.

Jesus Christ could hardly be said to have entered my picture yet, but He was working. Because of language and cultural differences, my parents never attended church in Nevada City, but they encouraged us children to go. For seven years I attended an Episcopal church but never came to a personal relationship with Jesus Christ. But the attitudes of commitment, loyalty, and sacrifice were being developed in me for His later use.

Although my father and mother were nominal Christians, my father was an alcoholic for a period of time. Conditions at home and in the family business went from bad to worse. Because Pop became so ill from his drinking, he was unable to work. We had to leave that cordial little town in the lovely pine foothills and settle in Oakland, in a small grocery store. Every able-bodied member of the family had to pitch in and pull his and part of someone else's weight. Pop experienced an encounter with God and suddenly, with medical help, quit drinking. And although he dropped that medical aid decades ago now, he never went back to the bottle. If the Son shall make you free, you are free indeed.

> Then Jacob called his sons, and said, ". . . hearken to Israel your father" (Genesis 49:1, 2).

It wasn't easy for me to adjust to big city life, but I did finish high school in Oakland. Although I had prepared for college I also developed a knack and liking for auto mechanics. Right after high school graduation a mechanic friend offered me a job in his garage. I soon forgot about college, what with difficulty competing for a place in the college of engineering with the many returning World War II veterans and my growing interest and advancement in auto mechanics. After one year my boss offered me fifty percent partnership in his business.

At that time my father felt strongly that I should go to college. We had come to an impasse, in fact; and he simply put his foot down and insisted that I leave the garage and matriculate in the university. At the ripe age of nineteen I acceded to Pop's wishes.

That parentally-determined change of direction trained my mind to think. It opened the door for eight years of engineering experience. It qualified me later for attending theological seminary. It gave me access to university students and graduates in Asia to bring the challenge for their preparation for the ministry. I'm so grateful that my mother and father—for it wasn't just Pop—stepped in at a time when I thought I saw success, and set me on another course that God was later to use in a way which neither they nor I could foresee.

One summer during my university days, I was employed in a local steel fabricating shop, building industrial equipment. After completing the fabrication of a large order, the company assigned me to deliver it to the purchaser some 1,700 miles away. As I drove along a narrow, curved, downhill pavement, the two and a half ton truck laden with steel equipment was performing beautifully. Suddenly the hood blew up, blocking my sight. As a result, I rolled the truck over, scattering all the equipment along the roadway and completely destroying the vehicle and equipment. I had moderate injuries but was grateful to be alive.

As I awaited treatment in the emergency room in the hospital, I realized the mercy of God in my being alive. I realized that up to that point, my life goals had been completely self-centered. Then and there I said to God, "If You spare my life, I would be living on borrowed time. I have been living for myself. From now on I will live for You." My priorities went through rearrangement. If anyone is in Christ, he is a new creature. Old things are passed away.

Meanwhile, my parents were being renewed. Although they had faithfully attended a Chinatown church, it was evident that Jesus Christ was making changes in their lives. They began reading the Bible, teaching it, living it. They spent much time in prayer for each one of us.

"Who can find a good wife? She is far more precious than jewels." God gave me a gem for my wife, a woman after His own heart. When we were married, Marge took a position as a literature research chemist while I continued in engineering as supervisor of a mechanical testing laboratory. As we grew in our marriage and in our Christian lives, we felt that God was calling us to train for the Christian ministry. This meant leaving our professions, packing up housekeeping, and relocating with our year-and-a-half-old son to attend theological seminary.

It took God's grace to make such a step, but seeking first the Kingdom of God appeared to us as a wiser goal. It was from that early background just outside the border of welfare that I was able to begin depending on the Lord for our day-by-day needs. As for Marge, I think her willingness to submit herself to my love and care, and fully support me in our calling in God's will, is just sheer "godly-womanness."

As Marge and I considered sharing our sense of calling with my parents, we wanted very much to have their blessings on our step of faith. While we worked in our professions, we were giving significant financial help to Ma and Pop (they had retired from their grocery business). When we told them about our calling, their immediate response was firmly negative. I asked them not to close their mind to it but to pray for us about it, for they in their retirement spent much time in the Word and in prayer. The very next day when we visited them they said, "Thanks be to God for His gracious promise. He has spoken to us through His Word in 2 Corinthians 6:10—'As sorrowful, yet always rejoicing; as poor, yet making many rich; as having nothing, and yet possessing everything.' God will meet our every need. You go and prepare to serve Him." How thankful we were for their openness to God and for their dynamic response to His Word.

As we completed seminary training we felt that God had given us a vision for China, a land closed to the gospel at that time. We desired to go to China Bible Seminary in Hong Kong to train Christian workers for the future of China. Ma and Pop wanted us to do some kind of ministry in the area nearby. As we continued to think and pray and plan to go to Hong Kong, my mother became very ill, so severely ill that the doctors had given up hope for her life. Then, in an unusual and miraculous way, she "turned the corner" and became well.

It was then that my parents realized the import of life: to seek first the Kingdom of God and His righteousness and trust Him for all else. As we left for our ministry in Hong Kong, my father gave us a verse of Scripture as their gesture of joy and blessing to us: "Bless the Lord, O my soul . . . who satisfies you with good as long as you live so that your youth is renewed like the eagle's" (Psalm 103:2, 5).

My parents felt that if they themselves being elderly and weak in health could only live day by day in the Lord for the rest of their lives, they would be satisfied. They themselves couldn't take God's Word to their people, the Chinese in Asia, but their "youth, renewed like the eagle's" could, for we were an extension of them to Hong Kong and China.

Repeatedly, over several decades, my parents made decisions that resulted in God's blessings to me: coming to America and moving to a grass-roots town, which freed me from the aftereffects of family immigration binds and allowed me to choose my own loyalties; steering me into the university to give me prerequisites for later ministry; responding to God's Word themselves to give me supportive blessings to do His will. Mundane decisions, deeply spiritual decisions.

12
Elisabeth Elliot

Elisabeth Elliot is a former missionary to Ecuador, the widow of Addison H. Leitch, theologian. She has written many books, most recently A Slow and Certain Light—Some Thoughts on the Guidance of God.

Who was in charge in our home was never in question. It was my father if he was at home. If he was not, it was my mother. It was never we children.

We were perfectly sure that both our parents meant exactly what they said. There were no empty threats or promises. "If you don't do this you will be spanked" meant that if we didn't do it we would, in fact, be spanked. It was also understood that no amount of whining, wheedling, or crying would result in any revisions or amendments. If we cried, we knew that we might be given "something to cry about." A small switch was kept in nearly every room of the house, on the lintel of the door, and often my mother's eyes, raised in the direction of the door, galvanized us to obedience.

A "strict" home? A "narrow" view of life? "Repressed" children? Yes to the first question. No to the others.

We are, all six of us, unspeakably grateful that we were taught authority, acceptance, the arts of listening and observation, and the necessity of biblical order. Beyond all this, we were loved.

We lived in a double house in Philadelphia for the first nine years of my life, during most of which there were just three children in our family. The house was practically *on* the street, which was a busy one with bus lines and plenty of cars, horses and wagons delivering bread, milk, and ice. Because my childhood coincided with the Depression, I remember hawkers yelling "Clothes props!", door-to-door salesmen with pitiful trays of shoelaces, pins, thread, and pocket mirrors, and what we called "poor men" who rang the doorbell and asked for something to eat. Sometimes we gave them a dime out of the tithe box in the drawer of the living room table. Usually my mother invited them to go to the backyard, sit on the sandbox, and wait for her to prepare a huge sandwich and a huge cup of coffee which she carried out in special dishes kept only for this purpose.

Because we were always in a position to help poor people we had no idea we were poor ourselves. I have since learned that my father's salary was something under $4000 a year. We understood that there was nothing extra for our own use. "We can't afford it" was an expression common at our dinner table when we questioned why we couldn't have new furniture like my friend Peggy across the street, or eat a whole Milky Way at a time as other kids did. (A single Milky Way or Hershey bar would be cut into five neat rectangles by my father's penknife.)

We wore hand-me-downs, some of them nice ones from rich people who were friends of friends of ours, but they never fit me properly. I couldn't fathom the wealth people must have if they could *discard* clothes like these. My mother also wore hand-me-downs and I was the only one who complained about hers. She accepted them with grace.

My parents' attitude toward money, material possessions, and their own place in life taught us a simple, humble kind of acceptance. Christianity was the thing that obviously mattered most to them. It mattered infinitely. My mother had come from a home where there were two maids and a butler. Her mother had had a reception room furnished in white and gold. My father's home was much more modest, but a home where Christ was the Head. Both my mother and my father were willing to leave what they had had and become missionaries. Five years later my father had answered a call to become the associate editor, under his uncle, of a religious weekly called *The*

Sunday-School Times. It wasn't a career that a man would have chosen for the sake of money. We learned that money belonged first to God. Tithing was strictly taught and strictly practiced in our home. We children received an allowance of five or ten cents a week, but we put aside a tenth for God.

My brothers all had paper routes, which taught them to value money and to keep accounts—as well as to face a sometimes irritated or cruel or hostile public in the shape of housewives who didn't want to bother to go upstairs for the money to pay the paper boy on "collecting day."

We learned to listen and to observe. We heard talk at the dinner table about Christian work and Christian people and churches and editorials and Philadelphia fundamentalism and the modernists, interspersed with quotations from the Bible and from Dickens and George Borrow and P. G. Wodehouse, from Matthew Henry, Jonathan Edwards, Alexander Whyte, and even from Robert Benchley and Gluyas Williams. We learned to pay attention to adult table talk and to ask questions and to look up words in a dictionary kept within reach of the table. We knew that dinner time was my father's time, and we expected him to do most of the talking although he often asked us about what we were doing.

Our pronunciation and vocabulary were constantly corrected and improved, and we were taught (mainly by example) to observe. My father often described in vivid and hilarious detail the people who came into his office, remembering what color their eyes and socks were and whether they had wide, flat thumbnails (a type to watch out for) and what part of the country their accents bespoke. Sometimes when we told a story he would interrupt to question us about details we hadn't noticed, which were, we began to realize, important to the total picture. He was an amateur bird-watcher and taught us to see birds we couldn't have seen by ourselves. He could imitate to perfection the calls and songs of about sixty different birds, and this sort of thing trained our ears as well as our eyes and minds. He sent us all into fits of helpless laughter with his descriptions of himself as a boy, "knobby kneed, with wrinkled black stockings and a shock of straw-colored hair over one eye."

Our home conformed to a strong biblical order. Nothing was

vague or loose. Our security as children lay in knowing what to expect and what was expected of us. Things were perfectly clean and neat, exactly on time, and entirely predictable. With six children my mother managed always to have clean bathrooms, a spotless kitchen, meals on the dot of seven, twelve, and six o'clock. My father could be counted on to leave the house at the same minute every weekday morning and to return (on foot from the train station) at the same minute in the evening. I think of him as wearing the same navy blue suit and carrying the same briefcase all his life.

If anything was going on at the church, we were there, and we were generally there together. We were expected to pitch in with housework, set and clear the table, wash dishes (in a precisely prescribed order—glasses, silverware, cups, plates, pots), empty trash, make beds, clean rooms, rake leaves, and help entertain guests. We could bring our own friends home, even to spend the night if we liked, and my parents regularly entertained visiting missionaries and preachers for dinner and/or overnight. We were required to be polite to our parents as well as to outsiders, to obey immediately ("Delayed obedience is disobedience"), to make no complaints about the food.

Of course, knowing perfectly well what was expected of us we expected a great deal of each other as siblings. We older ones saw to it (not always graciously and certainly not always successfully) that the younger ones snapped to it. I can't recall any teenage rebellion, really. Naturally we felt irritated at times that we couldn't do things other kids did, but we trusted our parents. I felt that their arguments against the use of makeup were a little flimsy and wished I could wear lipstick. We went to public school up through ninth or tenth grade; then five of the six of us went to a private Christian boarding school.

The order of our household depended on the godliness of the parents. Each of us knew, when he or she woke in the morning, that we had already been prayed for that day. My father rose at four-thirty or five to spend time in his study reading the Bible and praying. He had notebooks in which he kept notes on his readings and prayer lists. After breakfast we all gathered in the living room for the singing of a hymn (we sang straight through several hymnbooks without skipping around, all the stanzas, all the hymns), the reading of the Bible, and prayer.

It wasn't as though it was "easier in those days" to get six
children together in one place at one time and get them to be
quiet long enough to listen. It wasn't an easy thing to do, but it
was considered a thing worth doing and we did it. There were
fidgets and sighs and I can remember the pain of kneeling in the
summertime on a straw rug. I remember the impatience we felt
as we gathered for family prayers long before dawn on those
breathtakingly exciting days when we were leaving for the
annual tour to New Hampshire. But family prayers came first.

We listened to Bible reading again at supper time each evening, and again we joined in prayer. When we went to bed as
small children, one of our parents came to pray with us individually.

Last, we were loved. And the kind of love we were shown
was courageous. It took self-discipline on my parents' part to
discipline us. It took strong faith in God to stick to what they
believed. And, as I look back over many years, I now understand something of what it costs to prepare those you love for
suffering. It is always easier to try to shield, to urge a more
comfortable way, to grant the thing that is in our power to grant,
to excuse rather than to forgive. This is sentimentality, it isn't
love, and sentimentality is an idol—it is a man-made thing,
limited and constricting, and, like all idols, at last it is heartless
and destructive. Love, according to I Corinthians 13, "looks
for a way of being constructive," and this way usually involves
a cross for somebody. My parents had not evaded that cross for
themselves. They did not encourage us to evade it.

If the picture I paint seems impossibly ideal, I am sure that
my mother—who is seventy-five now and often gets questioned
on this subject—would be the first to say that she has no idea
how it all happened, no "secrets" to share. It was, she says,
only the grace of God. If the picture seems, as it will to some,
anything but ideal, and perhaps incredibly rigorous and austere,
I know that any one of the six of us children would be glad to
testify to the rollicking fun we have always had. We got together
again, thirty of us, in 1972, and for a week most of us were
laughing most of the time.

13

Walter R. Hearn

Walter R. Hearn (B.A., Rice; Ph.D., Illinois), after twenty years in biochemical research and university teaching, is beginning a new writing career with his wife Ginny. They preside over the Troll House in Berkeley, where at any particular time one might encounter six black cats, a gentle dog, Walt's teenage son and daughter, Ginny's mother, a great variety of people in their extended family, thousands of books, an assortment of unfinished manuscripts, and a big pot of soup on the stove.

When I was four, my mother took me with her to a school board meeting, set me in a nearby chair with a couple of books, and went about her business. When the meeting ended, Mother and I were surrounded by other board members telling us what a wonderful little boy I was to sit so quietly for such a long time. This happened more than once, and the story was incorporated into our family lore, to be retold many times as I was growing up. It seemed to account for my unusual interest in books.

I suspect that my parents were also unusual for the time and place in which they grew up. Even with little formal education, they were "upwardly mobile." But their move upward in society was strongly influenced by spiritual factors a sociologist might miss. They felt that whatever status they had, they owed to God. They wanted to honor Him, and wanted their children to honor Him too.

My father was born near Oxford, Alabama, in 1892. At eleven or twelve, after his father's death, he had to drop out of school to support his mother, a sister, and two younger brothers. They must have been desperately poor, yet my father looked back on his youth with humor and a sense of gratitude for their survival. Years later, if I complained or got the "gimmies" ("Gimme this, buy me that"), my mother told the "corn meal mush story." "Your father ate corn meal mush when he was twelve and was glad to get it. Now be thankful for what you have."

Selling newspapers around the railroad station where his father had worked, my dad learned the Morse telegraph code at odd moments. In something of a nonfiction Horatio Alger story, he took over the key when the old telegrapher had a heart attack (or passed out from drinking, I'm not sure which). The story of a twelve-year-old doing a man's job to keep the trains going worked its way up to the president of the railroad. My dad, teaching himself to use a typewriter (four-finger style) and write shorthand (his own way), became his secretary. For a while, he traveled about in the private railroad car that was the president's office. Eventually, but still in his twenties, my father held the high responsibility of train dispatcher on the V.S.&P. (Vicksburg, Shreveport & Pacific). The V.S.&P. never reached the Pacific, but it had discovered my dad as a "comer."

Dad left railroading during the transportation turmoil of World War I. After being rejected by the army for his undernourished physique, he came down with the influenza that reached epidemic proportions in both the military and civilian population. Called to the phone from his bed with a high fever during a crisis, he was violently cursed by his boss for being sick with freight cars lost and an engine off the tracks. Dad quietly said, "All right then, I quit," and hung up. Telling this tale, my father said he wouldn't work for anybody who would swear at him that way when he was well, let alone when he was dying of flu. And said it with that hearty laugh I loved.

Why is integrity, or "righteousness," so often associated with grimness and rigidity? My father had what seems to be a rare gift: a tolerant, easygoing personality combined with unimpeachable character. Because he was worthy of trust, doors opened for him in spite of his minimal education. He worked hard but never seemed driven to succeed. And if the ability to teach oneself is the hallmark of genius, he may even have been something of a genius.

My mother had developed strength of character mixed with a kind of softness herself. She was born in Garrison, Texas, the only daughter in a family of boys. Vivid impressions of her father remained in our family lore. Short, proud, and disdainful of others (especially his wife), "Papa Alf " was an unbearable tyrant when drink unleashed his anger. He gave my grandmother grocery money grudgingly but spent hundreds of dollars on Masonic uniforms and other pleasures for himself. His sons each ran away from home as soon as they had had enough. Papa Alf may have encouraged this as one way of cutting household expenses.

Even though my mother had few good things to say about her father, she came out of that unpleasant childhood without bitterness. She had become a Christian and taken refuge, with her mother, in the Baptist church. She was resolved to make her own home a place of love, joy, and peace, and she saw in my father a man with whom she could do that. She was fond of telling about their courtship: taking a trolley ride was a luxury and buying two five-cent ice cream cones instead of splitting one was a splurge. Since even Papa Alf recognized integrity, Jessie was permitted to sit on the front-porch swing with Brad after everybody else had been run off. Mother always smiled about sharing with my underweight dad the candy other suitors had brought her.

By the time they were married the oil boom had hit Louisiana and Texas. After leaving the railroad, my father and two other young men in Shreveport organized a petroleum production and refining company. My father was named treasurer. Mother claimed that years later one of the partners ended up in jail and the other committed suicide. At any rate, Dad became concerned about the ethics of some of their "deals," and my mother wondered about the high-living social environment Dad was being drawn into as a company executive. So in that Depression year of 1930, my father resigned to take a lesser job with an established oil company, a move that also meant leaving their beloved home in Shreveport (where I was born) for Dallas. After two years my father was transferred. My brother and I grew up in Houston, which we both think of as our hometown.

After Papa Alf died, my maternal grandmother lived with my mother and father, so I was raised in a three-generation family. I've seen elderly people grow lonely and bitter and I suppose "Mama" might have—if my parents hadn't drawn her so fully into our family life. My dad called her "Maw" and gently teased her out of preoccupation with the past or dread of the future. She learned to tease back in self-defense.

For fifty years my parents made Mama genuinely welcome in their home, even though her constant presence must have circumscribed their life. In a sense she was a helpless old lady who often isolated herself in the security of her own room, the newspaper confirming to her daily that it was the only place in the world for her to be. But she read her Bible there, following the verses with a gnarled forefinger, and looked things up in her outdated *World Book Encyclopedia*. She sewed a lot on a treadle machine and even taught me to embroider. Her genteel presence softened our family life, and probably softened me in the process.

She was a frail woman who could get a "sick headache" from the strain of the most casual shopping trip or from anything unexpected, yet she amazed us with her stamina in crises. When she was eighty she bought a dress "to be buried in," but ten years later she gave it away. By then it was out of style, she said. In her nineties, she survived an emergency appendectomy, news of the suicide of one of her sons, and her first plane trip (to his funeral). She lived to be 102, on her feet and mentally alert until 100. We knew she was beginning to fade when she sometimes forgot pleasant things. She had always been able to forget unpleasantness, a gift that may partially account for her longevity of body and mind.

I know I also owe a lot to my brother Dale for the directions my life has taken. I've sometimes wondered why I never rebelled against my parents the way my son and other teenagers seem compelled to do. One basic reason may be that I had my older brother to push against. Dale was twelve when we moved to Houston. As he began his years of adolescent exploration, I was a smart-aleck, six-year-old tagalong. I told on him if he wouldn't let me in on his mischief, and cramped his style if he did. I remember one night the police came because Dale and some friends had been chunking mud at cars. I followed when the boys took off down the dark alley, and then came back to report where they were hiding. No wonder I clung close to my parents when I was young. I needed protection.

Dale had a tremor in his hands, some kind of neurological problem that couldn't be corrected. His almost illegible handwriting made his years in school terribly difficult. School was easy for me, and simply by doing my best, I could be in the good graces of my parents. Especially to my dad, my "stick-to-it-iveness" was a virtue to be praised. Later, when I better understood the social dynamics of our family, I was ashamed of ways I had contributed to my brother's hurt. I always had mixed feelings about being called on to show off before company.

I can remember being sent out of the room to keep me from chiming in on sessions when Dale was being disciplined, but I can't remember ever being punished myself. For me it was punishment just to know that my father was disappointed in me. I had a tendency to mouth off and often needed to be corrected. To be called "smart aleck" by my father was so painful that he abbreviated it to reprimand me unobtrusively in the presence of others. If I goaded my brother or made jokes that weren't funny or simply rattled on without making sense, Dad would say, "Don't be an S.A.," or simply "S.A." and I would shut up in embarrassment.

My father had to travel a lot when I was young, "hounding" leases on which oil wells could be drilled. Mother ran the whole show in those years. In fact, I think she must have been pretty much in charge of the house and family all the time. Looking back, I suppose my father's work became more demanding when he left "the road." Working in an office in the land department, he must have had to interact with men of much more formal education than he had. Mother continually reminded us of Dad's accomplishments against great odds, of his reputation for integrity throughout his life, and that he was "head of the house." Actually, my dad didn't know how the house was run, I suspect. It was a family joke that he would starve before he would try to cook a meal for himself, even one that came out of a can.

My family was sometimes a disappointment to me: Dad wasn't a handyman who could teach me how to use tools, and Mother was such an indoor person that we almost never even picnicked. Our rare Saturday trips to Galveston Island (fifty miles away) weren't so much to go swimming in the Gulf of Mexico as to "eat out" at a seafood restaurant and buy buckets of shrimp off the docks (a nickel a pound in those days). I remember once driving along the beach on such a trip, my mother saying, "Oh, those poor people out in the sun!"

If my father couldn't teach me some things I wanted to know, he did teach me a general principle that was even more useful: anything you want to know can be learned from books. After hearing Marconi himself lecture on the new "wireless," Dad began to teach himself the principles of radio transmission and became one of the first amateur radio operators. Eventually the technical aspects of radio developed too fast for him to keep up, so he let his operator's license lapse. Copying code messages remained one of his major forms of relaxation. The other was printing.

In Shreveport my dad had been given a small Kelsey hand press and a few fonts of type. He was fascinated by typographic layout and began to design and print stationery and business cards for people as a hobby. When we moved to Houston, the sun parlor of the house we rented became the print shop. By that time we had racks of type cases, and Dale and I could both set type, lock up forms, and turn out things of our own. When I was in junior high my family built a home in Houston. My brother and I never had separate bedrooms, but the new garage had a separate print shop attached to it. My dad still puttered with the design of family Christmas cards, etc., I went through a phase of publishing a newspaper for my Scout troop, but it was Dale who became the printer in the family.

Before I was born, Dad had helped my mother sponsor a Baptist Young People's Union at the church, and even found time to be a Boy Scout commissioner. His battered Scout manual passed into my hands and I mastered it long before I turned twelve (then the required age). The first night I was old enough to join, I passed all the Tenderfoot tests and also all the Second Class tests, even though I still had to wait the required period to advance in rank. I could have passed the First Class tests too, but I waited for that until the day I became a Second Class Scout. I had learned it all from a book, in my father's footsteps.

When my brother's printing enterprise expanded to include a secondhand, motor-driven press, my folks were willing to have a new addition built on the garage-shop just for me. It became in turn a woodworking shop, a den for Scout meetings, a chemistry lab. I had dreamed of building it myself, but my father wanted to be sure it wouldn't detract from the looks of the house, so I didn't get the opportunity. (People thought our backyard rather strangely filled with buildings as it was.) Giving me that space of my own was a big expense for my generally frugal family. My impression is that Dad made only a modest income and that after we moved to Houston, he turned down promotions that would have meant another transfer. He invested heavily in life insurance, much of which was canceled when he suffered a crippling stroke just before retirement.

I never had a paying job in high school (or even in college, though I did earn scholarships), nor a regular allowance. The governing principle was that if I needed something or wanted it badly, I had to "make a case" for it. The pros and cons would be discussed at length. I would explain all the important things I could do with the new jigsaw or whatever it was, and cite things I was willing to do without, which could have been bought with the same money.

My mother was always happy to see her boys occupied at home. Home and church were the two areas where she felt secure. She was capable in both, a meticulous, well-organized woman. We often had company or relatives for Sunday dinner, followed by long sessions of recounting family lore. The "colored woman" who came a few days a week to do washing, ironing, and housecleaning sometimes helped in the kitchen but never did the cooking. These women were the only black people I knew in my segregated youth, by the way. Mother treated them with such respect and graciousness that I was hardly aware of any racial distinction. No one who used the word *nigger* was fully welcome in our home, even though that included some close relatives. Southern-style racism was only one of the evils my mother tried to shield us from. Profanity, vulgarity, drinking, and smoking weren't welcome either.

Mother was suspicious that the neighborhood kids would be a bad influence on me, and to some extent they were, I guess. I used to sneak off with my friend Billy to swim at "the big hole" in the bayou. It was just downstream from the sewage plant, but it was the only place in hiking distance where we could swim. I knew my mother was afraid of water and would say no if she knew, so I had to make up elaborate schemes to avoid lying. From Billy I also learned how to snitch lumber from new houses going up in the neighborhood to build flat-bottom boats for bayou adventuring.

Mother never had to worry that I would neglect my homework. She worried that I would get killed or injured or corrupted. Mostly my adventures were relatively mild: fighting rubber-gun wars with ammunition cut from inner tubes, digging "caves" in vacant lots, skating down the middle of the street holding a homemade sail just before the full force of a hurricane hit. However experimental I may have seemed to Mother, I was really cautious, even considered chicken by the rougher elements at school.

Once or twice in my experimentation I was terrified that I'd gone too far and might disgrace my parents. I prayed earnestly for help at such times and God seemed to rescue me. Basically I was a "Sunday school kid" and later a Boy Scout who wanted to be "morally straight" as well as "physically strong" and "mentally alert." My friend Billy, incidentally, loved to be around my family. We didn't fight or swear at each other.

Looking back, I see that my parents had a rather paradoxical influence on me. My mother in particular tried to shield me from discovering the world as it really is, or as she feared it was. But my parents also opened up the realm of books to me, leading me out of provincial isolation into worlds beyond their experience. That Boy Scout manual brought me leadership positions in Scouting and association with boys my mother wouldn't have approved of under other circumstances. For me, Scouting was a major escape from parental overprotection, providing in its adventures some physical and moral risks to face on my own. The direct experience of nature from outdoor Scouting supplemented my book learning and eventually helped influence me to choose science as a career.

Sometimes my father or mother would take me to the children's room of the Houston Public Library and leave me for the whole day. I started at one end of the nonfiction section and browsed my way around the room, devouring all the how-to-do-it books and skipping many of the rest. The usual gifts for my birthdays and Christmas were books, often ones I had particularly asked for. That may be one reason I've never been much of a celebrant of special days: my favorite way to spend Christmas was by myself, reading my wonderful new book. (Mother's annoyance at relatives who smelled of alcohol on such occasions probably played down large family celebrations. Also, my frugal attitude and lack of an allowance made gift-giving awkward for me.)

The book of books is, of course, the Bible. Although we never had family devotions, grace was always said at the table by my father or by a Christian guest. My father was a great conversationalist and raconteur, but he never discussed abstract ideas, so theology and most of the intellectual content of Christian faith passed him by. He attended a men's Sunday school class only rarely but supported my mother's efforts to get the boys dressed, away from the Sunday funnies, and off to Sunday school "with a quarter in one hand and a quarterly in the other." Mother regularly taught a class, younger married women at first and later women her own age, all of whom responded both to her teaching and to her love for them. She worked hard on her lessons, relying heavily on *Peloubet's Select Notes* and other helps, but focusing on the biblical passage itself. When I brought my questions about God to her, she would answer with Bible verses, never with arguments.

Our Baptist church in Houston was a big city church with an intelligent pastor and a largely well-educated, middle-class congregation. I usually liked my Sunday school teachers, and because I was well behaved, they usually liked me. Other kids I saw as hypocrites, misbehaving and goofing off in Sunday school. I began to appreciate hearing the denunciation of sin as part of the preaching of the gospel. Those kids needed it. Eventually I realized that from God's standpoint I was more like "them" than I wanted to admit. So I came to see that I had just as much need for repentance and forgiveness as the most obnoxious kid I knew, in or out of Sunday school. I acknowledged myself as a sinner, meaning it, and accepted Christ as my Savior when I was perhaps ten.

What did it mean to me to be "saved" when I was so young? I'm not sure, exactly, because my life might have been different from the lives of my peers anyway. In many respects I was an ordinary kid, but with a conscience. Did other kids also have consciences but manage to suppress them better than I could? I don't know. My parents' concern for integrity certainly sharpened my sense of right and wrong.

I think I accepted God's forgiveness with a great sense of relief, as though the pull of spiritual gravity had been reversed for me. I would continue to stumble, I knew, but ultimately I would fall upward into Christ's arms, not downward. As a Christian, I could pray for help even as a kid, and thank God for being my loving Father. I may have learned these traits as Sunday school exercises, but they were there when I needed them.

Puberty hit me hard, with all its sexual confusion and doubting and searching, but I think my environment must have made the agonies of adolescence less painful for me. Mother wanted home to be a peaceful refuge, not a battleground—not even a moral battleground. For all my dad's uprightness, I was never afraid of him. Because of Dad, no doubt, I still think of my heavenly Father as having a sense of humor and a friendly way with His children. I'm sure I was scolded for laziness, because I hated to mow the lawn and put out the garbage, my basic chores. I was devious about my whereabouts and careless about getting home at the specified time. But the fact that I barely remember such conflicts may be significant. I remember being terribly ashamed of my gross and gripping sexual fantasies, and of my cleverness at deceit. But even those stabs of conscience left no festering wounds.

Dark shadows are cast by the harsh beam of a spotlight. I've known Christian homes where there was bright light but also much darkness. In our home, the light was more diffuse. I grew up not so much in an atmosphere of rules and punishments as in an atmosphere of respect and trust. I learned to care about what I was becoming without expecting to be perfect. The security of my home taught me that there is ultimately nothing to be afraid of, even in myself. In Christ was life, and "the life was the light of men. The light shines in darkness, and the darkness has not overcome it."

So by the time I was sixteen and a freshman in college I was digging deep into philosophical and theological controversies, not out of an unhealthy skepticism but because I knew there must be a Christian answer to important questions.

14

Phyllis Royer Posey

Phyllis Royer Posey (B.A., Otterbein College; M.A., St. Francis College) and her husband Bill have two sons, Billy, 8 and Timothy, 6. She teaches foreign language and English in a rural Ohio high school.

The first thing my parents did right (as if they had any say in the matter) was to be born to honest, hardworking, God-fearing people. They were proud of their heritage and loved and respected their forebears. I can remember being taken to visit grandparents frequently, great-grandparents or great aunts and uncles occasionally. I usually went willingly because I found my elders interesting. Maybe that was because they also showed interest in me.

My lone living grandparent, Grandpa Royer, is today a surprisingly thriving ninety-five years old. I can remember his mother, who lived to be ninety-four. Grandpa's mind is sharp, although he is physically unable to do much that he would like. His eyes now lack the luster I recall from earlier years—but not his memory. He is a fascinating conversationalist, both as he recalls the past and as he discusses current issues. He keeps up with these dizzying times in a way that amazes us all.

Grandpa is a retired minister. He began and ended his official career with the denomination today known as United Methodist. But up until just a few years ago, he was still being called upon to preach special services and perform weddings for churches and individuals of many religious persuasions. He attributes his long and useful life to 1) the will of God, and 2) the indwelling Spirit of Christ. His faith has enabled him not only to endure emotionally (for example, Grandma's death over twenty years ago) but also to live without the excesses of the flesh that so many seem to find necessary.

A descendant of the noble Royers who escaped from France during the bloodbath following the French Revolution, his is also their religious heritage. In Germany, where they had fled, they came in contact with the devout "River Brethren." Converted, they became dynamic Christian people. I remember Great-grandma Royer with a black dress on her tall, heavyset form. She never wore anything but plain, dark clothes and always she wore the white gauze cap ("prayer covering") on her head. I remember her kindness too.

My grandfather, however, had not always been the paragon of virtue he appeared to my childhood eyes. This was a truth no one ever tried to keep from us. ("Honesty is the best policy" was an axiom practiced and preached by my parents, though we never learned some unvarnished truths until we were considered the appropriate age for them.) When Dad first told me Grandpa's conversion story, I was incredulous. Try as I would, I couldn't imagine him an unredeemed man, his temper flaring, the swear words flowing. But Dad could, for he had been seven years old when his parents attended an old-time revival meeting one night. Convicted of their sin, they went forward with their children to receive a personal experience of Jesus Christ. After that, things changed. At that time a farmer and schoolmaster in one of those little red schoolhouses of the past, Grandpa soon felt a call to the ministry. While preaching, he continued to farm—after all, he had eight children to feed.

I never knew my Grandma Heath, Mother's mother. But I know from my mom's recollections of her and their times at home that she was a Christian woman. The proud, red barn they built still stands on the dominant hill of their farmland; it reads "Mile A. Heath," and the farm is still in the family.

Grandpa Heath worked on the railroad with hard, tough men. Some of his ways may have been rough or crude, but underneath beat a "heart of gold." He was either converted later on in life after his wife died, or else he had been a Christian prior to that time but wasn't living it as much as he did in later years. I remember him particularly as he was ill with heart trouble before his death. He talked about looking forward to being in heaven. He wanted his favorite hymn played at his funeral, "When the Roll is Called Up Yonder."

With parents like these, church and the Christian way of life were an important part of my own parents' upbringing. My mother remembers a definite time when she gave her heart to the Lord. With Dad, it was a more gradual experience. So naturally my folks incorporated what they had known as youngsters into our early lives.

It seems to me that all moral training is spiritually derived. A permissive society, such as we have today, can lead only to anarchy. Such permissiveness is born primarily from the lack of moral anchors, which in turn derives from the lack of spiritual conviction. And everything begins in the home. Formal education is secondary.

In our home, my parents' spiritual convictions led to strong feelings about our formal education. The authority of the school was upheld. My parents were desirous of having each of us earn marks befitting our mental capacities. But their primary concern was that we learn to work hard and therefore insure "doing well" in life, which meant something like: Become useful citizens and good parents yourselves, and (in the process) fulfilled persons.

Mom and Dad's concern for our genuine fulfillment (born of self-sacrifice and discipline) was felt by us, and is still. Their philosophy was: Hold a sincere spirituality, turning to God and His Word often (life frequently is beautiful, but it is also often hard); get as much formal education as seems practical for you, but never stop learning in "life's school" (if you do, your mind is already "six feet under"); work hard and be thrifty; be as independent as you can; be kind and gentle to those less strong or less fortunate than yourself.

How did they go about handing this philosophy down to us? First, they presented a united front. Oh, I don't mean there weren't disagreements; I recall some very vocal ones. But always, they knew they were a team—and we knew it too. We were secure in that knowledge. Dad was a high school principal and he consciously used psychology on us. Mom's was more the "school of common sense" approach, but no less effective. Usually their ideas on how to handle us coincided, but not always. When there was a conflict, Mom ordinarily deferred to Dad—at least in our presence. They gave us affection as freely as advice and punishment, and they stressed that the latter two were because of the former.

They tried among other things to teach us the value of money and the importance of work. I remember saving my weekly nickel for what seemed an eternity, until I had two whole dollars to buy roller skates. I must have been seven or eight at the time. I helped with the dishes, ran errands to the country grocery store, and, as oldest, helped look after my younger brothers (my sister wasn't born yet). Each week I placed a hard-earned Indianhead nickel into "my jar" in the cupboard. The skates were highly anticipated, and it was a great day when I could finally hand over my hoard in exchange for that first heart's desire.

On one of my trips to the grocery, when I was a little older, I had a dime of my own money to spend. I was with Mom. I saw one of those Take-a-Chance boards set up on the counter. I don't remember what the prize was, but at the time it seemed attractive, and very cheap for ten cents—if I punched out the "lucky name," and oh, surely, I would. Mom tried to dissuade me, quoting that old adage, "You don't get something for nothing," and pointing out to me that my chances of winning were small. But I persisted, and my mom knew that, to some degree at least, I had to make my own mistakes. So she let me pay for a chance. Of course I didn't win, and I was extremely disappointed. "You see?" Mama said. That probably turned out to be one of the best coins I ever spent. It inoculated me then and there against any future case of gambling fever. I decided that my folks were right: work and thrift were the ways to obtain what one desired.

Mom and Dad took time for us. They listened to us. What we said was important. Mom didn't work away from home the major part of my childhood. I can remember her always asking me when I came home from school how my day was, what I had learned, etc. I was expected to give a full report.

Now I marvel at how my parents were able to take so much time for us. Dad was so busy as a principal that he practically had to live at the schoolhouse, or so it seemed. Mom was busy with the four of us, plus gardening, canning, sewing clothes from scratch, washing (in an old wringer-type washer), ironing (no "permanent press" then), cleaning. Yet she wasn't too tired to look out for our spiritual and emotional interests. Dad was equally concerned, but just not so available because of the nature of his work.

Teachers' pay then didn't stretch over the summer months, and in order to take care of us, plus pay for our three acres as quickly as possible (Mom and Dad had seen people lose their homes during the Depression and were determined it shouldn't happen to us), he worked many summers in factories. This was especially true during World War II, when male help was needed in war industry. Too, Dad gardened summers and did repair work about the place. Yet with all of this, they realized we needed more than physical security. Some of my fondest memories are of Mom sitting down to play a game or two of Monopoly, Scrabble, Chinese Checkers, or the like with us.

Mama didn't allow us to play card games, with a regular deck, that is. Grandpa preached against them. She wasn't really all that convinced that cards would send us straight to hell, but to keep peace in the family and "just because," it was better not to have a deck around, she said. We had plenty of other games, didn't we?

Once when we kids were old enough to have enough money of our own, we pooled it and talked Mama into ordering us a Ouija board out of the Sears and Roebuck catalog. It came, we played with it, and Mama watched. She hadn't realized what it was, she said, but now that she saw us playing with it, she was sorry, but it would have to go back. "Why?" we asked. Mama explained the dangers of becoming involved with the unknown world. Properly horrified at the implications of what we had thought just to be an innocent parlor game,* we acquiesced. We didn't want any evil spirits in contact with us! Now that we are into a more occult age, I am grateful for my mother's insight.

Along the academic line, I'll never forget the "multiplication table caper" I failed to pull off. One afternoon after school, in reply to Mama's usual query about my day, I informed her that we were having a multiplication table test next day. I had the gall to add that I thought them quite silly and useless and *I* certainly was *not* going to learn them. "I have news for you, young lady," my mother said firmly. And right after supper she sat me down to work, several hours it turned out, on the hated things. I cried and begged for mercy, but none was given. She drilled me and drilled me and drilled me some more. My head was swimming with figures. Finally, satisfied that I had some rudimentary knowledge of third-grade mathematics, she let me go to bed. The next day I did tolerably well on the exam. To this day, I can't say that I like math. But I did learn the basics, thanks to Mom's insistence and effort at this crucial point.

Through this experience and others, I learned to endure what I didn't like, no matter how painful at the time, in order to enjoy later what I did like. Today, as a high school teacher of English and Spanish, I have a master's degree largely because I learned early to "take my academic medicine."

Both as a teacher and as a parent, I work hard and I am willing to try new ideas. This, too, is a gift from my parents. Although Mom and Dad have long since retired, they remain young in

---

*G. K. Chesterton said: "My brother and I used to play with . . . the Ouija board; but we were among the few, I imagine, who played in a mere spirit of play. Nevertheless I would not altogether rule out the suggestion of some that we were playing with fire, or even with hell-fire. In the words that were written for us there was nothing ostensibly degrading, but any amount that was deceiving. I saw quite enough of the thing to be able to testify, with complete certainty, that something happens which is not in the ordinary sense natural, or produced by the normal and conscious human will. Whether it is produced by some subconscious but still human force, or by some powers, good, bad or indifferent, which are external to humanity, I would not myself attempt to decide. The only thing I will say with complete confidence, about that mystic and invisible power, is that it tells lies. The lies may be larks or they may be lures to the imperilled soul or they may be a thousand other things; but whatever they are, they are not truths about the other world; or for that matter about this world." Quoted from *The Autobiography of G. K. Chesterton* (New York: Sheed & Ward, 1936), p. 77.

spirit. Maybe that comes, to a degree anyhow, from a lifetime of working with the young. Certainly they adhered to basic principles and ideals learned in their own youth, but they adapted well to newer ways of doing things. This enabled them to communicate those ideals to their own and other people's children.

We lived in the country and our school was a consolidated one, but still friendly and small enough to give all your talents a workout. It was great, too, to have the physical liberty that went with our own little plot of ground plus the neighbors' adjacent farmland to roam about on. We lived all our lives in that spot. It's my parents' home still.

Through the years, Dad had many other job offers, for principalships and even superintendencies elsewhere. He thought all the possibilities over, but eventually turned them all down —largely because he wanted his family to know the stability of being brought up in one locality. He even refused the local superintendent's job because "the average job span for a superintendent is five years. They'd get tired of me here and we'd have to move. It's safer to be principal." So we remained on our own chunk of Ohio flatland.

But we were encouraged to go away from home when that experience would be good for us, if we were properly supervised. We went on 4-H trips and to church camps. But my fondest memory is the yearly visit I was allowed to make, one week each summer, to my cousin Barbara's in Dayton. A country girl, I was dazzled by the seemingly endless sidewalks on which to roller skate, the thrill of a nearby amusement center, the stores and local moviehouse. And when we were older, what fun it was to go downtown together unchaperoned to the shops and cinemas in the heart of the city. Downtown was *It,* exciting, throbbing with life. And then Barb paid me a return visit one week each summer. It was a heady experience in turn to introduce city girl Barb to the fascinations of rural life.

My desire to be an English teacher and a writer sprang from—I don't exactly know where. I learned to read early and our home was rich in books. We never had family devotions as such, but the Scripture was often quoted in our house, and we were expected to respect and obey it. When we didn't want to do our assigned tasks about the house, or when we wanted "extra pay" for them, Mom would remind us that we were given our food, clothes, lodging, and an already reasonable allowance. Then she'd quote, "If any would not work, neither should he eat" (2 Thessalonians 3:10, KJV). The commandments, of course, we often heard on appropriate occasions. "Honor thy father and thy mother"; "thou shalt not steal"; "thou shalt not bear false witness." When we longed for some material possession such as a classmate might have but which we couldn't afford, "thou shalt not covet" or "be content with such things as ye have" (Hebrews 13:5, KJV) rang in our ears. If we were in doubt about some activity, we were advised to "abstain from all appearance of evil" (1 Thessalonians 5:22, KJV). Or we heard the old adage, "If in doubt, don't." If we kids quarreled, we had to settle it before bedtime: "Let not the sun go down upon your wrath" (Ephesians 4:26, KJV).

If we became too gossipy, we heard "judge not, that ye be not judged" (Matthew 7:1, KJV). When we were spanked (by Dad) or switched with young pear tree branches (by Mom—and getting to pick your own branch was no help!), we often heard about the "rod of correction" (Proverbs 22:15). "Spare the rod and spoil the child." We always heard how much they loved us, and that this love was why we were being punished. We used to wish they wouldn't love us so much.

I could go on, but all verses were apt to the situation and extremely practical. They ended any argument. The Scriptures were authority. Who could fight against that? As we grew older, we sometimes tried quoting paradoxical Scripture back to "refute" a Scripture given, but of course it never worked. Mom and Dad were the undisputed Bible-quoting champs!

Mom was determined we should have the advantage of piano lessons, which she had wanted as a child and had been denied. She watched newspaper ads closely, and one day a truck brought an old monstrosity of an upright, with yellowed keys. But learn we did. Our first piano teacher was a funny, wrinkled, brown old fellow who dressed none too well. He drove an ancient Ford (about 1915) around to his pupils' homes. He chewed peanuts with his few remaining teeth all during our lessons. But he knew his stuff and was patient with children

—most of whom would rather be anywhere than at the piano. And, most important, he charged only fifty cents an hour.

My brothers were Dan and Jack, two and seven years younger. I loved them, but they teased me and I fought with them as siblings will. How I longed for a sister. Finally, when I was eleven, Dotty was born. She was my "baby sister" for years, fun to dress up and show off, and enjoyable to entertain. But due to our age difference, we never were the companions that sisters closer in age are. Dan and I had many good sister-brother talks while growing up. In high school, when I didn't drive yet, I won a camera for selling the most magazine sub-scriptions in my class. It was possible only because Dan drove me "all over creation" and patiently waited for me in the car while I did my selling.

I was between my junior and senior years of high school and attending a summer revival at our little country church when the Holy Spirit "got to me." I was sitting in the congregation that evening because it was expected of me to attend the special services with my family. I had always gone to Sunday school and church, and I'd even gone down to the altar once with Dan. We were baptized and joined the church at the same time, three or four years earlier.

So I had done everything prescribed. I thought I was a Christian. But as the speaker gave the message night after night, what was first a gnawing doubt gradually became a burden of sin and guilt so heavy that I couldn't shake it. One night when the evangelist called for Christians who wished to rededicate them-selves to come forward, I went. That's what I thought I was doing. But afterward, with a new feeling in my heart, I gradually gained assurance that this was the eternal presence within me of the Holy Spirit. Continuing to grow by Spirit-enlightened study of the Word, I realized a few weeks later that I hadn't truly been a Christian before at all.

Before my actual conversion, I had my heart set on going to Ohio State to study journalism. I had some kind of crazy young dream of becoming a real-life "Brenda Starr, Girl Reporter." With my salvation came a change in my career desires. Then I wanted to be a foreign missionary as passionately as I had ever previously wanted to be a newspaper-woman. I wanted to share "the good news" or "the best news." And being intensely interested in Spanish-speaking peoples because I had studied that language in high school, I thought it was to them I should go.

Now, looking back, I can see that my new career plans were nearly as much "of myself" as my old ones. Yet I honestly did want to take the gospel to others. But I replaced my glamorous newspaper dreams with romantic unrealistic dreams of the mission field. Almost everyone thought it was terrific that I wanted to be a foreign missionary. Not much was said about service "in Jerusalem," my own home area, and beginning at once.

This change in career wishes at that stage of my life, however, did change my entire life, because I went to a private school instead of a state university for my undergraduate education. For my new plans, I needed a church school. My parents wanted me to go where I wanted to go and do what I wanted to do. They were supportive of me, as always, although going to a private, church-supported college was a financial drain for them. They stressed that I'd have to work harder to help earn my own way. And Mom finally got to put her business college course to good use and went to work. She held an office position for a while, and later became school secretary in that same rural school where Dad was principal and where we children went.

"Where there's a will, there's a way" was something I often heard. If we were poor (or lower middle class), ours was a genteel poverty. We never thought of ourselves as poor. Somehow, if you wanted it enough, there was a way to make your dream come true. "Giving up" was foreign to our natures. We were humbly proud and resilient, because that was the example set for us.

15
Robert W. Smith

Robert W. Smith (A.B., M.A., University of Southern California; Ph.D., University of Wisconsin) is chairman of the Department of Speech and Theater at Alma College in Michigan. Married, the father of three, he has contributed to various scholarly periodicals and recently edited the book Christ and the Modern Mind.

The scene: the First Methodist Church, Madison, Wisconsin. The occasion: a Sunday morning in spring.

I was walking out the door with my future wife, returning to the campus of the University of Wisconsin. I introduced myself to the associate pastor who had preached that morning, and mentioned his hometown and my parents' names. Though it had been many years since he had seen any of us, he immediately recalled the earlier relationship. Thereupon he introduced me to friends of his with, "The best thing about this guy is his parents."

He was right. I took no umbrage at living within the lengthened shadow they have cast as a husband and wife team, now for almost sixty years.

I had parents and grandparents who took God's claims seriously, so that viewing life from a Christian perspective was part of my domestic culture. I don't know when I became a believer, but I know it happened, and irrespective of the heritage I enjoyed. ("God has no grandchildren," an old tract was titled.)

This atmosphere gave me a clear sense of who I was. Somehow Mother and Dad's warm relationship with each other and with us, along with our knowledge of a personal Lord, spared us the "identity" crises that presumably many young people in the last few years have experienced. My extrovertish father early set the pace for us to reach out without waiting for others to move to us.

Perhaps another factor that brought me safely through childhood and adolescence was family Bible reading. My wife and I were unusual, I find: when we were dating we frequently prayed together. We had a Friend in common, a fact that cemented our relationship. It was natural therefore that after we married we should institute the practice of reading the Scriptures and praying. This we have continued on a regular basis, now with three children, even though at times the path has resembled portions of the Pan Am Highway: rocky, uncertain, crooked, and not always well-executed.

Mother and Dad years ago had set the pace. Nearly every evening Dad would take his Bible—a Bible storybook when we were very young—read usually a chapter, and then each of us, sometimes stumblingly and repetitiously, would pray. If they neglected to introduce the variety of means of corporate worship we might have needed—for example, group singing or Christian poetry—and if they neglected more recent translations of the Scriptures, still they clearly instilled within me the desirability and necessity of such family gatherings. The King James Version often failed to speak to me at the close of a day of school or play. I often stretched out on the floor and fell sound asleep before Dad's "Amen." Yet the long-range effect was positive.

Bible reading and my parents' example primed the pump in other areas. Take tithing. I can't recall when I first began to set aside a tenth of my income for God. Perhaps it was in elementary school when I earned fifty cents per week with a commercial bill-passing route, or maybe it was when a colleague of Dad's would ask us children to hold a hat into which from a distance he would toss nickels, dimes, and occasionally a quarter. Whatever we caught we kept. But no matter what the source of income, Mother and Dad reminded us that a tenth of it belonged to the Lord. Though poor themselves, they gave back to Him this portion. It was natural for us children to do the same.

Though born in the affluent mid-1920s, I really grew up in the Great Depression. A friend of Dad's talked him into leaving a manual laboring job with the local power company to become a life insurance salesman. That's a great business in times of plenty, but it's about as productive in hard times as selling swimsuits to Eskimos, especially when first breaking into it. The realities of tight money meant that Dad—and Mother —worked hard to feed and clothe three children. They skimped, they borrowed, they gardened, they mortgaged to meet their obligations. Many nights Dad worked, calling on clients to sell a big or small policy. Mother, at the same time, washed and ironed for several families to supplement the meager income we had, sewed in a garment factory, and clerked in a grocery store. (Perhaps as a kind of bonus God has given them in recent years good health and the opportunity to travel widely at home and abroad.) In their war on poverty they had little to offer but blood, toil, tears, and sweat, and they never surrendered to "relief," as welfare was called in those days.

All this taught me that money must be used responsibly. While it was not the essence of life nor even the most important part of it, nonetheless it was a reward for labor duly given.

And so in elementary school days I began my first regular job, a weekly trek through snow and rain to deliver those commercial fliers to households in the city. I finally worked up to 300 bills per week, with a take-home pay of seventy-five cents. I held this job into high school, along with a daily paper route; both were mine for several years. Mother and Dad had set the example of hard work, so that today I see my profession as a sacrament to God, a way of worshiping the Creator who Himself continues to work. These jobs and others taught me responsibility, a quality I needed to learn early in life.

Not only did I learn discipline by example, but my life was broadened by enlarged social contacts. Our house was an open house. Not only were we children encouraged to bring our friends home, but frequently guests of the whole family sat at our table. While unable to provide delicacies, Mother always had ample.

I particularly enjoyed those times when families pooled their prepared dinners and we all shared. I learned that good times with friends need not cost a lot, require unusual work of Mom, nor threaten one's inner security. It was a natural response to friendship. These gatherings further helped us see that other Christian families existed, people of modest means but in whom Christ was alive and well. Intellectually unsophisticated, not in the Social Register, still paying on their mortgages many years after they contracted for their homes, these friends nonetheless were genuine people and I delighted in them.

Never by precept, always by example, Dad taught my brother and me to be helpful to our wives and affectionate to them. Whether it was aiding Mother in cleanup after friends had joined us for dinner, or in my parents' affection before us children—hugging and kissing—we saw what love meant. Sometimes we children joined in, five of us with our arms around the little knot of humanity.

It follows that we did many things together. Baby-sitters were either unknown or too expensive. One of the greatest vacations we had was a couple of days at the 1934 World's Fair. Or was it those three days at that Indiana lake when Mother had to take along bedding, food, and utensils to stay in a cottage? We picnicked, frequently visited relatives, and played games together. In short, they gave us not things but themselves.

As a Christian man I am beset with all the problems of egotism, pride, and self-centeredness that most Christian men battle. Often I "know" I am right in marital disagreements, parent-child differences, or professional matters, only to learn later that I was incorrect in my earlier evaluation or reaction. The temptation is to pick up where I left off, without any indication of sorrow.

But Mother and Dad taught me differently. I learned as a small child to say "I'm sorry," not in the casual way one hears today, "Sorry about that," but in a manner calculated to heal the wound I had caused. Perhaps I said it sometimes when I didn't really mean it, but I learned that one doesn't lose face when he admits error. It does bridge troubled waters. It taught me that others, too, have feelings. Not all the world revolved around me.

Responsibility. *I* was accountable to others and to God for my actions and words. I couldn't blame society or anyone else. And if I didn't bring home good grades in school, especially following in the train of two bright siblings, it was my fault and not the teacher's nor my peers'—nor the temperature of the classroom nor the tempting spring weather outside. I had a mind. I wasn't bereft of decision-making powers. I need not follow the crowd. And I had better understand that. In later years that sort of training has helped me a thousand times.

Upon leaving home for the Navy and college, I met friends who cast some issues in a different light. Under their influence I modified several of my Christian views. But as wise parents, Mother and Dad didn't try to compel me to return to the position in which I was raised. We talked about the issues to be sure ("eternal security" proved the most troublesome difference). We argued at times, but I never saw wrangling and bitterness in them. Significantly, today I view myself as an "Arminio-Calvinist" rather than the hard-line disciple of the sixteeth-century Geneva theologian I was in my early twenties.

Now, for many years, such matters have not come up during our visits. Separated by hundreds of miles we are united by a bond too deep for such challenges. Christ is real to each of us. It would make little sense in these adult years to hassle over such questions. Yet I needed to work through that argumentative stage, difficult though it may have been for them, to become a man in my own right.

But areas outside the home left their print on my life. I think of the organized church, for example. One of the most difficult situations of my married life, with short delightful exceptions, has been to find a satisfactory church-home. A chronic malcontent? Perhaps. Not until college days and with friends in Inter-Varsity Christian Fellowship did I learn what it meant to use my brains in worshiping God. I was raised in a fundamentalist, demonstrative church which emphasized feeling and whose pulpit provided meager sustenance for hungry souls. So I never was taught how to think through problems that troubled me. It was enough, it seemed, that I had made some sort of commitment at some time in the past. Nor did the church introduce me to good literature which spoke to the needs and desires of teenagers.

But the refreshing reality of this situation is that years later, long after I was married, Mother told me that she and Dad didn't like all the shouting, weeping, and loud preaching either. Yet they never complained about it before us children. In retrospect maybe they should have pointed out to us that God can be worshiped also in other ways. Undoubtedly they wondered when they saw many young people dropping out of that church how it would affect their own offspring. But today their three children are committed to the Savior, trying to work within the organized church despite its spiritual myopia.

When one sees churches of the 1970s at the two extremes of the theological spectrum—strong on social gospel but with no personal commitment to Christ, or strong on personal redemption but with no concern for the American Indian, black, or Chicano—he wonders if anyone brings them both together.

Dad and Mother did. Whether it was Dad going to the city jail to talk with the current inmates, getting up at 5:00A.M. to distribute New Testaments to departing servicemen, taking a class of church boys to visit their black counterparts and reciprocating as host later, sharing their limited supply of fuel wood with a poorer neighbor, spending hours (with Mother) refurbishing a mission church; or whether it was Mother's feeding destitute men who came to our back door during the Depression, helping at the Neighbor House, or preparing Christmas baskets for the poor, my parents could never close their hearts to people's needs. Their multiple-leveled concern for others was consistently lived before us.

They did far more than their share in bringing into their house an invalid parent when a brother declined to assume his responsibility. That did more to impress me with the need for a home atmosphere for the elderly, sparing them the lonely, cruel hours of a nursing home, than perhaps any other single act. Years ago I made clear to my parents, and to my wife's widowed mother, that when they can no longer satisfactorily care for themselves they are most welcome to share our home. Welcome? No, wanted!

I have suggested some areas in which Mother and Dad might have done things differently. Hindsight is always twenty-twenty. They weren't perfect parents, but none of my friends had better ones. If we weren't introduced to good Christian literature—I never read *Pilgrim's Progress* or saw modern translations of the Bible until years after I graduated from high school—nor to art and poetry, music was a vital part of our home: each of us children played a musical instrument and were encouraged to master its skills and literature.

Perhaps too they should have noted in a gentle way the weaknesses in our church and its practices, for we grew up thinking that most of the truth was somehow embodied in our denomination's doctrine and practice, seasoned with Wesleyan theology. I've often marveled that I, like so many of my church friends, didn't turn my back completely on God. Surely the prayers of my parents moved Him to keep His hands upon me.

Clearly, parents live on in the lives of their children; the good need not be "interred with their bones." The lamps they light by precept and example show their children better than anything else the way to go. Or so it was with me.

Supposing then that I have become a Christian man, it is in large measure because of Mother and Dad: their patience, kindness, generosity, prayers; their living for Jesus Christ. I am touched by their understanding and guidance when my own rebellious, critical spirit made life difficult. And so, again, I thank them.

16
Anne Fillin

Anne Fillin and her husband both hold part-time jobs in order to devote their energies to volunteer work: a day-care center, the United Farm Workers, and a Sunday school class.

As a child, I always felt out of it when the conversation turned to parents. Everybody else I knew, it seemed, could complain about how horrible their parents were to them, but I could only keep quiet—I really liked my parents. I think they did a lot right in raising the nine of us (I was the oldest).

We still stick together as a family. (Two of my brothers, a sister, my husband, and I recently celebrated my pregnancy with a trip to the ice cream parlor.) I attribute this to the strong sense of "family" taught us by our parents. We did many things as a family: assisted at Sunday mass, went on family picnics and camping trips, helped other people out when we could, and basically grew and learned together with our parents.

Our religious life was especially family-centered. I fondly recall many family rituals, a number of which were centered around the dinner table. Dinner itself was a sort of ritual. Everyone was expected on time. Thanks were offered to God before anyone started to eat. (At first our parents taught us a traditional prayer, but then, as we got old enough, we took turns giving thanks in our own words.) During the meal, conversation was to be directed to the whole table. Only one person was allowed to talk at a time, but everyone got a turn. When we finished we each had to ask to be excused from the table by our parents.

Among the rituals centered around the dinner table was Advent, the preparation for Christmas. We were always reminded that the "Christmas season" does not begin until Christmas Day, school parties and advertising to the contrary. The Advent season is a time of preparing. During these four weeks before Christmas, when we were rushing around buying presents and checking lists, the dinner hour became a special time. We made an Advent wreath of evergreen branches around four candles, one for each week in December. At the beginning of the meal, we took turns lighting the candles (one the first week, two the second, etc.), and leading the singing—usually "Come, O Come, Emmanuel." After dinner was over, we took turns blowing out the candles.

Another Advent custom that started while I was in high school was the "Kris Kringle." Sunday night, after dinner, each person drew the name of another person for whom he was to be Kris Kringle that week. The idea was to prepare surprise presents, perform some kind deeds without his knowledge, or do the person's job for him without saying anything to him (very difficult). We children had—and still have, I suppose—a strong tendency to look at Christmas in a selfish manner: "What am I going to get?" instead of "What am I going to give?" This custom to some extent helped to counteract this tendency.

Christmas itself is celebrated in my parents' home with even more ceremony. Christmas season starts on Christmas Day and goes on until the Feast of the Three Kings on January 6. My father brings in the Christmas tree on Christmas Eve, and after dinner everyone gets to decorate it. The littlest ones put on the unbreakable ornaments before their bedtime and help to put up the crèche without the baby Jesus (He hasn't been born yet). Later the adults and the older children finish trimming the tree, and go off to finish wrapping presents or to rest for a while before midnight mass.

At eleven or so, my father takes the older children to midnight mass. My mother stays home to finish up and takes the younger children the next day. As we arrive home after midnight, I bring my mother the good news, "A Child is born to us." She responds, ''Unto us a Son is given.'' Then one of us is chosen to place the Christ child in the manger. The next morning, someone always remembers to look for Him in the midst of receiving presents.

While putting up the crèche on Christmas Eve, we always put the three wise men as far away as possible. They get moved up a little each day until they ''arrive'' on January 6. During this time we give out cookies, etc., to our friends and neighbors. Shortly after that date, the tree is stripped and taken down, and Christmas is officially over.

Ritual was important in my parents' house only as it involved each of us. Although there were nine children, our parents saw each of us as an individual. We knew that each was important to our parents by their constant small demonstrations of concern. My mom's ability to listen to each of us has always amazed me. Even when she was busy, she would take time to listen to our stories and answer our questions. My father helped us with our homework, played with us, and encouraged deep conversations.

This concern for the individual person wasn't confined to our family alone. It seems we have always had at least one extra person staying at our house either short- or long-term. I had an ''older brother'' for a year, who taught all of us to pluck chickens (he was raising them for a project); and an ''older sister'' later on who introduced me to dating. A friend of my parents always brought a game or two when she visited us, or got us reinvolved in a game we already had. We learned that every person had something to offer.

My parents also encouraged our concern for other people. Through high school and college, I had the opportunity of friendship with an older French woman. She was confined to her apartment with bad legs for most of the time we knew her, and really enjoyed visits from us children. We took turns having dinner in her small apartment. She taught me a lot of French, and I really enjoyed her stories of France, but I found it hard to make time to go and see her. Much as I enjoyed these visits, I'd often have put off calling Madame if my mom hadn't reminded me of my obligation and of how much my little visits meant to her.

We also had opportunities to give to people as a family.
During the flood in Santa Cruz in 1955, my father went into
town to see what he could do to help, and the rest of us cleaned
up the whole house in expectation of housing some flood victims. Though no one showed up, we had the opportunity to
work together for someone else.

For two summers while I was in high school, all of us went out
to the prune fields in the Santa Clara Valley with a Migrant
Mission Program, to teach what we could and to spend some
time with people with another life-style. We found much in
common with the children, though they lived in a different
world. They had to work all day in the fields with their parents,
which showed us how easy our lives were. My mother made a
good friend with whom she was able to discuss many things
important to both of them. Others always have something to
teach us as well as needs we can fill.

We also spent a lot of time with other families through the
Christian Family Movement. We would gather at a park or a
farm with full picnic baskets, ready to share talk, food, fun, and
always a religious celebration. These masses were the best I
remember. They were held outside, so we children felt a little
more free to move around and make some noise. The whole
congregation were our friends, and that made the atmosphere
more joyous.

My parents' relationship with God is a joyful one. My mother
has often quoted, "Believing in God is knowing that all the rules
are fair and there will be wonderful surprises." She became a
Catholic at age eighteen. When she was preparing for baptism,
the priest instructing her was constantly surprised that she had
no questions. She believed and was willing to accept whatever
was necessary for baptism. Since I've known her, however, she
has been learning and growing. She has always tried to answer
our questions to the best of her ability, especially in the realms
of religion and our personal lives. When I entered college, she
told me, "You are officially on your own now. We'll always be
here when you need us though." Although we don't always
agree, I still have much to learn from her, and I hope that I can
continue to learn and grow as she has.

My father was raised a Catholic. Like my mother, he has

continued to grow "in wisdom and grace." I look at him today and don't see the same person I remember when I was ten years old. For one thing, at that time we knew him as a harsh disciplinarian, whereas now he tends to "discuss" behavior problems with the children still at home.

He is very involved in Bible study and in ecumenical discussions. When I was about sixteen, our family, along with two priests and six other lay adults, were privileged to be the first Catholics (in our area, at least) to be invited on a Lutheran retreat. The incident I most remember is hearing my father describe the Catholic belief in the consecration of the Eucharist in a way I had never heard or thought of before. He said that the consecration is the opening of a window onto eternity, onto the eternal sacrifice of Christ on the cross. I felt proud and happy to be present.

My parents have taught me that God is love, that He teaches us to love, and that He asks love of us, both for Himself and for the people with whom we come in contact. They have shown us love in their concern for each of us and for others outside the family. Believing that God's vocation for them is parenthood, they have made our family something special, a warm support for us in all our ventures. They have also taught us the joy that comes from serving others. I pray that I can continue in what I have learned and can pass some of their love and joy on to my own children.

17
John White

*John White, M.B., Ch.B., is associate profes-
sor in the Department of Psychiatry, University of Manitoba, where he teaches medical
students and psychiatric residents in addition
to his research and clinical work. For many
years he directed the work of the International
Fellowship of Evangelical Students in Latin
America.*

My parents taught me to honor them. I don't mean that they
drummed respect into me, but that somehow they imparted to
me a sense of certainty in life that I would not possess without
honoring them. I cannot explain this stabilizing effect. I can
only be grateful for it.

My attitude to my parents sprang more from watching them
than from "the way they handled me." They respected my
grandmother. They brought her to our home during the Depression and cared for her until she died years later. The day
Grandma arrived was a festival. My parents were as delighted
as I was. During the years that followed I never heard them
complain that she was a burden, nor did I see any hint of
impatience or lack of courtesy towards her. For at least a year
she was bedridden, and though her memory failed, our affection
for her never did. I learned respect for my parents by watching
their respect for theirs.

In the same way I learned not to gossip. Our next door

neighbor, Mrs. Kingsley, had a sharp ear for scandal and a tongue that added spice to it. Her voice pierced the walls of our terraced house, and many times I would hug myself in delight at her revelations. My parents heard it too, but the only comment they made was to lament that the walls were so thin.

One day I stood at the back door as Mrs. Kingsley grew red with indignation over the sins of the woman across the street. My mother stepped forward and took her gently by the arm. Vividly I can see it in my mind. My mother, tiny and quiet, was holding Mrs. Kingsley's elbow. Mrs. Kingsley's eyes glittered with fear from their bed of corpulence. "Come," my mother was saying, "why don't we go and tell her how you feel? It would be so much better . . ."

Not everything I learned came from observing my parents relate to others. Some lessons were quickened by the warmth of their kindness to me. I have a very special feeling for a walk my father took with me one day when I was four. Magic warmed the English damp as we ambled hand in hand through his favorite woodland. He would grip my hand and point when he saw a rabbit or a bird, and I would quiver in silent ecstacy as I saw it too. But the greatest miracle of all was an acorn. He showed me how you could take it out of the cup and how you could put it back again. His hand was big and the acorn small.

Why is the memory vivid? Why are my emotions powerfully stirred by so trivial a matter? I have no idea. I only know that none of his impatience with me during the years that followed ever erased it. When I try to think of a specific instance of his impatience, I'm at a loss to do so. Yet my mind ever comes to rest on the joy of that particular walk. I found myself not long ago showing my children acorns and wondering whether it would mean to them all that it had once meant to me.

My parents tried to "bring me up" well, of course. My mother had a thing about learning to be independent. She insisted I "fight my own battles," sometimes with disastrous results to me and to my enemies. She also sent me on a journey to my aunt when I was seven. I was to travel by bus to a certain railroad station (which I had never seen before) in the city. I was to buy a round-trip ticket to Altrincham and ask the way to platform number two. There would be six stations before

Altrincham and I was not to get off the train until I saw the sign saying "Altrincham." Auntie Jennie would be there to meet me on the platform. I must ask my mother some day whether she felt nervous about it. She showed no trace of anxiety when she waved good-bye to me at the bus stop.

I really can't say whether the experience made me independent. Certainly I was hugely excited and exceedingly proud. Certainly too, I have had an enormous appetite for travel since. Perhaps it did teach me not to be afraid.

Not all their conscious attempts to train me turned out well. My father wanted me to understand the innards of a car. Dutifully I studied diagrams of cylinders, pistons, and spark plugs, and learned enough to satisfy him. But for the rest of my life I have closed my mind to all forms of mechanics. I am filled with repugnance whenever I lift a hood, and helpless dismay whenever anything in a car goes wrong.

My father's attempts to warn me of the horrors of war had likewise paradoxical results. He meant what he said when he told me that it was unspeakably evil. Yet I shivered with delight at his stories of Flanders, World War I trenches, of night patrols in no-man's-land, of live hand grenades tossed back into German lines, and of close friends blown to smithereens. War remained horrible, but became fascinatingly so. Pacifism was for oddballs and cowardice was unthinkable. I resolved in desperation that when war broke out again, I would get myself killed as soon as possible so as to get the terror over with quickly. Surely that way would not be cowardly.

For all his war experiences my father was sexually naive, and it bothered me to feel that in my teens I knew more than he did. I did not like to be patronizing towards him. An awkward sense of embarrassment grew up between us and I was foolish enough to imagine myself in some obscure way his superior. The feeling brought me no happiness. Yet World War II completed in our relationship what stories of World War I had begun. The German blitzkrieg bombings on Britain were increasing in tempo about that time, and I was able to observe my father's cool and competent behaviour as an air raid warden. My respect and admiration grew again.

Then my own turn came to leave home as a teenager for

overseas battle fronts. On the morning I left, my father, to my surprise, embraced and kissed me—something he had never done before. As I walked at dawn through bombed ruins to catch my train I felt oddly lighthearted, as though the universe, in spite of the evidence all around me, were somehow on a stable footing. That one little demonstration of his affection had an extraordinary effect on me.

I so wanted him to be strong that it needed only a little strength on his part to reassure me. A few months later when I became a junior Naval Officer, I was haunted at the Royal Naval College at Greenwich by a senior Naval Officer whom I suspected of being homosexual. He made no overt suggestion to me but persisted in pressing me with invitations to the ballet and to have a meal with him in his London flat.

My father responded promptly to my plea for counsel. His letter was so full of sound advice and common sense that it won for him forever the place of leadership I really wanted him to occupy. I knew with irrational certainty that though V2 bombs were falling around us, the war would have a happy outcome.

My religious formation was well under way before World War II began. I was only eight when my mother took me to an evangelistic campaign in a huge marquee. The smell of fresh wood shavings and sweat is still fresh in my nostrils. I cannot remember what the red-faced man said. I do, however, remember asking my mother as we left the tent what "substitutionary atonement" was. As well as she could, she told me. I doubt that I understood the explanation. What I did know was that when she finished, she would be overjoyed to hear me say, "Well, then I'm saved!" And I was right. My announcement was received with the warmth and respect I felt it merited.

And curiously enough I was saved. I was trapped into the liberty of the Kingdom. Powers greater than I began at that point to shape my life. The loving warmth in our church nourished me, while its ignorance and bigotry failed to blight me.

My parents undoubtedly helped me to avoid being withered by ultraconservatism. They tempered blind bigotry with a gentler approach. "No, we would never forbid you to go to the movies," I remember my mother once saying, "though it would grieve us if you went." Yet when in junior high school I had to write an essay on "My Favorite Movie," my mother risked the wrath of the leading brethren and took me to see two films, both of them aseptic tributes to Queen Victoria's long reign.

I was more grateful than she would ever know for her instinctive understanding of my plight, and my unsophisticated soul lapped up the glamour of the black and white production. The fact that my mother herself enjoyed both movies gave us a bond we could share with no one and at the same time rid me of false guilt.

I know that my parents made mistakes and weren't always as strong as they should have been. I see them in retrospect to have many strengths and weaknesses. I have no wish to analyse them or to take their measure. I throw my psychological yardstick away and am content to know that they were my parents.

The strength of my feeling for them was never clearer than on the morning of Christmas Eve 1940. All night long, bombs screamed down to devastate our city. Fires were so bright that one could see to read anywhere in the streets all night. On my way home from church I had been trapped in an air raid shelter over which a burning factory had collapsed. I had escaped to run home, only to find that many houses in our street were in ruins and our house badly damaged. My sister was in our air raid shelter, and I managed to get my confused grandmother in too. My father's voice was never far away, directing other men who dug in the ruins for victims. But where was my mother? No one seemed to know anything except that she had set out earlier that evening in the direction of the church.

An hour before dawn the air raid died down and gunfire became only sporadic. Rescue work ended as the last of the victims was freed. Dawn began to break as my father and I left the shelter to set out in different directions and search for my mother.

The streets seemed suddenly quiet and empty. At one point I had to scramble up the outer edge of a large bomb crater. As I paused on the rim to decide how to proceed, I heard the soft sounds of someone scrambling up the outer edge of the crater on the opposite side from where I stood. A moment later I found myself staring at my mother's face, as she slowly stood upright and looked back at me. Neither of us spoke for a full minute.

Never did the fragility and the extraordinary strength of our family bonds seem so apparent as they did in that moment. Fragility, because any one of a thousand bombs could have destroyed them. Strength, because fear never would. I wanted to cry with joy as I stumbled over the shifting rubble to where she stood, but I made no sound.

"I am fine, I am just fine," she was saying. "The Lord really has been very good."

18

Hazel Matzke

Hazel Matzke, married to a Wisconsin post-master and mother of one son (attending the university), formerly worked for her hometown newspaper. A joyful Christian and now a school secretary, she is active in the United Methodist Church.

"But Mother, you promised!" As I tried to think of how to explain to my young son why unexpected circumstances prevented me from keeping my promise, I suddenly recalled a lesson I'd learned as a child: not to insist on doing things merely for selfish pleasure.

One of our favorite forms of entertainment was family outings on hot summer evenings to a beach on Lake Michigan. During the middle 1930s we didn't often have money for extras, but one year I managed to persuade Mother that all I wanted for my birthday was a bathing suit. The day I got the suit, I insisted on going to the lake for swimming, even though I knew my parents were both tired and would rather stay home.

Having listened to my pleading all during supper, they finally gave in and took the whole family to the lake so I could wear my new bathing suit. After playing in the water a few minutes, I suddenly realized that it wasn't much fun—seeing how tired they were and knowing I had added to their burden by insisting on my selfish way.

Our family lived in Zion, Illinois. We were part of an independent religious organization known as the Christian Catholic Church. The founder of the church was also the founder of the city, and most of the people living there had the same religious convictions. One of the basic beliefs was faith healing by laying on of hands. We never visited a doctor; in fact, there was none in the city. We strictly followed the moral code of no smoking, drinking, dancing, movies, etc. No business places were allowed open on Sunday. Church services took up most of the Sundays, with Sunday school from 9:30 to 11:30 in the morning and worship from 3:00 to 6:00 in the afternoon. Our total life was religiously oriented, since schools and businesses (bakery, candy factory, printing house, radio station, curtain factory, bank, stores, etc.) were owned by the church. I attended parochial school from preschool through grade four.

"The Passion Play" was organized and produced by members of our church and was given each Sunday afternoon for three months every year. It was considered an honor to have a part in the play and I felt quite grown up when given a part (I was a member of the crowd scenes).

I don't recall that we had many family rules when I was a child. I was the second oldest in a family of seven children, so I was expected to help with the household chores as well as with the care of the younger children. Chores were assigned on a rotation basis to those old enough to do them: washing dishes, getting milk from a neighbor, making beds, dusting, etc.

Two of my brothers had paper routes, and I frequently filled in as a "sub." We often trudged the route, several miles, after dark on the coldest winter evenings. I complained a lot, and often threatened to refuse to help, but secretly I liked the feeling of being needed.

My parents didn't seem to worry about us or question our activities. Rather, they always expected us to do the right thing and not get into trouble. We never wanted to disappoint this trust, so perhaps trust is one of the greatest things that parents can give their children.

One of the best qualities Mom and Dad have is to listen to and be interested in young people. My friends were always happy to have Dad join our group as we played, knowing that he added to the fun and enjoyed being with us. We had simple pleasures: playing checkers, playing the old windup phonograph, playing paper dolls with the girls, playing hide and seek outdoors, listening to the radio. There has been no generation gap in our family: even now, the grandchildren want to play with Grandpa.

Whether or not to go to Sunday school and church services on Sundays was never a question. The whole family went, and parents as well as children were involved in church activities. Religion wasn't just "woman's business." Dad was always the religious leader in our house. It was important for boys as well as girls, men as well as women. Family devotions were taken for granted, with children participating by taking turns at reading the Bible chapters, and all praying in turn, beginning with the oldest and going to the youngest. My religious commitment came naturally to me, over a period of time. There never was a sudden awakening, but rather a gradual awareness of the love of God and of my need for it.

Our family then left Zion and moved to Monroe, Wisconsin, to a rural environment. There I felt quite lost for a long time. Gone was the secure feeling that everyone else believed as I did. During my high school years we went to a small United Brethren church, where few young people were active. It seemed to me that now I was "different" from others in school, and this was *not* a pleasant feeling. Since we lived on a farm several miles from town, we didn't participate in many extra-curricular activities after school. The friends I had, thought it queer that I didn't attend dances, know how to play cards, etc. I clung to my beliefs, but didn't attempt to share them, for fear of being laughed at.

I found the thought of dating quite frightening. I was afraid I wouldn't be asked, and afraid that if I were asked, I'd be expected to do things I didn't wish to do. As it turned out, I didn't date until after high school, but those were still very anxious days. Should I refuse a date, or go out and possibly compromise a religious conviction? I wasn't a strong enough Christian not to mind the social stigma of "being different." If others sensed that I was a Christian, I was completely unaware of it.* Many times I agonized over the experience of "denying," what I believed. I often withdrew when I felt that a situation would require a commitment I didn't care to make. Many times I wished I weren't a Christian, since it was painful not to be part of the crowd. My immature faith greatly needed strengthening.

After graduation it was a joy and relief to me to find there *were* others in the community who were Christian. Also, I gradually changed my thinking to the positive side of Christianity, rather than living by the "don'ts." During this late-teen period I found the "larger Christian community" and learned that we were all one in Christ, even though we might have differences in beliefs.

But to return to the way things were among us seven children. We were seldom left with baby-sitters. We either went on outings as a family group, or on rare occasions stayed home with the two oldest in charge while our parents were gone. We could always count on the folks to help invent fun things to do. On many evenings during cold Wisconsin winters, all the neighborhood children would come to our house for their turn at riding on a long sled that was tied behind our car and then slowly pulled across vacant lots at the edge of town.

As a child I needed time away from organized play, time to be alone to think, dream, and learn to feel comfortable with myself. Some of my happiest memories are of long summer afternoons spent under a tree in a field, with a book and a peanut butter sandwich. Mom never insisted on knowing what I had done all afternoon, as long as I had first taken care of my duties at home. I read all the novels by Grace Livingston Hill that I could find, some several times. Other books were mostly romantic novels. Most girls as preteens seem to live in a romantic dream world. Since Mother was afraid that so much reading would weaken my already poor eyes, she finally had to limit my library books to four a week.

Members of large families get used to being teased, but Mom always seemed to understand when it was important to our

---

*The editor of this volume, a high school classmate, *did* recognize this.—*Ed.*

pride not to be. When I had just received my driver's license, I was proudly backing the car out of the garage one day and turned the wheel too sharply. The front bumper caught on the side of the garage door and pulled part of the door loose. Seeing how bad I felt, Mom finished backing the car out, and later when someone asked what had happened to the door, she simply didn't tell anybody. I was forever grateful to her for saving me from much teasing about my driving ability.

Praise is important to children—not praise for everything done, but special praise given for special efforts. A gentle word from Mom like "Done with dishes already? That's good," or "The lawn looks nice since you mowed it," or "You were a big help in weeding the garden—you must be tired now," made a youngster feel appreciated. I remember feeling very important when I was asked to stay home from school to help cook for large threshing or shredding crews. I loved to feel that I was contributing to the family's needs. And family ties are often strengthened by emergencies or sudden needs that arise. During World War II we all helped by taking care of a big garden, gathering milkweed pods for use in flotation gear, and accepting shortages in gas, rubber, etc., without complaint.

The lesson of helping others, reaching out to share burdens, was one we learned by example. In a small rural area it perhaps was easier to offer help and sympathy to neighbors. I always remember families and neighbors helping each other in any emergency. Many times we helped with farm chores, offered food, or just spoke words of encouragement. Once when a neighbor woman (the mother of several children) died, my mother took food to the house and offered to have the children stay with us for a while. During the 1930s many men, out of work, traveled around the countryside seeking employment or food to keep alive. No one was ever turned away hungry from our house. We always had bread, cheese, milk to share.

As in all families, we had disagreements, misunderstandings, quarrels. Many times a sense of humor was the key to overcoming these things. On the whole our family life was happy, and as a parent, I have followed many of the same ways of raising my own child. I believe that a family grounded in Christian faith will always be able to accept and love all family members, regardless of shortcomings, and will remain close to each other. "Faith, hope, love—but the greatest of these is love" (1 Corinthians 13:13).

19
Donald Heinz

*Donald Heinz is currently completing his
Ph.D. in the area of religion and society at the
Graduate Theological Union (Berkeley) and
enjoying life in the Bay Area with his family.
He anticipates a teaching career or some sim-
ilar ministry in the church.*

I grew up in Dubuque, Iowa, in the '40s and '50s. The boundaries and horizons of my life weren't Tom Sawyer's Mississippi
River and irresistible islands and caves, but those ancient
strongholds—family and church. I was the third born of two
boys and two girls, all four years apart. My father endlessly
tried to convince us that we were our own best friends and ideal
playmates. In his mind, no utopian playground existed quite
like our own backyard.

Church was four blocks away, the place where almost all the
adults I knew gathered on Sundays, the focus of our family's
outside activities. We sang and prayed there, heard the choir,
and ingested strong sermons about God and Lutherans. (Along
with a short-lived parochial school, church eventually included
a two-year obligation to do my stuff in confirmation class three
times a week in seventh and eighth grades.) It wasn't at all a
forbidding place, but one where (as at home) we learned that
God loves us and who we were. Acceptance and identity are no
small gifts.

When I was a little boy my father often took me for walks on summer evenings after supper. He held my hand very tight, walked much too fast for me, and urged me always to hold my head up high. He told me in many ways that we were Heinzes and should always be proud of it. Twenty years later a speech professor at seminary suggested that some people might take the tilt of my head as suggesting a lack of humility. I never forgave him for that comment.

We rarely had soft drinks in our home. When my father would bring home a six-pack of Pepsi and a giant bag of potato chips, it was a real occasion. We would all gather in the living room, my mother usually by the register where it was warmest, and have a great party. My father would insist on serving us—pouring the Pepsi into the glasses with ice cubes and putting the chips in a nice bowl—never out of the bag. Other times we would have popcorn and large, red, freshly washed apples. I never liked them as well as Pepsi, but I humored my father into thinking I did.

I can't recall eating any evening meal with any member of the family absent. Eating together at this time was a kind of ritual that celebrated the meaning of our family, especially for my father. We always prayed together before and after meals. No one was supposed to touch the food until we'd prayed. We talked about our day at school, what new jokes the coach had told us, what was going on at church, who had called that day, how work was going. There was nothing formal about these evening meals, but I think they must have been important to our family unity and our sense of who we were.

My father was adamant about all of us being present for that meal. We could play away from home during the day, but we were all to be home at supper time. Once my brother was late for supper, after having been in a fight and getting his bike wrecked. When he walked in the door, my father was furious. The rug flew up and my brother flew down, with my father somewhere in the middle.

If my father sounds like an unloving authoritarian, that isn't true at all. He made funny noises in our ears, kissed us extravagantly when we fell down, dried between our toes after baths, tucked us in and said good night innumerable times when we went to bed, almost as though reluctant to leave us. He always came in before he went to bed to see if we were breathing okay. Sometimes we refused to breathe while we knew he was listening to us.

If along with his love, my father taught me discipline, pride, and responsibility, my mother provided that softness and steady accessibility that all children need. She was a Hannah, continually bringing us before the Lord. She could tell us endless nursery rhymes, march around the room with us to music on the radio, welcome us home from school each day as if it was a big occasion, give us the spoon to lick when she was baking, take us on her lap. She held us and herself together while my father was away in Italy in World War II. (He was drafted as a man of thirty-five, the father of four.)

Mother was a strong, independent woman. Although certain kinds of decisions were my father's to make—how money was spent, how much freedom we children were allowed—just as many directions were set by my mother's will. She guarded the course my brother and I set out on when we decided to leave home after eighth grade and begin preministerial training at a Lutheran high school and college 200 miles away. My father at first was inclined to lament both of us leaving home and neither entering his grocery business. But my mother stood firm and eventually went to work to help pay expenses. She always made more pajamas for Lutheran World Relief, sewed more carpet rags for Ladies' Aid, taught Sunday school more often, and served in Lutheran Women's Missionary League longer than my father was ready to grant she should. She was generous and a burden-bearer for many. Her commitment to the church knew no bounds. She also never forgot to provide me with a weekly and tremendously welcome small check for spending money while I was away at school and even one summer after high school when I went to California. I never would have asked her for this.

My father was also active in the church. He served as elder year after year. Some of my most self-defining experiences are connected with the church, the other pole of our lives. I recall the Thanksgiving when we didn't have a car. Fortunate to have a lovely early Iowa snow, we loaded our three boxes of food and clothing for Lutheran World Relief onto a sled and pulled it the four blocks to church. I vaguely recall my parents arguing most of the way about our being so late (the ushers would carry everything to the front when we got there), but mostly I remember the excitement of this family project. My mother recently reminded me that the chief argument was over my father's insistence that we take back streets and alleys. Heinzes shouldn't be seen by the whole community bedraggedly pulling a sled to church.

The pastor was almost like a member of the family. He was a rather stern individual and I was mostly afraid of him. Still, he stopped by often and was a close friend to my parents. I recall my mother occasionally lamenting that some waspish tongues in the congregation accused our family of trying to get in good with the minister. Those were the days when people still wanted to, I guess. When the pastor was over in the evening, he would always have a glass of beer, ask for a salt shaker, and then pour a little into his beer—a practice that never ceased to attract our curiosity and comments after he left.

Only when I think about it now and look around me does our devotion to the church seem unusual. Suddenly my family life sounds like those good old days I sometimes tell Christians today about, when they wonder why the church isn't the force in people's lives it once was.

When I was about ten my mother succeeded in inaugurating what was to become a permanent practice of family devotions. There was nothing original about these every-night-after-supper events, but somehow they too were reminders of who we were. We all took turns reading.

As I look back on my upbringing now, in view of the concerns my wife and I express as we raise our family, I am amazed at the "significant" things my parents apparently did wrong. Sex education was nonexistent. I remember my desperate quest to get to the bottom of the baby question. This included sneaking into our Fibber McGee closet to root for a *Life* magazine photo essay on birth that my parents had hidden away. My father also had a quick temper and there was not a little hollering in our house. I recall many parental arguments in front of us children, sometimes lasting for hours, usually about money and hard times. We scarcely ever got allowances, and my father often borrowed them back when he did give us one. I was pretty immature and insecure socially from being relatively secluded, and have had to work hard to overcome that. I suppose the family was sometimes a retreat for me from new friends or sports. Yet that all seems relatively unimportant now.

I remember when my mother slapped my face in second grade, the only time ever I think, for telling her to shut up when she reminded me to hook the gate as I left for school. I remember them both standing unwaveringly on certain family rules and principles. Certainly one ingredient in that family atmosphere was respect. Certain kinds of language were unacceptable. Certain tones of voice brought an immediate "Don't speak to your mother like that" or a "Here, here!" if we were berating our brothers or sisters.

Mostly I recall a feeling of security, and emotional warmth in our "interpersonal relations" in the family. Lots of singing, lots of verbalizations of feelings (before people wrote books about the necessity of that), lots of physical contact: kisses, hugs, lap-sitting, handshakes, and embraces—when I thought I was too old for kisses. "Go to your room" was a command I never heard, though spankings were certainly not unknown. We weren't a family where parents and children separated after the evening meal to leave each other in peace, except, of course, when we went out to play. We were a lot of sunshine for each other, I think. And evensong.

Family conferences weren't unusual. My father would call us all together to talk about something important. There were also father-mother conferences, which were a favorite joke among us. My father would come home from work, ask my mother to come down to the basement with him, where they would discuss something important and apparently highly secret. Meanwhile we kids would carefully open the cellar door, sit quietly at the top of the stairs, and listen to the whole thing. My father took all this in good humor, as I remember.

I think we were so secure in our parents' love that to this day we find it easy, natural, and obvious to love them. The expressions of regret, siege, and anger we so often hear expressed about parents, or the upcoming visit of parents, are simply unknown among the three of us (my older brother, an Army chaplain, was killed in Vietnam in 1969). We aren't full of authority hang-ups. I find it normal to respect older people on principle. Apparently my parents left me with few unresolved conflicts in that area to work through. If they were somewhat strict, they never stifled us.

They were interested in what we did and said and were especially affirming of our school lives. When my brother and I would come home from high school, college, and seminary we were welcomed with a certain respect and pride over our preparations for the ministry and the education we were getting. Yet my parents never played up to us, and we never lectured them. We knew the difference between having some superior education and knowledge and the positions we all held in the family.

Part of our family unity was a sense of responsibility we all had for each other and for tasks in the home. None of us escaped a long period of doing the dishes, though I can remember warm summer evenings—the night air irresistible, and the call to hide-and-go-seek unrefusable—when my mother would quietly take my place in putting the dishes away after my big sister and brother had washed and dried them.

My father, too, took his role in family tasks. He always washed the dishes after our big Sunday dinner. He was always involved in setting the table or making the salad for supper. He also added his own touches to housecleaning, usually to his satisfaction alone. Even though we kids fought like cats and dogs, my sister occasionally scalding my brother with hot water while fighting over the dishes and I often pommeling my poor little sister, we learned a love and respect for one another that has lasted. When we get together we often remark at the disintegration of many brother-sister relationships among our relatives and friends and find it inconceivable that this could occur among us.

Today we are scattered around the country, but our strong sense of family identity still exists. We know what we mean to each other. We love to get together and reminisce endlessly about the way things were.

To love and be able to be loved, to be a son of the Church, to be responsible, to have respect, to strive for excellence, to have a little more pride than I need (and too little selflessness), to be secure in the human community and committed to it, to care about life and the human condition and the larger course of mankind: these are the legacies from my parents and from the Church.

As I write I wonder whether I have described a family my two sisters will recognize, whether their portraits would have been different. I wonder whether I have described a family my parents will recognize. I know about the social construction of the human personality. But I also believe that with the birth of each child an ego or soul came into our family which had its own independent and lonely life, but also shaped our life together. One of those souls now selectively remembers "what they did right."

20

Arlene Keller Hatfield

Arlene Keller Hatfield, married and the mother of three small daughters, received her B.S. in elementary education from Iowa State University. She and her husband Larry, an artist, now live in California and are involved in starting a Christian day school.

I spent my first months in an orphanage in a small Illinois community. My mother and father were overseers of a church-related orphanage, so this was where my first experiences occurred. My mother, busy with another daughter (Anna Mary, twenty months old) and other children in the orphanage, nevertheless breast-fed me and gave me the love and attention I needed. In 1946, when my father's alternate service for the military was completed (in that orphanage), our family moved to central Iowa, where I grew up.

We lived with my father's parents on a 200-acre farm owned by them. Our nuclear family of five lived in the "summer house" which was attached to the rest of the house. We ate one meal (the big noon meal) together with Grandpa and Grandma, but ate alone as a family for breakfast and supper. My grandparents moved into this farm home when they married in 1910 and lived sixty-two years together there. I have many fond memories of living in this "extended family" situation.

My grandfather, with a gray-white beard halfway to his waist and his hair cut one length at the neck, was not only a biboveralled farmer but also a Brethren minister (formerly "Old Order River Brethren"). He would sing songs of praise to his Lord while doing his daily chores of slopping the pigs or separating milk and cream in the "separator room." Above the noise of the machinery would come his words, " . . . saved by grace."

While she sat in her favorite rocking chair peeling apples for a pie, Grandma told my two sisters and me stories and poems she had learned by heart as a girl. She wore long dresses, black stockings, high-topped shoes, and always a "prayer veiling" or white cotton covering on her head, in keeping with the tradition of her church. She was a poet herself, a petite woman with a big heart, who always wanted to share with others whatever she had.

Today I feel appreciative of older people, and realize their contributions of experience, wisdom, and maturity, because of my early closeness to godly grandparents. My mother's parents also lived in the community. (They are at present still living there, and have been married seventy-six years.) Five of their twelve children lived close by with their families, so I had a large group of cousins, aunts, and uncles with whom to identify, along with dozens of second and third cousins. I belonged to a close group of people who cared about each other's lives.

Daddy and Mother were open in showing their affection for one another in front of us girls. Many times I remember hearing him say "I love you" as he gave Mother a hug and kiss. He would also tell us, "I married the most wonderful woman in the world." Each of us children was looked upon as an individual given to our parents by God, cherished and special.

My father was strongly influenced by his own Christian family, and as a teenager had committed his life to Christ. He needed brain surgery around this time, and his entire life thereafter was altered because of the effects of the scar tissue. He had great love for God and served Him with his whole body and soul, but he was physically curtailed by recurrent attacks which took long periods of time from which to recover. His desire to serve the Lord was channeled in ways that stronger people often overlooked. He was self-employed as a door-to-door salesman. So when his health permitted he spent time talking to people all over the community in the course of his work. He found many opportunities of sharing his faith in Christ with people, and even started a Bible study group in some homes in which our whole family participated. He had concern for needy people. He conducted a regular service once a month for local county prisoners, who otherwise had no spiritual contact, and also at the county home for the elderly and disabled. He always included our family, so I became part of these ministries. I saw how his love for Christ was worked out in his love and concern for others.

One important quality that Daddy had was a great love of giving. Even though we often didn't have enough money to pay our own bills, he generously gave to the Lord's work and to people in need. This was a conscious choice on his part. He took God at His Word, trusting Him to provide for us as he was seeking first God's kingdom. I remember time after time when these sacrificial gifts of his led the way for the Lord to bless us with specific things we needed. This reality of God at work in our lives was instrumental in strengthening my own faith.

My mother also grew up in a Christian family, though she came to understand her personal need of the Lord and His grace to her as a young woman. Soon after her marriage to my father, Daddy started having convulsions, and she began to understand even more God's perfect plan in bringing them together. With Daddy's increasing physical limitations, Mother found wisdom and courage from the Lord to help him in his life and work, both with the family and the outside community. She helped to bring us children into a closer bond of caring for him and each other in times of physical and financial hardship. Her joyful attitude prevailed throughout all her daily tasks, as she sang hymns and gave thanks to God no matter what the circumstances. She taught me the importance of a singing heart. I marvel at her strength as she encouraged and nursed my father, especially during his last years of increasing failure before he died in 1968 of a malignant brain tumor. I wish now she could have felt more free to share her own emotions and discouragements with her children. I remember only rarely seeing her cry—and how unsettling it was for me. I somehow wasn't expecting her to be so "human."

Mother was very thrift-minded. She sewed almost all of her children's clothes, much of the material coming from prettily decorated cotton feed sacks. She raised a vegetable garden and canned and froze enough to keep us eating all winter long. It was a thing I took for granted.

Each child in our family had chores to do. One of mine was to go out to the cold, dark, corncob bin and shovel corncobs into a basket and bring it into the house to use as fuel for Grandma's cooking stove. It wasn't so cold and dark if I did my job earlier in the day, but if I waited too long, it was a bit scary with the possibility of mice scampering past my feet! We were responsible for cleaning our own rooms as we got older. I remember doing dishes with Anna Mary each evening. I dried, she washed, Mother cleared the food away, and it was a time of visiting and sharing.

With little money, our family enjoyed simple entertainment. We played games together such as Authors, Bible Travel-log, and an old favorite, dominoes. Without a TV, we found active ways to fill our time. We would sing together around the piano, with Anna Mary playing hymns by ear. She, Faithe, and I sang together as a trio for church and even on a local radio program on which Grandpa Keller preached every Sunday. Our parents encouraged us in this, and Mother made us dresses alike. We spent several years singing for others as well as ourselves.

A special event each year for us was Drake University's presentation of Handel's *Messiah*. Our family went, even when we were small. I learned to appreciate the beautiful music and words from the Bible. Those passages are so intimate to me that I appreciate them as old friends each time I hear them.

Daddy loved sports and taught us the enjoyment of running. He played softball and Ping-Pong with us, and I could beat even the boys at school. Reading favorite books was a family recreation too. Going on a picnic with just our family or with friends was also common, even if only to our tree grove or to the neighbor's creek.

Daddy was fascinated with the stars and used a small but powerful Traveller telescope to study constellations. We spent many evenings together under the stars. We even slept outside on hot summer nights. Daddy would share facts he'd been learning about the planets and stars, and we learned to appreciate the Creator of the heavens.

As long as I can remember, our family had devotions together every morning, where we'd read a passage of Scripture and each member of the family would pray. God's "making Daddy better" or giving us enough money to fix the car were direct answers to prayer. We lived in the reality of His working in our lives.

At the age of nine, at an evangelical film, I came to a point in my life where I accepted His grace and love for me. The church my parents belonged to was very Bible-oriented and seriously committed to living totally for the Lord. Our family was so a part of the community of believers that I felt as if the other families and people in the church were as close to me as my relatives. Spiritually we were sisters and brothers in Christ.

In the rural setting it was easy for different members to work together in the fields or gardens, and not only in church service situations. Although I had some good friends at school as a child, my closest friends were in the church. Today I also see the importance of a close-living and working Christian community and am involved in one here in Berkeley, where a growing number of Christian families are renting or buying homes in several inner-city neighborhoods.

Sunday school and later the young people's group helped to reinforce what my family started: a strong emphasis on Bible knowledge and memorization. Each week we were expected to quote some new verse we had learned in front of everyone at Sunday school. We also had Bible quiz teams for teenagers in which we studied a particular book of the Bible and were in competition with other church teams to answer questions. Aunt Ruth, Daddy's sister, coached us and encouraged us to memorize large portions of Scripture. Our teams did well in competition and had opportunity to travel to Pennsylvania and California for national playoffs two different years. This motivated me to hide God's Word in my heart, and I still remember a lot I learned then.

My father knew the Bible very well. He played a game with us children where we would read a verse anywhere in the Bible, and he'd try to tell us in what book it was found. We, of course, didn't do as well when it was our turn.

Private devotions were encouraged by our parents as well as by our church. I don't remember when I first started having them, although I must have been around ten years old.

When I was twelve, our family moved into a house of our own in Dallas Center, Iowa, the closest town, which had a population of around a thousand. This marked a change in my life in a number of ways. I now attended a different school and met new friends. We had been fairly isolated from events other than church, but now I could easily walk to basketball games, friends' homes, the roller skating rink, or bowling alley where young people gathered. My older sister had friends over to our house, and I began to see that life held many more exciting possibilities than I'd dreamed.

I appreciated my parents' willingness, at the expense of others' disapproval, to allow change. In this small rural community, our church tradition had strongly emphasized the Christian's separateness from the world. This included many areas, especially what you wore and the activities you participated in. Taboos which were "worldly" seemed to have the same significance as Christ's direct commands to His followers, although in reality they were founded on a certain religious culture and were important for its perpetuation in the midst of a changing world.

My mother and father allowed us children to break out of many of these traditions. One example was in the area of school activities, especially sports. I was allowed to try out for the girls' basketball team, a very big sport in Iowa. It meant I had to wear shorts and was devoting a great deal of time to practicing and playing a game that wasn't "spiritual." I made the first team for two years, and Daddy came to all the games that he could and cheered me on.

I was about fifteen when I began to date. The boys I went out with were old friends in my small school class of less than forty. We had a lot in common, and my parents knew who they and their parents were. I knew the high standards my parents had, and I truly wanted to be a Christian teenager. They encouraged me to put Christ first even in my friendships with boys. I wanted to do this, but it seemed pretty vague to me a lot of the time when dealing with specific situations and emotions. The biggest thing that always stayed in my mind was the importance of my future marriage partner being a believer too. I looked forward to a marriage for keeps during bad and good times, just like my parents' marriage. Although Mother and Daddy never told me I shouldn't go out with any particular person, I always knew they were praying for me and were concerned. Mother would never go to sleep before I came home, which sometimes would be very late. I knew she was awake and praying as she lay in bed, which certainly had a big influence on me. I'm so thankful for my knowledge at that time that God's will was best, and that He was in charge of my future. I felt I could lean on my parents' faith and prayers for me, even when my own faith was small and circumstances weren't the way I wanted them.

Our biggest tensions arose over dates that conflicted with church activities. For the most part my parents held firm in my attending church services on Sunday and Wednesday evenings. Even though I often disliked this and felt it was unfair, I appreciated their stand. I knew what commitment to the Lord meant to them. It wasn't a convenience thing.

Because my parents, neither one, had had the opportunity to finish high school, they both had a great desire to see us girls do well in school and go into any educational field or vocation we chose. We were greatly encouraged to take studying seriously and to do our best. I had grown up liking to read, as all of our family did. I enjoyed learning very much and found it fairly easy, so I didn't feel any pressure from my parents to do better than I could. My parents preferred I consider our church college in Pennsylvania, but because of the finances they couldn't really make that an alternative for me. They weren't able to help us girls at all financially, but prayed and trusted God to provide for our education.

My two sisters and I all made it through college on scholarships, grants, and working. We all had high regard for our purpose in being in college. We weren't there just because our parents paid out the money and it was "the thing to do." I chose to go to Iowa State University, which was very reasonable financially and close to home (about fifty miles). I still could come home on occasional weekends and holidays. As a college student, I still considered my family very important, knowing they were interested in each area of my life. My appreciation for them has grown from the time I left home for college to the present.

21

Thomas H. Stebbins

Since 1957, Thomas H. Stebbins has been a missionary in Vietnam with The Christian and Missionary Alliance, serving as evangelist and church planter. Most recently, as field chairman, he has directed the work of approximately eighty missionaries there.

I was born the youngest of seven children in the ancient imperial capital of Hue, when Vietnamese emperor Bao-Dai was reigning in the height of his glory.

Mom and Dad, missionaries in Vietnam from 1918 to 1960, were frequently invited to official receptions at the palace. If at all possible, my father would attend these functions as a representative of the Mission, always dressed immaculately with his straw hat, white shoes, and sometimes a cane or umbrella. Tall, bald, and stately, he looked so distinguished that on several occasions he was mistaken for the French Governor General. Of course the little French official was outraged when he learned of the mix-up. And Dad, true to form, had a good chuckle. After all, he was an ambassador, wasn't he? "We are Christ's ambassadors. God is using us to speak to you" (2 Corinthians 5:20, TLB).

During the eight years I lived in Hue I watched many times with deep admiration as the emperor paraded down the main boulevard, carried in his royal sedan chair and flanked on all sides by his highest-ranking mandarins. On one occasion I accompanied Mom and Dad into the palace grounds for an audience with the emperor. Shaking his hand was the most thrilling moment of my boyhood.

Dad was born in New Haven, Connecticut, of old-time Methodist parents. His father drifted from the Lord and separated from his wife when Dad was an eighth grader. Dad quit school and worked at many kinds of jobs to support his mother and two sisters. By 1915 he had become quite successful as an automobile salesman. About this time his mother was told that she was dying of tuberculosis. She attended a camp meeting where Dr. A. B. Simpson, founder of The Christian and Missionary Alliance, prayed for her healing. When she was miraculously healed, the family joined the C and MA, my Dad's faith soared, and he dedicated his life to be a missionary. Though offered a pay raise and promotion as car salesman, he enrolled at the Missionary Training Institute in Nyack, New York, of which Dr. Simpson was also founder and president. Two years later Dad sailed for Vietnam where he was to serve for forty-two years as a pioneer missionary with the Alliance.

Mom was born in Barbados, West Indies, the second of six children, to pioneer Alliance missionaries who founded the Christian Mission there in 1890. Ten thousand West Indians were won to Christ and four thousand baptized, before the family returned permanently to New England for the education of their children. (It was a decision my grandfather regretted the rest of his days: the West Indies work fell into the hands of poor leadership, and his children, except for Mom, drifted away from God.) Mom grew up in New England where her father served pastorates and was dean of the Boston Bible Institute. Early in life she heard God's call to missionary service. Like Dad she studied at the MTI but graduated two years earlier. Then for two years she worked in the South, teaching school and witnessing to blacks, whom she had come to love as a child.

Though Mom and Dad had seen one another at a distance, they met for the first time aboard ship to Vietnam. Together with other missionaries they studied Vietnamese at Danang until 1920, and then were married in South China. They enjoyed a honeymoon sailing back down the Mekong River. Their love for one another, daily expressed through the years, was a marvelous example to me of what a Christian marriage should be. Especially remarkable were their constant efforts to keep their relationship harmonious. If any disagreement arose, it seemed that each outdid the other with earnest apologies.

But my first recollection of our home life was a furlough spent in Boston. I can still see our family of nine—three boys and four girls—sitting around the living room or lying on the floor while Dad read the Bible and led the family in long prayers. Seldom did anyone else read or pray, and I did feel that he could have kept his prayers a bit shorter for the children's sake.

Mom and Dad believed in praying about everything. When any member of the family was ill, Dad anointed that one with oil while the rest of us either laid our hands on the sick one or lifted our hearts in faith together. I don't remember any of us seeing the inside of a hospital, except once when I broke my arm. Every day I saw Dad also reading the Bible alone (he tried to read it through once each year). This I'm sure was the secret of his faith. "Faith cometh by hearing, and hearing by the word of God" (Romans 10:17, KJV). And it was my parents' faith in prayer and in the Word of God that more than anything else undoubtedly influenced my life for right.

Added to Dad's faith was Mom's love. She loved God supremely, she loved everyone she met sincerely, and she loved her children with special sweetness. And somehow she found balance in her love for all. She was faithful in her missionary ministries, yet she never neglected her children. She always had a kiss any time of day for each of us, a story and prayer for each at bedtime. She spent long vigils in prayer for the salvation of each one of us. Mom loved everyone so much, in fact, that she couldn't stand to hear anyone criticized without rallying immediately to that person's defense, enumerating his strong points. One time it exasperated my father. He was telling her at the supper table how much he wished my oldest brother would write a letter home. She promptly began to vindicate their son: "After all, wasn't he terribly busy? And he never was good at expressing himself." As she went on like that, Dad impatiently interrupted: "Mary, if I criticized the devil, you'd find something good to say about him too!" "Why, Irving," she retorted, "the devil does have 'stick-to-itiveness'!"

For me to have been born in a missionary home and to have
spent my first eight years on the mission field was a joyful
experience. I'm not sure which I spoke more fluently as a child,
English or Vietnamese; which food I enjoyed more; or which
people I loved more. My first playmate was Luong, the cook's
adopted daughter, whom the cook's wife bought one day (no
doubt from an unwed mother). When Luong had been brought
home and given a bath, it was discovered that she was cross-
eyed. The cook and his wife begged Mom and Dad to pray to
God for her, that she might be healed and have straight eyes.
Several days later they came into the house shouting, "Look!
Luong's eyes are straight! They're perfectly straight!"

I enjoyed traveling with my parents in their various evangelistic ministries. Dad's faith, coupled with hard work, made him a
successful pioneer in many worthwhile projects. The earliest
one I remember was the building of Vietnam's first house
trailer. He had decided that a trailer would make it possible to
plant many more churches in central Vietnam, for he could take
his wife and youngest son right out into the villages and live
among the people for long, uninterrupted periods. Incidentally,
this firsthand opportunity to see my parents active in their
evangelism had an indirect influence later in my willingness to
obey God's call to serve Him as a missionary in Vietnam.

But to back up a bit, when Dad announced that he was going
to use a trailer, many people (even some missionaries) were
pessimistic: "It won't fit on the French ferries!" "Your Ford
will never have enough power to pull it up the mountains!" And
so on. Dad had already thought of all those problems and set to
work building his trailer. Every day before the workmen com-
menced, he gathered them together for prayer, asking God's
help.

One day one of the workmen, unknown to Dad, deliberately
hammered a rotten piece of wood in a strategic spot. Before the
day was over, that workman accidentally dropped his hammer
right on the rotten wood, breaking it and revealing the deception. And so it was that when the trailer was finally completed to
specifications, Dad crossed the ferries with inches to spare and
drove up to Dalat, the highest mountain in the land. He was
even invited to park the trailer in the palace grounds for a special

reception by the emperor. (It was on that occasion that the emperor shook my hand.) Everywhere we went in the countryside our black Ford and silver trailer were called "the black and white elephants."

Nor will I forget, as we traveled into the interior, watching Mom's love for the people among whom she worked. The Vietnamese have told me that she spoke the language poorly, but that she loved them. That was what endeared her to them. I can still see Dad preaching to a group of interested villagers, while Mom was slipping quietly from person to person, giving the sick her special homemade remedies: turpentine rubs for colds, tea for sore eyes, cheese for boils, olive oil for internal upsets. Thus Dad's messages with Mom's help became "sermons in living color." The love of Christ was illustrated right before the people's eyes.

At the age of six I said good-bye to Luong and left with my parents and older brothers and sisters for the missionary children's school, 5,000 feet above sea level at Dalat. The nine of us squeezed into our tiny '37 Ford for the two days' journey down the coast and up the mountain. When we arrived and crawled one by one out of the car, someone remarked that surely we kids were climbing out one side of the car and in the other. They couldn't imagine how nine people could possibly have traveled that far in such a cramped car. But missionaries spend their whole lives packing and traveling, and Dad was a master at organizing his big family and making us fit into whatever situation we met. Our heartrending childhood sorrow at our parents' departure was short-lived. By the next day we were wrapped up in the multitude of activities and studies with forty or fifty other missionary children.

In the summer of 1941, several months before Pearl Harbor, the Japanese invaded and took Vietnam from the French without on shot being fired. Some missionary families fled from the country while others who stayed behind were interned in concentration camps. With three teenage daughters, Mom and Dad wisely chose to evacuate. A year later at our furlough home in Nyack, Mom led me to Christ.

As World War II dragged on and we were unable to return to Vietnam, Dad was invited by the U. S. government to take a post with the Office of War Information beaming "free world news" by shortwave into Vietnam. Dad packed his family of nine into our '39 Buick and started for the West Coast. About two-thirds of the way across the country the car broke down and required a major overhaul. For several days he had to accommodate us in a motel, feed us in restaurants, and pay for the car repair. When at last we reached the Oakland Bay Bridge to San Francisco, we had only a few pennies left for the toll. Mom found some postage stamps in her purse, and with a chuckle counted out pennies and stamps for the man in the booth. We children were embarrassed to tears. But not Dad. He held his head high and drove off, reminding us that he was *not* a poor missionary; he was an ambassador of the King, a joint heir with Jesus Christ. His rich God wouldn't let us down. When we arrived at our destination, a letter informed Dad that his rich aunt had suddenly died, leaving him several thousand dollars. This optimistic faith in God and confident attitude gave a buoyancy to our home that carried us through many difficult days.

But my father wasn't perfect. During those war years in the homeland I learned that he wasn't very good in handling money, for instance. Having so many mouths to feed, he always seemed to be behind or in debt. "I'd rather spend money for good food than for doctors' bills," he used to say. So we were well-fed, but he never had a dollar in the bank. Indirectly this caused me to resolve early in life that I would never owe any man anything, and would do everything possible to be a better steward with God's money.

Further, Dad made mistakes with my two older brothers during those war years at home. He seldom took time to play with them, to talk "man to man," or to show them much individual attention. He told me later that it was because he'd grown up in a home "with just ladies," his mother and two sisters, and that he didn't know how to relate to his sons the way he could to his daughters. But when my oldest brother enlisted in the Army and fell into sin, and when his next son joined the Merchant Marines and began to show the same waywardness, Dad suddenly woke up and began to spend time with me, his youngest. He took me to baseball games, coached me in tennis almost every day, played croquet with me by the hour. He showed me the need for hard work, honesty, and perseverance: I cut lawns, shoveled snow, caddied at the golf course, delivered newsaapers. And when he demonstrated faith in me, I listened attentively to his counsel and tried to follow his example, working hard to please him.

One day in 1949 Mom and Dad announced that they were planning to return to Vietnam. They gave me a choice of returning with them or going to Hampden DuBose Academy in Florida. Looking at a yearbook of this Christian academy, I chose to stay. Dad took me to the Greyhound bus that would take me away from my parents for five years and stood in the terminal with tears streaming down his cheeks. It was the first time I'd ever seen him weep. I resolved that I would live up to his faith in me and somehow succeed.

Those junior and senior years at the Academy made a man of me. For the first time in my life I was on the honor roll. I read through the Bible, I sang in the male quartet, I lived a consistent Christian life. And during that time, God called me into His service. Word of Life evangelist Jack Wyrtzen was speaking from Ezekiel 22:30: "I sought for a man among them, that should...stand in the gap before me for the land...but I found none." Jack emphasized the need for *men* on the mission field. I was thinking: "Lord, Grandpa and Grandma were missionaries. Aunt Hester was a missionary. Mom and Dad are missionaries. Three of my sisters are missionaries (Harriette in Vietnam, Ruth in Cambodia,* Betty in the Philippines). And Anne (later in Indonesia) and George (Vietnam) are training to be missionaries. Let me stay at home to pray for them and support them." Just then Jack (coincidentally, I'm sure) pointed a finger straight at me and said, "Some of you fellows are sitting there saying, 'Lord, send my sister!' But God is saying, 'I'm looking for a man!' " Right then and there I gave Him my life for missionary service. Dad had always said, "Tom, I hope that one of my sons will be a preacher. But unless

---

*Along with four other missionaries, my sister Ruth and her husband Ed Thompson were later killed by the Vietcong at Banmethuot, during the Tet offensive in 1968. When I phoned the tragic news to my dad, he replied with grief in his voice but faith in his God: "Well, my Ruthie has her martyr's crown."

God calls you, I wouldn't ever want you to be a preacher just to make Dad happy." He and Mom were overjoyed to hear of my new purpose in life.

It was also during those high school days that Dad's faith inspired me to trust God for the miraculous. On one occasion a mother of two students from Atlanta came to visit them and suddenly became seriously ill. That evening we were to have a Bible study which she very much wanted to attend. She believed that God could heal her in time, but where could she find "elders to anoint and pray for her" according to James 5? She asked the leaders at the Academy if there were any Alliance students who could pray for her. John Ellenberger, son of missionaries in Africa, and I were requested to help. "John," I asked, "have you ever prayed for the sick?" "No," he said, "but I've seen my dad do it." We agreed to pray just as we'd seen our dads pray, and surely the Lord would honor her faith if ours wasn't strong enough. That night she was at the study completely well. Our youthful trust in God was greatly encouraged.

Returning to Vietnam, Dad was appointed to Saigon. Because of Vietminh activity in the countryside he wasn't able to travel outside the capital. Obviously plenty of work could be done there, with only one Vietnamese church for the entire population of one and a half million. When Dad announced to this church that he was going to start a second church, its executive committee paid him a visit and begged him not to "split the church" this way. "One church is plenty for the city," they insisted, "and that church should be united, not divided." But Dad believed that God wanted many churches in Saigon. When he replied that a second one would be started in his home, the men were very unhappy with him. And when he requested a national pastor to shepherd the new growing congregation, he was given a pastor "under discipline for becoming involved in politics." Dad encouraged that worker and together they saw the church grow rapidly. When Dad left for furlough five years later, several churches had been planted in the city. The original committee came to the ship just before his departure to offer their apologies. "They just had never seen more than one church in a city," Dad remarked to me later. "You couldn't blame them."

During his last term, Dad had a dream of a large canvas tent being used to preach the gospel up and down the coast of Vietnam. The next day after prayer he sat down and wrote a letter that was sent to hundreds of praying friends: "If anyone would like to donate a tent for our work in Vietnam, please let me know. I believe God can use a tent to the salvation of thousands of souls." This letter fell into the hands of a Methodist lay evangelist whom Dad had never met, but who was retiring from tent evangelism. This man had been asking God what he should do with the tent he'd just bought.

Having completed college, I sailed for Vietnam with my wife Donna (the youngest daughter of Alliance missionaries in the Ivory Coast) and our first child Jennifer. We brought the tent with us for Dad. For three years we had the joy of serving together.

After retiring, Mom and Dad couldn't just sit in rocking chairs. They moved to Maryland where they pioneered the founding of an Alliance church which today is thriving to the glory of God. While visiting in homes there, Mom fell and broke her leg, an injury that ultimately led to her death. On Christmas Eve 1964, she slipped into the presence of her Lord. A letter from her reached me in Hue a few days later: "Tom, I'm going home for Christmas." Seven years later my father joined her. He was found on his knees before an open Bible.

Mom, the loving homemaker; Dad, Christ's faithful ambassador: these two pictures remain uppermost in mind when I think of my parents. And to answer the question, "What did they do right?" I would reply, "They left me an example of faith and love." The seeds of these two graces have borne fruit in me, and in my brother and four sisters who have also chosen to take the gospel into all the world.

22
Dawn Frasieur

Dawn Frasieur and her husband are students at the University of California (she in history, he in ecology). They have recently taken time off from school to work at full-time jobs and to spend a summer in France with a North Africa Mission training program.

We have seven people in our family: my parents and five children, of whom I am oldest. I have one sister, two brothers, and a foster brother who joined us when he was fifteen.

We have lived most of my life in California, although we moved around a great deal. That might have contributed to our closeness as a family: we didn't begin to develop community ties or lasting friendships until we began staying longer in one place, which happened when I was in high school. I am married now, but my family is near—so I can see from a different perspective those forces still working in them that did when I was younger.

It's been hard for me to crystallize what life with my parents was like and what it's meant for me. When I first began to think about "what they did right," their appreciation for us as individuals with different gifts stood out most in my mind.

This was especially true of schoolwork. My sister and I did well academically, enjoying things like memorizing and writing essays. Our two brothers were into writing, acting, art, poetry. They enjoyed creating. All of us were encouraged to learn, to develop good study habits, to do well in school. At the same time, we felt great freedom and lack of pressure because of our parents' refusal to place value judgments on our abilities. They themselves are more study-oriented, for example, yet they accepted the boys' creative gifts with as much praise and encouragement as any academic achievement.

My parents knew how to give praise for more than just measurable achievement, like a good test score. They made an effort genuinely to appreciate less tangible achievements: a picture, a play, even active imaginations, in specific ways. Rather than being content to comment on how pretty or interesting something was, they tried to mention the use of color or words or whatever—which indicated to us that they were actually dealing with what we were producing, not just praising for the sake of praise. This took effort on their part. Specific insights into these creative endeavors did not come naturally to them.

Neither were we pushed beyond our capabilities. They cared enough to be sensitive to what we individually could and couldn't do. Dean, for instance, enjoys history: reading, thinking, and writing plays about it. The schools he attended were usually more interested in factual knowledge of history. Yet my parents understood the disparity between the teachers' expectations and my brother's gifts, and helped him not to be discouraged. They were honest with him about the discrepancy, and they encouraged him in his interests.

This attitude in my mother and father has been good for me. First, it has freed me to love and appreciate my brothers and sister without feeling inferior or superior to them. I can be excited about my sister's interests, even when she excels me in aptitude. I need not be jealous of my brothers' abilities or concerned with placing value judgments on them. For me, part of loving my family means appreciating them as unique human beings (and that includes my parents). The relaxed, noncompetitive atmosphere my mother and father fostered in our family helped free me to love them in this way.

In addition, now that I'm older, I've been able to accept my own limitations more easily and to encourage others who find it difficult to accept themselves. I have found that struggling with worth, self-acceptance, and limitations is common even among Christians. Several times I've been able to share my parents' example of treating differences as "special gifts" with friends who are troubled, feeling they have little to give to other people or to the Lord.

My parents are strictly conservative theologically. They are open and loving in life-style. That openness and love helped them integrate my foster brother into our home when he was already a teenager. It has helped them adjust to children who now have less "Establishment" orientation than they have.

When I was little, my father would tell me stories every night—sometimes fairy tales, but usually stories from the Bible or teachings in fundamentalist doctrine (like creation versus evolution, or "once saved, always saved"). I grew up knowing that Jesus was my Savior, loving Him, grounded in all these doctrines, and dogmatically believing them. I led my brother to the Lord, so I've been told (I can't remember).

When I was in high school I constantly "witnessed" to my best friend (a Catholic), mainly by arguing points of doctrine, like whether you could pray to saints. I was very doctrine-oriented (as are my parents), and I hadn't really worked through what Jesus had done and what it meant for Him to be Lord. Now that I'm beginning to study some theology on my own (and in different ways than my parents have), I'm thankful for always knowing that in my family Jesus was there, part of us. He was someone my parents loved, who was able to meet our needs, as well as someone to whom we were responsible.

My parents created this atmosphere in our home through their words and life-style, rather than through regular family devotions. Those just never seemed to work for us, maybe because we didn't try hard enough until we were too old to develop the habit. Though my parents regretted our lack of this type of regular sharing, we did have times (and still do) when the family was called together to discuss specific problems. These family conferences helped us not only to recognize the presence of Christ and our dependence on Him, but they also contributed to a climate of trust in which we children knew that our parents had confidence in us as persons.

At such conferences—which might take place at any time of

the day or night—my father, who was the usual instigator, would share a particular problem with us. My mother might add her insights, and we then could discuss it together. We would always pray about it, a few of us or all around the circle. Sometimes, especially as we grew older, these get-togethers were uncomfortable. At times we would be involved in something else and were upset at being called away from it to meet with the family. Occasionally we got restless and daydreamed through half of what was said. Rarely did we have an open, sharing discussion to which we all contributed.

I realize now, though, that these meetings did draw us together. When there were financial problems, we knew about them, though we weren't necessarily told every detail. We might need money for food that week—and our parents trusted us with this information. We were treated as part of a body: all of us were affected by crises, and all of us could help. We knew that they didn't see us as mere recipients of parental decision-making. Yet my parents weren't in favor of the kids getting jobs; we were to focus on doing our best at school.

When other personal crises arose, we could see our parents' faith clearly in these meetings. More than just trying to live our faith individually, and occasionally talking about it together, praying together (even when we didn't feel like it) helped us to share our walk in the Lord as a family. It was also good just to hear ourselves being prayed for by other family members.

My parents, especially my father, also trusted us enough to share weaknesses with us. Dad had problems with his temper, and he called some conferences just to ask our forgiveness for an outburst and to pray together about it. I know that this is how Christ wants us to act: to be open about our sins and to confess them to each other. Sometimes those sessions were embarrassing, but that was probably because we didn't fully understand the place of confession in the Christian life. It has never been easy for *me* to say "I'm sorry" or to acknowledge my wrong attitudes and actions to Dad or to anyone else.

I am learning, though, to be open about my sins and shortcomings with other Christians, including my husband. As I grow in my willingness to ask forgiveness when I have wronged someone, I have my father's example of obedience to what the Lord asks of us.

Because my parents believed the Lord to be so much a part of our family, when they thought it was God's will that something be done—for instance, that we move somewhere—they did it. I remember how much this attitude helped me when I decided to attend the University of California. This school was not their choice (they didn't want me to lose my faith from exposure to "godless learning"). They wanted me to go to Bible school for a few years, or at least to a community college. We were at a low point financially. But when they realized that the university was my choice after I had thought and prayed about it at length, they trusted my discernment of what I should do. They trusted the Lord to work it all out and to provide all I needed. It was difficult, but they helped me through discouraging times by their confidence in me, their faith in the Lord ("He's always taken care of us before; He will now"), and by encouraging me to trust in Him too.

I had a friend in high school who always shared everything with her mom, just as she would have with a girl friend—even what boys she liked. The relationship was good for them, but I remember thinking it was the strangest thing I had ever seen. I just couldn't relate to my mom as that kind of "pal." Yet I did know that I could come and share my vision and plans for our church youth group and she would be as excited as I was. Or I could explain in detail exactly how my friends and I had spent our day and she would listen. Or if I felt like crying, she would let me sit with her and would hold me, and not push me if I didn't feel like telling her why. Now that I'm older and away from home, we can still talk together about important things, including the ways I am working through Scripture. Even when I disagree with some of her theology, she listens and treats me as a responsible person. She trusts my love for the Lord and knows I want to follow Him.

The testings through which my family went were oriented around my father and his strong faith, probably because he was very specific and vocal in his trust in God. My mother's influence tended to be one of loving support and encouragement. She especially tried to help us understand how God had chosen to lead my father. She did so by encouraging us to love Dad and respect him even when we were struggling with his ideas and decisions. She also prayed with us, quietly reminding us (and we needed to be reminded countless times) of all that God had done for us both through my father and in many other ways.

God has chosen to work in a special though not unique way in my father. Dad is a man of great faith. He is much less interested in logically analyzing circumstances than I am, for instance, and is much more oriented toward earnestly seeking God's will through prayer and reading the Word, in every aspect of his life. God has then led him not only through the Scripture and through clear conviction, but also through dreams. For example, twice when my foster brother was younger and struggling with tough emotional problems, he ran away from our home. Both times God revealed to my father in dreams exactly which part of which cities he was in. Twice Dad was able to find him and to encourage him to come back to our family.

What seems to me the most exciting instance of the Lord's special guidance showed both His great power and loving care for His children. Four years ago, when I was a sophomore in college and still at home, my dad had been praying about where we should go for our summer vacation. He had a dream that he believed pertained to it, and decided it meant that we should go back East. We kids were skeptical. A weekend of camping would have been more in keeping with our money situation at the time.

Several times in the days before we left and one last time a few hours before, Dad called my great-aunt in Washington, D.C. He'd been trying to reach her for months, but her mail had been returned, and the phone would ring with no answer. The last time he called, his cousin (her son) answered. He was surprised, because he'd asked that the phone be disconnected and the house had been empty for several months. He was there only that one afternoon to move her things. He told my father that he and his wife had taken his mother to Florida to live with them and invited us to visit. This little incident confirmed my father's remarkable faith that this trip was what God wanted for us. As we left, he was more excited than ever about being in God's will.

When we arrived in Florida, we were informed that my great-aunt had been rapidly deteriorating mentally and had been moved to a rest home. Dad went to visit her that day and she didn't recognize him. She thought she was home in Virginia, and she hardly remembered her family at all. After Dad spent several hours with her, talking to her, reading her the Bible, and praying with her, everything came back to her. Then she was able to have a wonderful talk with him about the Lord, about what she was feeling, and about how she yearned for Christian fellowship (she and my father were the only Christians in that family). When we all visited her later, she knew us immediately and was able to talk and share with us. Before we left Florida, Dad was able to arrange for some pastors to drop in on her so she could have fellowship. She has since died, but never after our visit did she again slip into that withdrawal.

My impression is not with what my father did. His aunt needed someone who would spend time, who knew and loved the Lord as she did. Of course it helped that he was a nephew who was close to her in a human way. Yet God brought them together in such a magnificent way. I won't ever forget how God displayed His sovereignty over human affairs and how much He loved our aunt. My father's faith allowed God to accomplish what He wanted to do.

I know that these experiences of God's special leading aren't repeatable. I don't yet understand them fully. God has not tried my own faith in such major ways. Neither has He chosen to work through "direct revelation" with me. It's an area I'm still uncertain about, though it has forced me to be more open to His working in perhaps unexpected ways in some individuals.

Although Dad's experiences are somewhat different from those of many Christians, his example of living faith in the Lord is something I can hold on to. His honesty with us about the times he doesn't trust God enough has helped me to see him as a human being who sometimes makes mistakes. It also convicts me of my own far greater failures to trust Him. I still struggle with His sovereignty in my life. I still have many problems in growing up and in becoming a disciple of Jesus Christ. Yet I have my parents' example of taking God's power, guidance, and care for our problems seriously. From my two earliest examples of Christians, I have seen how much He will do when He is trusted like that.

23
Jerry D. Albert

*Jerry D. Albert (Ph.D., Iowa State University)
is a biochemist in southern California and a
Fellow of the American Scientific Affiliation.
(The ASA is a 2,000-member professional organization of scientists who are Christians.)*

Almost as early as I can remember, my parents made me aware
of the presence of a Higher Being. An invisible, personal God
listened to and answered my prayer requests, watched over me
to keep me from harm, and was displeased when I was disobedient or otherwise naughty.

The first table prayer they taught me was "Come, Lord
Jesus, be our guest." My mother taught me the bedtime prayer,
"Now I lay me down to sleep," and the song, "Jesus Loves
Me, This I Know," and listened to me pray and sing every night
before sleep. This bedtime routine began when I was about four
years old and continued until I was about eight, after which I
was encouraged to pray on my own.

My own prayers were quite naive. In my preschool and early
elementary school years my special prayers included requests
for particular toys as gifts, such as an electric train and a
bicycle. I regarded God as a powerful magic genie who could
grant wishes or make things happen if I was "good" and asked
sincerely and often enough. My prayers would go something
like a bargaining encounter, with a lot of hope on my part that
God would come through and grant my wish: "If You give me
this, or let me do that, or make that happen . . . then I'll really

believe that You are the greatest God, and I'll always worship You and believe in You." Later, during my preteen years, I had doubts about my faith, especially in times of personal failure, since I mistakenly connected personal successes with faith in God—and wrongly connected God's favor and keeping of His promises with my being "good."

My mother suggested that I pray for help to think clearly before taking examinations, starting in about junior high school. I took her advice and became convinced that prayer always helped me in these tests by putting me in a frame of mind to do my best, while placing my fears and anxieties in God's hands. Under the influence of my parents, I also prayed for restoration to health when I or others I knew were sick.

My mom and dad encouraged me to read God's Word, and at age twelve I began a concerted effort to read the Bible regularly. I was encouraged to attend an instruction class for confirmation with my friends at our neighborhood Lutheran church in Milwaukee, Wisconsin, where I learned the basic doctrines of the Christian faith and teachings of the Bible. I had been baptized shortly before my confirmation at age thirteen, when I publicly committed my life to Jesus Christ. The catechetical doctrines I learned weren't particularly relevant to my life and personal problems as an early teenager, but they did give me an understanding and appreciation of Christianity and Christian theology. Learning these doctrines seemed to bring my faith into sharper focus.

I carried a New Testament with my schoolbooks in my duffle bag while in high school. I tried to read passages in my spare moments, e.g., while waiting for or riding a bus and sometimes while waiting for an athletic contest to begin or for the return ride to my high school. My dad remembers an incident when he entered a locker room after one of my state sectional wrestling matches. He asked one of the boys where he could find me and was told by another boy that I was in front of my locker reading my Bible, on the other side of their lockers. Another boy said to the one who answered my dad that maybe *he* should start reading the Bible, since he had lost his match and I had won mine.

In my freshman year at Occidental College in Los Angeles,

my dad remembers that I had to study very hard to keep up with assignments. He felt that I was afraid I wasn't meant to be a chemist (my declared major) when I started to talk about going into the ministry and asked for advice and direction from Lutheran pastors. One evening I asked him and my mother what they thought I should do. Their response was that I should pray about this decision, and they would also.

A turning point came before the start of my second year at Occidental, when I was forced to stay in bed after injuring my leg while working at a service station. Several days on my back allowed me to think about my purpose in life and my future directions. I asked God to use me in whatever way He wanted, but to give me an indication of what my role in life should be. It seemed that the answer He gave me at the time was to try to do my best in my second year as a chemistry major, and if that attempt didn't go well or if I lost interest, He would show me another direction more clearly.

In the spring of my second year, I was asked to work on an organic chemistry project that extended through the summer. I began to see chemical laboratory work as a feasible career for myself, besides being fun or fulfilling, and not merely as an academic exercise in demonstrating some chemical fact or principle. At some point in my last two years of college, as scholarships and awards in chemistry came my way and I became active in student chemistry groups, my dad remembers that I told him I thought God wanted me to be a chemist, since everything seemed to be working out toward that end in my favor. "Whatever you do, do all to the glory of God" (I Corinthians 10:31). Those words of Paul inspired me and helped me to realize that I didn't have to preach and lead people in worship to be fulfilling my service to God.

I was concerned to find a wife who shared my Christian faith. I wanted us to serve our God together in the same church, as well as to be able to work out problems of marriage (and later of family) in a Christian context and with Christian resources and insights. Judy and I met after a church service, shortly before I had to return to graduate school at Iowa State University to begin my second year. We got to know each other a few months later at a New Year's Eve party at the same church while I was home for the holidays. We continued to correspond during the winter and spring quarters. Then we were together almost every day while I was home in June, and when she visited me in Iowa before and after her sister's wedding in August. In the fall our correspondence was frequent, and we decided to get married when I came home for the December holidays.

My parents taught me another principle that has helped me cope with the world: to strive to do my best or to make the best out of every situation. I remember an incident from my model airplane building days that made an impression on me. I was anticipating my satisfaction and pride in completing my best model ever, when I ran into trouble putting on the final touches. As I tried to place the insignia decals on the wings, they slipped around in my inexperienced fingers, tore easily, and folded under. I became frustrated and was about to give up in disgust over my failure to complete this "perfect" model. But my mom, who was working in the same room, heard my cries of despair and came to the rescue, calmly showing me how to patch up the messed-up decals to make them look as if nothing wrong had happened and encouraging me something like this:"Always try to do your best. But if something goes wrong, make the best of it that you can. Don't give up. You can't expect to do everything perfectly."

My parents encouraged me with their praise to do my best in school. My dad also inspired me with his pep talks to do my best in sports. Thoughts of his athletic prowess, along with my own keen competitiveness and desire to win, motivated me. Although it was difficult for me to accept defeat, my parents also put much effort into teaching me to be a good sport in losing. Gradually I came to realize that joy in competition could come from putting forth my best efforts in participating and enjoying the contest itself, the outcome of which might or might not be victory for me. (My seven-year-old daughter is going through the same stage I once did, considering that winning is the only purpose in playing a game, and that joy comes only when you win.)

My parents have also given me the provision of physical needs, always a place to call home, and the security of being part of a family no matter what.

24
Margery B. Berney

Margery Ann Black Berney is a sixth-generation Californian (her ancestors arrived by covered wagon from Illinois to homestead in pre-Gold Rush days). Credentialed to teach secondary physical education, she, her husband, and two daughters are themselves now relocating from the Berkeley area to a new world, southern California.

I'm doing something now that I've prayed for and dreamed of for ten years: I'm leading a neighborhood Bible study. It has come into existence after many small steps of faith in the lives of my neighbors over the years. Yet these steps have brought openness and response to Christ, and at the same time trust of me and my words about Him.

My husband and I live in my childhood home. I have had many grand thoughts of what Christ could do in this integrated and multinational neighborhood in which I grew up—if my faith and my neighbors' response to Him were to grow. Our studies have been times of genuine interaction. We learned that Jesus Christ is the friend of social outcasts, a category into which we all fit to some extent. He changes our condition: He mollifies our alienation and we become different people in His power. My neighbors are hungry for Him and enthusiastic about Him.*

---

*Once they were committed to the study—that is, after five weeks or so—I loaned each member my copy of Gladys Hunt's *It's Alive–the Dynamics of Small Group Studies* (Wheaton, Ill: Harold Shaw Publishers, 1971). It gave each one personal vision for what could happen in a neighborhood Bible study of this sort.

This story really begins for me with the accidental death of my handsome, tall father when I was eleven months old. My sisters were four and five years old. We grew up as a family of women; even our dog was female.

Mother taught school for our livelihood, so we had a stable home with a regularity of schedule that I now admire in my mother. Our day was like this: hot cereal at seven, cheese sandwiches with half an apple and a spiced cupcake for lunch, supper at six—with dishes done after every meal. Every week we washed and did yard work on Saturday, and ironed and made cupcakes for lunches on Sunday afternoon.

Breaks came at Christmas, Easter, and summer, the latter two the best. We climbed nearby Mount Tamalpais at Easter and went camping in the Sierra Nevada mountains in the summer. In some ways the school year was to be "endured," while family growth came during the breaks, when we could relate to and enjoy each other without a schedule. Mother loved roughing it. In college she backpacked by herself into virgin areas of the Sierra and ten years later she began taking my older sisters car-camping in Yosemite. She took us when we were babies, right on through to the time we were in college.

I recall many facets of our summers with joy; for example, our early afternoon "rest periods" when Mother would read through novels such as *The Yearling* and *Lassie Come Home*. After rest time we always went swimming. It was a treat to get ice cream cones (five cents per scoop) on late Sunday afternoons. We had no refrigeration.

To be out in the mountains provided time for the necessary healing in my relationship to my mother that the school year tore down. There, she was available to us. In the unhurried atmosphere she was able to show her appreciation of us and to share her love of nature. We swam, hiked, and backpacked in the mountain air and sun. I remember how relaxed she was, with no commitments other than her family. She smiled more. She sang fun camp songs and taught them to us. Around campfires at night with camping neighbors, we played word games. Mother was a cheerful presence at these gatherings and often initiated the fun.

There was time, too, for the one-to-one conversations that

every child desires to have with parents. Mother shared her desires and joys and listened to each of ours. Those were days to enjoy one another and our surroundings. As a result my own pleasure in life received a good shot in the arm during our summers.

Mother enjoyed life and was fiercely independent. We girls had needs, but they were never discussed. She had ideas of what she wanted us to be. No man measured up to our father, so she raised us by herself.

The joy of the present is that my sisters and I are strong believers in the Lord. My second sister is a translator with Wycliffe Bible Translators in Peru. My oldest sister is the mother of six children in Pennsylvania. I am the wife of a man who has served for thirteen years on the staff of the Inter-Varsity Christian Fellowship. Yet our background belies this depth of commitment, except for the working of God through a number of individuals as we came in touch with them.

Our home church was by and large not spiritually alive: belief seemed nominal, though a few older women were believers. The gospel was partially preached, with the "unpleasant side" ignored (sin and the need for personal salvation). Although Mother took us faithfully to this church, its influence in our daily lives was minimal.

What brought about the change in us? As I look back, the Lord's special interest in our family seems obvious all through my growing-up years. Scripture teaches that God takes a special interest in widows, orphans, and the foreigner. So though those years were fraught with setbacks and bad choices that still affect me somewhat, God was seeking me.

Child Evangelism Fellowship had an initial and very large role in directing all of us. Mother knew the woman who taught the class my older sisters attended. To get to my class (in the fall of third grade) I had to take a bus from school that didn't go in the direction of my home. It was a long walk home afterward and I remember a couple of times when I arrived at dusk.

The first time I heard the gospel, my heart responded. I was needy and I knew it. The teacher was loving and maternal. She was young and soft-spoken. I was attracted to her demeanor even more than to her message. She served wrapped caramels in a little dish as we left, and that too was appealing to an eager, hungry, weary seven-year-old.

Three years later, when I was ten, a neighbor one block from my home ran a Child Evangelism class. Again I overtly responded, though I knew in my heart that I wasn't "saved." This neighbor then wanted me to take a copy of the Gospel of John and read it. I wasn't a very fast reader—I was poorly motivated to read anything of any length—and I thought the Bible would be difficult and therefore uninteresting. No one shared any excitement with me about its contents. Why should I read it just because I was asked to? Obviously my "commitment to Christ" didn't go very deep.

In grammar school I sensed lack of social acceptance from some children. Yet I freely shared my desire for a father with the fathers of my school friends and others. Their reactions varied: some genuinely cared, others used this information to exploit me. Home was a retreat in some ways. There I was accepted for who I was, but I was really lonely—a loneliness that stemmed from certain hours of "regular neglect." I was alone after school from 3:00 to 4:30, and after 7:30 on many nights. My mother had many evening meetings that she attended: church, lodge, and later D.A.R. functions. My older sisters were baby-sitting other children away from home as I approached the age of ten.

When I was eleven, my mother permitted me to attend our Child Evangelism neighbor's church, so I was immersed in a very conservative Christian culture on Sundays. Yet I seemed to take my code of ethics from my home. The church stressed "No movies, drinking, smoking, or dancing." My mother's ethic agreed in the no smoking and drinking but diverged in the blanket prohibitions of movies and dancing. The church also emphasized attendance and Scripture memory, and I participated fully in these two expectations.

Later this neighbor took me and three other teenage girls and a boy to a Mount Hermon Baptist conference for a week of greater exposure to her teaching from the Word. One experience in particular showed how she cared for me. The girls and boy had gone off one afternoon leaving me alone. I was used to that from my older sisters, so even though I felt alone it wasn't too painful. Our hostess had come back and had seen me watching my friends bantering together happily down the hill from our cabin. She noticed my resignation and my reluctance to join them. Later that day she called the girls in and told them how unkind it was to have done that. I had never before had anyone feel my loneliness to such an extent. The girls each came to me personally and apologized for "skipping out."

The next day she talked to us about God's love in the Cross. She explained how He was able to forgive even our secret sins, and I responded in my need. Today I feel that Child Evangelism Fellowship is still a winsome, loving witness to many young lives in our community and is having keen influence. The exposure I received at an early age caused me to be open to Christianity as I grew up.

When I was in high school my big sisters got me to change from the Baptist to the Presbyterian church. I went to a large church in Berkeley and participated in Sunday morning classes. I also went to a retreat with this church's teen group but never felt accepted by them. My feelings of inadequacy remained strong. Here were guys and gals who seemed to me to be able to relate socially to one another, but nobody knew quite how to include me. I was frightened by the money they represented. They had such nice clothes and some went to private schools.

At that retreat I didn't feel that any one person was a real friend. Some of the girls at times tried to include me, but all I saw were cliques that said, "Do not enter into our relationships to any significant extent." After the retreat a Scottish fellow seemed interested in me, but I rebuffed him and then recoiled inside at being so cruel. I cut off these thoughts though and went on my not-very-merry way. I stopped going to the group.

Yet at that retreat I again responded to the call to commitment by a Young Life-type speaker but doubted whether I could make it stick. I appeared to be a Christian but had no power in my life. I had the jargon and even lived the part, but my weaknesses were blaring.

My mother did nothing to hinder all these Christian influences from outside our family and church. Although a believer from her childhood, she was "asleep" in many ways because of the sickness of our church. A year before she died, I knew for certain that she was alive in Him because we both participated in Bible Study Fellowship. When she studied God's Word, she came alive. It was like water on a dry and thirsty land that then bore beautiful flowers. The seed was in the ground waiting to grow, and the Word of God, backed by His Spirit and the fellowship of His people, ripened the fruit of the Spirit in her. She blossomed with His attributes of love, joy and peace. I was twenty-three when she died.

When we were young, our mother moved too fast to be very affectionate. I went from baby-sitter to all-day nursery school and then to all-day kindergarten. I entered first grade almost a half year earlier then I should have. I was a difficult child and at times they barely coped with me. I ran everywhere I went. I was curious and must have worn out my baby-sitter. When I was four, I repeatedly disobeyed my mother when I was told not to cross our street. I wanted to please her and was very apologetic, but the attraction of the other side caused me to continue this disobedient pattern. She daily spanked me with her hand for this disobedience, and she felt annoyed when I wanted affection from her immediately afterward.

When Mother and my sisters went out at night I went to sleep petrified that someone might break into the house. Even though one of my sisters baby-sat in the corner house from ours, this was small consolation to a child with vivid imagination. (Now, at times of aloneness in my marriage, when my husband travels, I have literally felt the warmth of God's Holy Spirit surrounding me. Satisfaction of my deprived need of affection has come in this way and has set me free to love others.)

Mother's pattern of discipline should be mentioned. She gave up spanking before I was five and only returned to it when really angry or disappointed later on. Her pattern was more one of withdrawal of love. She almost had a master's degree in psychology from Cal, so this was a manipulative pattern to cause us to conform to acceptable patterns of behavior. My home duties were to clean my room and make my bed. I remember many Saturdays sitting in the mess I'd made that week, unwilling to clean up. I frustrated my mother, but I didn't seem to desire to change my procrastinating attitude. I have since learned that manipulative pressure on children when they are young creates a reaction of procrastination as they grow up. My mother's withdrawal of affection when we didn't please her seems to have created patterns in us as adults of resistance to authority on the one hand and an attempt to please for the sake of security on the other. Emotionally we were each driven to God, but it has affected our ability to rest in Him.

While we were growing up, we heard only of our father' virtues. Now God the Father is very holy to me and can seem personally very distant. Again I must say that the Spirit's healing through other human relationships over much time has allowed my sisters and me to grow.

I became a Christian at Campus-by-the-Sea, then IVCF's camp on Catalina Island off the southern California coast. I was seventeen, about to enter college, and my sisters, both Christians by then, talked me into going. At that camp the Lordship of of Christ was burned into my being. The Mount Hermon retreat when I was thirteen had taught me that Jesus was Savior, but this camp allowed me to know Him as Lord.

In the following years I was involved in IVCF camping to the hilt. At camp I received short newsy letters from my mother once a week, but I rarely answered. I really didn't know if she wanted to hear what I was learning and experiencing. Perhaps I would have been "hard put" to communicate it to her. I am a freer spirit in the Lord now. My spontaneity as a youngster is still with me but is tempered (I hope) by growing emotional maturity made possible because of Him.

I married at the age of twenty. My husband is full of faith and wisdom. We have two little girls and I am trying to love them as fully as I can. I am home—and choose to be nowhere else. I am a more direct authority figure than my mother ever was. I discipline my children when they require it and let them know the reason. I also hold them close immediately afterward, to be reconciled with them and to reassure them that the discipline is over.

The four of us are moving from my childhood home this year, and the Bible study with the neighbors reflects my desire to leave the Lord Jesus in their lives. We are a small group. Not all whom I invited have come, but I've been around long enough to know that that's often how it is in the Lord's vineyard. Small steps, slow progress, but reality and joy.

25

James E. Berney

James E. Berney has worked with Inter-Varsity Christian Fellowship for thirteen years in the San Francisco Bay area. He, his wife Margery, and their two adopted daughters, Christine, 8, and Sara, 2, plan soon to make their home in the Los Angeles area, continuing to be involved with IVCF.

During the summer of 1973, I spent a week at Inter-Varsity's summer training at Nyack, New York. There I led a discussion group with eight students about their relationships to their parents. Incredible problems surfaced.

One student had come without her parents' blessing; she cried about leaving home without the sense of their care. One fellow told about never having a serious conversation with his father without hearing, "Here's some money. Hope this takes care of your needs." Another young woman talked about the conflict of living with one parent, yet finding more love from the other separated one. She expressed great concern for her younger brother who was more emotionally caught in the division than she was.

As I listened to their problems and the feelings expressed, I realized that Jesus Christ was the common factor who enabled these students to function in a practical, concerned way for their parents. In a productive and loving manner, they were handling problems far beyond my personal experience.

I grew up in a stable, rural home, the product of a Christian heritage on both sides. Mother's parents were in the Methodist pastorate for some fifty years, and both were godly people who prayed daily for their children and grandchildren. Grandfather had churches in small towns in Montana and Wyoming, and in spite of a large family saw to it that all received a good education and opportunity for personal advancement. I didn't know these grandparents very well. Much of my Methodist heritage never came through to me, first because of the distance factor, and second because my mother was never able to bring its special influence to bear on our family.

Methodist ethics, such as honesty, integrity, cleanliness, and discipline, fitted right in with my father's background, although the church backgrounds of my parents were greatly opposed in ecclesiastical practice. One had pastors and the other didn't. Since my present vocation with Inter-Varsity Christian Fellowship has caused me to appreciate other church traditions, I deeply regret not knowing these grandparents better. I wish I understood more of their joys and disappointments in life in relation to their vocation.

My father traces his Christian heritage back to Switzerland, where his grandfather became a Christian through the evangelistic efforts of John Nelson Darby, one of the founders of a Christian movement called the Plymouth Brethren. Grandfather Berney settled in the farming village of Springdale some twenty miles east of Portland, Oregon, because of the vigorous Brethren assembly there. Brethrenism was a reaction in early nineteenth-century England to the coldness in the Anglican Church, and Darby was asked to leave the priesthood because of his evangelistic zeal.

The mainstream of this movement has always been merchants or professional people, which in turn has given it a social stability that allows its "priesthood of all believers" ideal to function vigorously without professional clergy. These two factors, family social stability and corporate church responsibility, have led to development around the world of a multitude of outstandingly gifted Brethren leaders over the past 150 years. Through the assembly in Springdale this developmental process began to take shape in the lives of my younger brother, sister, and myself.

As children our contact with itinerant Christian preachers and missionaries was broad. These preachers and missionaries stayed in our home because it was large enough to host families overnight. Nonetheless, church meetings bored me and I never could understand why anyone felt any interest in participating. My cousin and I would sit in meetings snickering quietly. We nudged each other in the ribs whenever the older men would publicly "Amen" to show their approval of some point the speaker had made. Their behavior amused us greatly.

Some people, however, caused all of us to respect their Christianity, especially the Fred Elliot family of Portland. Mrs. Elliot was my father's first cousin, and their four children all involved themselves in Christian service. "Uncle Fred" was an itinerant Brethren preacher and "Aunt Clara" was a doctor. The Elliots combined great fun and interest in people and things with a practice of Christian faith that continually amazed me (and still does to this day). As I was growing up, our families had constant contact. They seemed to me to be guarantors that real Christianity could be enacted in this life.

I remember the day I sat at breakfast as a freshman at Oregon State and read that some missionaries were missing in Ecuador. I felt at the time that one of them was probably Jim Elliot, the family's youngest son. My assumption was true: he was one of the missionaries martyred by Aucas in Ecuador in early 1956. (Jim Elliot's story is told in two books, *Through Gates of Splendor* and *Shadow of the Almighty,* by his wife Elisabeth Elliot.)

A sense of lostness came over all of us. Yet at no time was there outward despair. We all realized the tremendous commitment that Jim had to Jesus Christ. His ending seemed consistent with his whole life-style.

I realize now that a more subtle thing happened to us all. Some of us subconsciously shrank back from total commitment to Christ. We carried on as before in our Christian practice, but we hoped that one young sacrifice to the spread of Christianity was enough. When one of my cousins became serious about following Christ, it provoked a subtle reaction from some other family members about getting too fanatic. I realize that I have certain fears about this yet, and I believe my parents have had some anxiety about my own vocation.

My background therefore was one that in many ways had the best of both worlds. One was farm life at home with my parents most of the time, which gave tremendous stability for family growth. The other was contact through people with much of the world, which gave us a cultural vision greater than most rural families had.

As I look back on my upbringing I see that my parents attempted to combine two aspects of rearing us that are hard to hold in tension. The first was loving concern for their children. The second was allowing each child to grow up as a separate and genuine person without dominating him or her. Granted that my parents sometimes failed, as I do now with our two girls, they still function even today as a loving but hands-off model.

Yet they had goals for their children. They wanted us to serve the Lord and be people of integrity, doing good and being reliable. This has down-to-earth application on a farm where animals need to be cared for. Father expected us to do the chores regardless of circumstance. Real sickness was the only valid excuse. Athletic involvement in high school frequently caused us to arrive home after midnight from faraway basketball games, yet Dad expected us to be up early the next morning taking care of our chores before we went to school. We all were part of the team, and each had to carry out his job if the family was to function in harmony.

Along with hard work went lots of fun and good times. We went swimming in a nearby river almost every summer afternoon after the day's work. We spent winter evenings all together with either Mother or Father reading to us from a good book. The eight-book series by Laura Ingalls Wilder (*Little House in the Big Woods*, etc.), describing her family life on the midwestern prairies, was our favorite. A county bookmobile stopped at our farm each week during the summer, and we read practically every book in stock.

Another favorite time was taffy-making. We made a big mess when we pulled it with our fingers, but the results were delicious. Picnic outings were weekly during good weather, to the Oregon ocean beaches or the nearby Cascade mountains.

When I was a senior in high school, Father was ill most of the winter. It was up to my mother, brother, and me to take care of the farm. Practically, it meant taking care of about thirty milk cows. Mother was the one who got us up every morning at six to milk before we went to school. Her management at this time was remarkable, helping us to function during Father's illness.

My realization of how much my parents cared, along with our great times together, gave me a special desire to please them. There was little resentment of our life-style. I do remember one such incident, though. When driving the cows to the barn in a terrible downpour, I vowed I'd never choose to live in a rainy climate. I knew that my father wasn't exactly fond of the rain either, and at that moment, both drenched, we probably affirmed some common bond of not appreciating our lot as we milked.

My parents' patience with us also prevented resentment. As we grew up, my brother and I were full of mischief, lazy, and at times uncooperative. Instead of nagging us, Father would remind us in a firm voice of what he had asked us to do. Often he would take the lead in showing us what he wanted done. His example of integrity and hard work meant more to us in the long run than all kinds of exhortation.

Hoeing corn was anathema to us boys. Not only did we lack ability to see weeds, but we tended to uproot tender young corn plants. But Father never gave up on us and usually got productive work out of us in the long run. Both parents had great faith in God and what they could do with His help in rearing us. I believe this gave them great patience with us. "Love is, first of all, patient" (I Corinthians 13:4).

Looking back, I am impressed with their willingness to give us as many varied experiences as possible. They trusted us into the hands of others, especially relatives, for vacations. We usually spent a couple of weeks each summer with cousins, uncles, and aunts, and were at various times under their leadership. We also were allowed to participate in structured camping programs run by Christian organizations. All of us worked for other people as soon as we were old enough.

Such experiences helped us understand other family situations and what the expectations of others were. These experiences provided a mixture of fun and some rude awakenings. I learned, for instance, that not everyone had my father's pa-

tience in overlooking bad work habits. (One time I was asked
not to return to pick strawberries because I had engaged in a
strawberry-throwing war.) In general these new experiences
were positive and led to a conviction that the world was trust-
worthy.

Similarly, Mother and Father encouraged us and helped us to
make decisions on our own. They respected our individual
decision-making process and would do all they could to help us
on a course that we had decided upon. I remember coming
home from college and telling them that God was leading me to
go to a month-long leadership camp at Campus-by-the-Sea,
which would prepare me to become a better president of the
Oregon State Inter-Varsity chapter. This meant taking a month
at the beginning of summer, which in turn meant that it would be
harder to find a good-paying job during the rest of the summer so
that I could go back to school. The folks felt that it was right for
me to go to CBS and stood with me in my seeking a job.

I then got a job through an uncle in construction in Seattle
—which lasted two weeks. I found I couldn't join the proper
union and that forced the end of it. Although this promising start
ended in frustration, it resulted in my finding a second, better-
paying job in Seattle, related to my engineering skills, which
proved eventually more satisfying.

In the long run my parents' greatest gift to their three children
was allowing us to come to our unique understanding of the
Christian faith. While growing up, I personally had few intellectual doubts about Christianity. My problems were more in the
area of lacking confidence that God accepted me. I remember
strong pulls repeatedly to go forward at evangelistic meetings (I
had initially done so at the age of eight at my first Christian
camp). In retrospect this seems to have been a problem of my
own lack of self-acceptance, rather than of God's acceptance of
me. Brethren theology lays heavy emphasis upon the future,
sudden, and silent Rapture of Christians by Jesus Christ. My
lack of assurance brought on nightmares that Christ had come
and left me behind. Not until I heard a powerful explanation of
justification by faith at Campus-by-the-Sea late in my college
years did this problem start to go away.

IVCF gave me an adequate theology to help me understand

myself and the world around me. This was anchored in a context of loving concern that eventually proved powerful enough to establish in me personally much of the life of Christ that I saw so clearly in the Elliot family. So in the long run it was a group of people outside my family and assembly that significantly contributed to my Christian growth.

This never seemed to threaten my parents, because they had a deep sense that they didn't know everything about Christianity. They needed Jesus Christ and they knew that their children needed His resources too. Regardless of my good background, I needed Jesus Christ just as much as those students I talked with recently at Nyack.

My parents gave me the best foundation they could and then turned me loose to discover my needs. They rejoiced as God answered. For their loving foundation and releasing freedom I am profoundly thankful.

26
Sandi Hedlund

*Sandi Hedlund attended the University of
Washington and Seattle Pacific College,
worked for seven years for Young Life Campaign, and spent over a year traveling around
the world. She is presently on the staff of an
urban Presbyterian Church in California.*

My parents, known as "Mom and Dad" to quite a few more
people than just their own four kids, did a lot right—a lot more
right than wrong. Our home was grounded in love, in tangible
ways that I'll try to recall specifically, but also in an intangible
atmosphere about the place.

We had a big old house in several acres of trees and trails,
with a view I love and can have any time I close my eyes and
dream a bit. The "snow-capped mountains" of the Olympic
peninsula (to quote a phrase that we picked up from an aunt's
prayer and that we kids chanted—"Thank you for the snow-
capped mountains. Amen"—to close our own prayers). . . the
diamond-bright water of Puget Sound, with our little ferry from
Edmonds traveling back and forth . . . the huge trees almost
hiding our house. I know that the best setting is meaningless if
love isn't the aroma that fills the house though. Love has to be
the essence of a home where children can begin to discover and
develop their gifts and become whatever they want.

Discipline was quite strong and definite in our house. With
four children of their own, a nephew, three foster kids who lived

with us for about seven years, and often other foster children for a few weeks or so—plus, of course, all our friends and neighbors—no one would have come out sane without discipline.

Luckily Mom loved kids. I think that people in our non-denominational church vaguely thought of our family as "out in the country somewhere with a big house" and passed all requests for temporary housing for children our way. Temporary sometimes grew into long-term. For the most part, we enjoyed having lots of kids around, boredom was unheard of, and we all got plenty of attention and love from Mom and Dad and each other.

I don't remember my parents' turning many away, but I do remember a couple of boys whose stay was rapidly cut short when they continued jumping from second-story windows after Dad had said to stop. Mom and Dad accepted the fact that we would make mistakes, but to repeat something we'd been corrected on meant we did it on purpose, and disobedience had its consequences. Usually the consequences were of the "to make you stop and think next time" variety—such as helping pay for something we'd ruined, thoroughly cleaning, weeding, or polishing a job poorly done or left undone, or the temporary taking away of a privilege.

We each knew the rules: that we should treat each other with consideration (with kindness, Mom would say), that we should have our weekly chore done by Saturday night (vacuuming, cleaning bathrooms, and dusting for the girls; outside jobs feeding chickens, cutting wood, burning trash for the boys), and we knew there would be trouble if we goofed off.

I think we were more afraid of what Dad might do if we were bad than of anything he actually did. Just the thought of his anger usually brought us into line, but sometimes a spanking hurried us along. The words "I don't want you out riding Patchee for one week" were the most dreaded discipline for me. That pronouncement brought forth more tears and frustration than anything else could have. Patchee was my pinto quarter horse and almost constant companion. If I was late to dinner (my usual problem), it was because I was out riding and oblivious to time. I must admit in fairness to my folks that my sad face and promises to change were usually rewarded with an early reprieve. Maybe from the standpoint of "exact retribution" or the importance of sticking to one's word, the reprieve wasn't valid—but from the standpoint of grace and love, I learned the beauty of forgiveness. Again, the underlying knowledge that we were loved and precious to Mom and Dad made even what might at the time seem unfair discipline or strictness something we could handle.

Our greatest motivation for pleasing Mom and Dad was the amazing amount of trust they bestowed on us. They believed in us. They expected us to act responsibly with the cars, our friends, our bodies, our decisions. To violate that relationship of trust hurt everyone involved. It just wasn't worth it.

I'm not sure when I became aware of the "humanity" of my folks. Probably younger than my brother and sisters, since I was the youngest and had them to tell me all kinds of things. But once I knew that Mom and Dad made mistakes—even still sinned!—my care for them as people, parents or not, began to develop. I'm sure that this has been significant in our relationship now as adults. We are honest with each other, and we are friends. We enjoy being together.

We have always been quite close as a family. I think some of the things that encouraged this were our mealtimes together (even though I was often late), holidays, the sense of humor, puns, etc., that we shared, and the often spur-of-the-moment weekend trips we made to the ocean. With Dad commuting quite a distance to work, and all of us busy with lots of activities and friends, we could have grown apart. When Dad would come home from the office and say, "Let's pack up tonight and leave early tomorrow morning for the ocean," everything but the *early* sounded great. Through these times together, packed into a tent or squeezed into a one-bedroom cabin, we came to know one another's thoughts and dreams. Ideas came into expression easily while we walked on the beach looking for sand dollars or sat around the wood stove trying to warm up and dry out after digging for clams or playing circle tag.

The evening was usually spent singing rounds, laughing, playing games. In the dark, trying to get to sleep, we sometimes heard good stories about Mom and Dad's courtship or Dad's exciting childhood (exciting because so different from our own). In this way we "met" uncles and grandparents we didn't get to know in life, or to know very well.

Insistence on simple gifts for Christmas and birthdays was a wise move on the part of my folks. We didn't lose the value of the birthday of Jesus in the midst of the wrappings quite so much. This was also true with fairly simple birthday celebrations for each of us. The best part of the birthday was choosing the meal and kind of cake, and then everyone's eating it together. Presents were fun or practical for the most part, with creativity sometimes coming to the fore. When we did get large presents from Mom and Dad, such as skis or the horses, it wasn't for a special day, it was a considered decision. What came across to me from this was that these gifts weren't something I deserved, or something to make a day meaningful. They were Mom and Dad's way of sharing what they could financially in what was important to each of us.

I am thankful for the heritage I have from my family. For certain the most important truth they showed me is that God knows and loves me. We had a good base in the gospel, the good news that Jesus died instead of us, that God forgives us in Jesus' name, and that we can come to Him with anything. Dad came from a fundamentalist background, where the truth came through. But the experience of the permeating love of God grew with maturing years in his life. Mom had little background in the church or with Christianity until she met Dad (they worked for the same company). Her understanding of the Lord grew into a deep capacity to give love and comfort. Her favorite Bible verse is, "This is the day the Lord has made. Let us rejoice and be glad in it!" The joy of living day by day, not for the future nor in the past, is a special treasure from her to her kids.

In our "expanded family" we used to spend time together each night in "family devotions." When we were small, all eight or however many kids there were would choose songs, have contests with quiz games, "Bible drills," etc. This was fun, but the best part for me, and I think for most of us, was the continued reading aloud of some story or book by one of the older members. We read different series of books, and the characters and places became almost part of our lives. The boys in *The*

Sugar Creek Gang series gave us lots of laughs, and lessons too. *Pilgrim's Progress* was pretty much over my head, but parts of it made an impression, especially his humanness and struggle against temptation. We also read short stories from Christian magazines that usually gave a contemporary touch.

One especially good series was C. S. Lewis's *The Chronicles of Narnia*. The books appeal to all age levels. Lewis deals with the character of God (His love, guidance, and judgment) and with the nature of man (his sinfulness, disobedience, and repentance). They provide a way for kids to begin to grasp the reality of the unseen world as well as the possibility of meeting life with enthusiasm and confidence because we have a Friend who is with us in pain and joy.

Also in our devotional times as a family, we learned to listen to God's Word as more than just past history, to memorize verses, and to pray. The consistency of these times together over the years, and Dad's belief in the reality of God and the importance of knowing the Bible, encouraged discipline in my Christian growth when I moved away from the family. Even when we were in high school and older, we continued to meet in the evenings to read and pray.

Much of this early training, however, didn't really come together for me until later. I was able to go to a camp run by Young Life, Malibu-in-Canada, where I realized that other people besides my family believed in God. This was an eye-opener that helped me over my "be cool" stage of early puberty. All my family except my brother went to Malibu one summer when I was just out of the seventh grade. I was too young to go as a camper, but I went as a guest with my folks, who had been invited to sit in and observe this teenagers' camp for a week. We also took with us about thirty kids from the high school, friends of Karen and Jan, my sisters.

This time was significant for each of us, Mom and Dad included. The active, freeing, reliable love of Jesus reached right through those in charge: from the speaker, counselors, and staff to the work crew kids and to us. There we also discovered the modern translations of the Bible, Phillips in particular, which enlivened our view of Scripture and the fun of reading it.

For all of us from that point on, Young Life became an

organization we enjoyed and came to know well. Those thirty
kids were the beginning of a weekly Young Life Club meeting in
our home, crowding the house one night a week for the following year with kids listening to a clear presentation of the gospel.
One highlight of high school for me came a couple of years later
when my closest friend became a Christian. Having peers to
pray with and to rely on in the hassle of the average day in high
school was a joy. It also cemented relationships for a lifetime,
and more!

Involvement with Young Life in high school led to greater
participation in the organized church. The church we had attended since we were small had changed a lot with a new
minister who wasn't Christ-centered. We discovered that many
alive, warm Christians we met attended a church in the university area. So Mom and Dad were willing to change churches to
have the family worshiping together in a church that proclaimed
the gospel. This was a healthy change, helping us out of the
teenage-oriented Young Life world into the total family of the
church.

From my home life I've also learned to appreciate the wisdom contained in books. Many days, especially rainy ones, no
one would see me for hours while I read through books in the
den. Dad had bought the complete works of Dickens and
Shakespeare, beautifully bound, plus several other classics,
from an uncle who was in need of money during the Depression.
These, the *Book of Knowledge,* horse stories, mysteries: I had
to know what was between the covers. Mom and Dad encouraged me to read—everywhere but at the table. Once I had my
nose in a book, nothing else seemed real. With books on so
many subjects available at home, my curiosity about a variety of
topics and ideas was aroused. This helped me develop an interest in subjects at school—not enough to have great grades,
but enough to learn something from what I studied.

The "peopleness" of our home, Mom and Dad's respect and
enjoyment of the variety of personalities living together in our
house, have given each of us the desire to stay deeply involved
in peoples' lives. There's no way we can feel satisfied doing a
job where contact with others, involvement in their thoughts
and feelings, doesn't take place. Much of this stems, I'm sure,

from the way I was loved and respected as a unique individual from the time I was small, on through the stubborn years of being a teenager, and into the years of responsibility as an adult.

27

Bernard J. White

Bernard J. White, an Oregonian, has taught in the Midwest for the past ten years, most recently as assistant professor of biochemistry at Iowa State University. He and his wife Linda, who assisted in writing this chapter, have five children.

I would like to introduce you to my parents, a strikingly handsome couple in their seventies, living in their five-bedroom Victorian farmhouse (where I grew up) in the center of Portland, Oregon. They are lean, erect, quick-witted, and continually amazed and amused at the varied life and life-styles surrounding them.

My parents are two of the original ecologists. They were frugal creatures of the earth with a love and appreciation of people, natural things, and the environment—before it was the fashionable thing of the '70s. Through my growing-up years of the '40s and '50s, I learned firsthand lessons of love and loyalty, of "making do," of making decisions and living with consequences, of sharing simple pleasures, and of enjoying the magnificence of God's great earth.

Dad retired nearly ten years ago from his lifetime job with the First National Bank, his last position that of manager of the branch closest to home. In the world of finance all day, he continued the role at home and was the staunch keeper of the books. Many a time it was I who confessed to a department store charge but couldn't produce the sales receipt, or to a long distance phone call that wasn't recorded on the extra sheet he placed in the phone book for that purpose. My brother, sister, and I had before us a shining example, not only of budgeting but of accounting for each and every penny. Responsibility was expected at an early age, in the hope it would become a trait deeply imbedded in our character.

Mother has lived almost seventy years in the same house. Her Irish father was a successful merchant at the turn of the century on the bustling, rapidly growing east side of Portland. He built "our" house on the (then) outskirts of town. Shortly thereafter his wife died, and my mother and her younger sister were sent into the city on the trolley car (a two-mile distance) to St. Mary's Academy boarding school for their education. Under the guidance of the Holy Name sisters, my mother learned self-discipline tempered with service to others, values that were to filter down to her children.

On weekends their little family would reunite, with Grandfather bringing gifts and surprises for the young ladies. There would be outings and parties and a sharing of the lessons of the week. Soon the house was the scene of many youthful gatherings, a place where guests were always welcomed and made to feel comfortable, a tradition maintained today. After a year of college and a tour of Europe my mother succumbed to the charms of the handsome, athletic junior banker, and in January 1929 the two were wed, just months before the stockmarket crash brought the U. S. into the throes of the Depression.

As austerity gripped the nation, the patter of little feet and the chatter of little voices were heard in the big house. My sister Sheila, my brother John, and I (the youngest) were born within four years. Dad, whose former place of employment had closed its doors in 1929 never to open again, was now cashiering at First National. Meanwhile, Mother supervised daily activities—or perhaps "refereed" would be a better description. The orchards Grandfather had planted around the house were slowly becoming a neighborhood and soon on the land across the street stood the public elementary school, bearing his name, Kennedy School.

My parents are complex, interesting individuals, yet their life together has stressed simple, uncomplicated dedication to the needs of others. Both devout Catholics, they believe that God is served by serving others. Knowing and practicing the Catholic faith was an item of highest priority in our home. While most of the neighbors were still asleep on Sunday morning, the "walking Whites" would set out for church. (My parents still walk, but to "accommodate" them, a new church was built only seven blocks away, instead of the twelve blocks we walked.)

Afterward my brother, sister, and I would join other children who attended the public schools for an hour of catechism in the choir loft. There the good sisters explained and drilled us in the beliefs and practices of the faith. I lived in holy fear of these mysterious sisters in the flowing black and white robes, and prayed I wouldn't be called to recite something I didn't know or couldn't understand.

The first major religious event in my life that I recall (I was baptized in the hospital shortly after birth) was my first Communion. All the catechism lessons of the second grade were preparation for this great event, the reception of the body of Christ in the Holy Eucharist. As the time drew near, the religious significance was somewhat obscured in the flurry of selecting the proper white attire and practicing each step with the other class members. The sunny spring Sunday finally arrived. Inwardly shaking with fear and excitement, wearing a white suit with short pants and with palms pressed together, fingers pointing toward "heaven," I approached the altar rail and received my first Holy Communion.

Faith was the mainstay, the source of inner strength and calm to our family, but pious religious practices were more often done individually than together as a family. We were urged when first arising to pray the Morning Offering, a prayer offering the joys and sorrows of the coming day to God. As often as not we forgot the formal grace before meals. From Mother we learned of her day-long prayer, an ever-conscious awareness of God's presence revealed in her one-to-One conversation with Him. She called for His help through the various trials of each day, thanking and praising the risen, glorified Christ for His abundant blessings. Praying the rosary and meditating on the mysteries of our faith was part of our religious practice, but was something we most often did in the privacy of our bedrooms. When we were little, Mother or Dad always participated in the ritual of our night prayers, an examination of conscience, an act of contrition, and prayer of thanksgiving. Later they assumed we said them . . . and sometimes I remembered.

During Lent it was family practice to attend daily mass together, beginning with the distribution of ashes (a smudged cross on the forehead) on Ash Wednesday and continuing for forty days. We were routed out of bed at 6:30 A.M. each day, and the brisk hike to church in the morning's chill was just about enough to keep me conscious through the half-hour Latin service.

Lent was a time of sacrifice and denial, of "sharing in Christ's suffering" prior to rejoicing in the glory of His resurrection. Mother's strong willpower and encouragement set the tone for us. We were urged to "give up for Lent" something we dearly loved. Most often I would try to live without candy, but temptations rarely were overcome for longer than the first week if my friends offered some. I also attempted positive behavior, such as making my bed, eating all the food on my plate, and being agreeable to my brother. I can remember marveling at my parents' strength of will in fasting—eating only one full meal a day and nothing in between. How I dreaded adulthood and having to fast, finding it hard to see how doing without snacks, candy, desserts, etc., could possibly be good for body and soul. It was hard enough not eating meat on Fridays.

On Friday nights during Lent my dad always took us to devotions at church. With the priest and two altar boys leading, we prayed together the Stations of the Cross, which portray the passion and death of Jesus. "We adore Thee, O Christ, and we bless Thee," the priest intoned, and we responded, "Because of Thy Holy Cross Thou hast redeemed the world." When Easter finally came, I must admit, we did rejoice. The scent of lilies filled the church, once again the bells rang, and we raced home to revel in the delicious (so long denied?) candies, chocolates, and jelly eggs.

I grew up thinking that belonging to a church meant participating. Both my parents freely gave their time and talents to parish activities: cooking and serving at church suppers, ushering, visiting the sick, delivering food baskets, supervising fund drives, counting and recording the collection, keeping the official calendar of events.

With the public grade school bearing my grandfather's name just across the side street, my practical family entertained no thought of the children attending the distant parochial school, much to my pleasure. Parading to church on a Sunday morning was not nearly so enjoyable as shuffling across the public school grounds on a "holy day," headed for church while the other children were busy at work in their classrooms. On those days, arriving tardy at school with a written excuse from Mother, we were even prouder to be Catholics!

Living close to school had its drawbacks. Never one to awaken early, I was known to emerge from bed at the sound of the first bell, dress quickly (the bedroom had no heater), grab breakfast on my way through the kitchen, dash across the street and be in my seat before the tardy bell rang. My family knew all the teachers, and vice versa. Following two more serious and predictable siblings, I was never quite what they were expecting—redheaded, freckled, with an imaginative tongue and impish grin. In retrospect, I think the reason my mother often invited the teachers home for special luncheons was in payment for putting up with my talkative tirades.

My most vivid memory, and one that has influenced me tremendously, is of family togetherness. Both parents and children were simply expected to share the work load and then share the fun. Along with many other families we worked our "victory garden" during World War II. The task of weeding, watering, and picking vegetables was a joy, in my estimation, compared with the weekly duty of cleaning out the chicken house (not a house exactly, but the back part of our huge garage). A wartime endeavor, the end of chicken-raising was my own personal reason for rejoicing on V-Day. Besides the produce of the vegetable garden, together we reaped the fruits of the pear and cherry orchard and picked so many blackberries that by the middle of August I'd wish never to see or eat another one again—until the middle of winter when we devoured Mother's hot berry cobbler in minutes.

When it comes to reminiscing about chores, I immediately

think of our kitchen, the hub of all activity. I recall it with ease, because it hasn't changed in the past thirty years—in fact, in the last sixty years. The black cast-iron wood-burning stove, the focal point, is remarkable. In my youth it cooked the food, heated the kitchen and all the water for the household. Today it is used for cooking, heating, and trash burning, besides being a prime conversation piece. (In honesty I must add that a gas range now shares the cooking 50-50.) Being the youngest, I had the easy job of gathering pine cones from under the many trees in our yard to use as fuel, and as I grew older of chopping wood. Our own children now listen with disbelief when I tell of the Saturday night bath in a huge tub, in two inches of water, warmed in the tea kettle on the wood stove. We were all glad when Dad decided that an electric water heater wasn't such a farfetched frivolity after all.

Sundays were always special days. After church and breakfast we would often pile into the 1939 Chevy—how vividly I remember that historic car, since it was our family car until 1952—for a Sunday drive. Living in the Pacific Northwest we had many vistas beckoning us: mountains, beach, the Columbia River gorge, or just the ol' swimmin' hole of the little Washougal River. We usually packed a picnic lunch and enjoyed a leisurely day running, hiking, or swimming.

My growing-up years were filled with abundance not of material goods but, more important, of attention; not of presents from my parents but the presence of my parents. In those days fewer mothers worked outside the home, and we expected Mother to be there to greet us after school and to guide our weekend activities. But we also had a father who enjoyed, encouraged, and entered into family activities.

In those years before family rooms with wall-to-wall carpeting, cozy fireplaces, and color TV, people needed more resourcefulness for their leisure time. The Ping-Pong table in our yard became the neighborhood gathering place for so many years that even today deep trenches remain where players' feet wore away the soil. Dad was usually out there too, playing with us. Besides Ping-Pong there were continuous rounds of softball, football, basketball, croquet, kick-the-can, and hide-and-go-seek. We were encouraged by both parents to entertain our friends at home. No wonder our house was the scene of a yearly Halloween party, a kids' club in the musty cellar, a dancing group in the dining room, summer campouts in the yard, dress-up and talent shows, Kool-Aid stands, and practically everything within stretch of the imagination.

Discipline at our house wasn't synonymous with physical punishment, even though Mother's distinct preference was the hairbrush. There were times when I wished it *were* physical, just to get it over with.

One episode I recall—one my dad likes to tell, often—is the time my brother John and I started a fire in the backyard. We were playing "house" outside, as five- and seven-year-olds do, and in arranging the toys, boxes, etc., decided that the discarded fireplace screen belonged in our "living room." Since it was old and wobbly we leaned it up against the foundation of the house. Naturally a fireplace screen required a fire, so we diligently collected some papers, wood scraps, and sticks, sneaked some matches out of the kitchen, and successfully lighted a fire to lend a warm atmosphere to our home.

We were suddenly surprised by the appearance of both parents, who quickly doused the flames and ushered us firmly into the house for a severe scolding. Dad then told us to come along with him, and we soon found ourselves at the neighborhood fire station. Mother had called ahead to alert the firemen that two firebugs were approaching and to prepare a good stiff lecture. We were properly interrogated and humiliated and after many agonizing minutes we departed with promises never to play with matches or fire again.

We had sufficiency but not excess. People who lived through the Depression retained habits of frugality, and my parents were no exception. They never threw anything away. Every cent was spent with caution. They chose never to buy a brand new car, but to be satisfied with a series of secondhand ones, a pattern my wife Linda and I have repeated.

The idea of recycling is nothing new in the White family. My parents, withstanding any pressure to keep up with the Browns next door or the Greens across the street, first sought necessary household articles in the classifieds. On the other side of the coin, my dad's dictum, religiously followed, is: When buying something new, patronize the local merchant instead of discount chain stores, and never buy on credit. Both Mother and Dad have deep commitment to the local scene.

In spite of the fact that my parents have strong convictions of their own, both are unusually tolerant of others' ideals, attitudes, and behavior. They never force their opinions on others, but state their own beliefs and feelings without hostility. Perhaps that's why today they have such a wide circle of friends and an open, positive relationship with their children. In looking back I'm aware that they didn't always agree with each other, and at times these diverse opinions were expressed. What a tremendous feeling as a child to have a parent on your side, not both "against" you.

From an early age my parents allowed us great freedom, but with it came responsibility for our actions. With the joys of freedom came the sorrows of making mistakes and taking the consequences. I remember Mom often telling me, "Use your own head, Bern!" Having begged for a dog, it was I who cared for our golden retriever Judy (and an endless succession of cats with kittens). If I wanted a paper route, it was my decision and responsibility. When an activity conflicted with delivering *The Journal*, I had to arrange my own substitute, and not ask Mom and Dad. When I began frequent weekend skiing at Mt. Hood and participating in musical and theatrical productions, my obligations at home didn't shift. During high school I took an evening job as desk clerk at an athletic club. My parents pointed out that my main responsibility wasn't to earn money for college, but to earn grades so I would be accepted for college.

My first big streak of independence didn't show itself until Holy Week of my freshman year at the University of Portland. I was in Pittsburgh with the debating team, scheduled to fly back to Portland on an Air Force plane. I wanted to see New York City and my sister who was there working for TWA. I called home for approval. Dad said no; Mother said yes, if I could pay for it. So, after spending Good Friday afternoon in a Pittsburgh church, I caught a plane for New York, met my sister and her friends, and spent the weekend sightseeing. I arrived back in Portland feeling guilty about not spending more of that Holy Friday, Saturday, and Sunday in church praying. Now I understand that experiencing new people and thoughtfully evaluating new situations as a Christian are also ways of serving God. But I grew up a lot that weekend. I had tried my wings and they worked.

As a college sophomore I was selected with another student to appear on a weekly program on Portland's first television channel. The format was for the students to pose ethical questions and discuss possibilities, with a theologian from our university available with "the answer." I enjoyed the challenge and acclaim, and now recognize how much of that honor was due to earlier parental input in moral decision-making.

My parents are celebrating their forty-fifth wedding anniversary this year. That alone is an inspiring accomplishment. But more inspiring than the longevity of their marriage is the way they have lived it.

28
Marge Stromberg

Marge Stromberg, who graduated in Christian education from Bethel College in Minnesota, is a wife, mother, part-time nursery school teacher, secretary, gardener, bookkeeper, and helper in her husband's design office. She is involved in the C.E. ministry of a Baptist church in Chicago as librarian, women's Bible class teacher, and assistant to her husband in directing the Sunday Bible school.

Growing up on a small farm/ranch in northern Wyoming is a bonus hard to equal. People there have a rugged individualism that's not found everywhere. Most people are sons and daughters of original settlers to the area of many nationalities: German, Russian, Welsh, Danish, Norwegian, Swedish, Scottish, Indian. Though there weren't the close ethnic clans one finds here in Chicago, all were intensely proud of their achievements.

Our family name, Johnston, is English; my Mormon relatives traced it back twenty-three generations to George Washington's maternal grandmother. Dad was born in Missouri, along the Mississippi. My grandad traded his job as mail carrier with his brother who had homesteaded in Wyoming, moving there when my dad was about twelve. My mother, whose parents came from Kentucky, was born on Gooseberry Creek, an area where the only way to travel at that time was by horse.

It took a lot of back-breaking work to turn that barren land into a productive valley, and each farmer was immensely concerned about his farm and its appearance. Since my father didn't have to go away from home for his job, I knew what he did every day. In summer he often worked fourteen-hour stints without complaining. I frequently helped in the field, driving the tractor during haying season while my dad and a helper picked up hay bales. During the fall our main crop was sugar beets. After school I helped where I could, often getting rid of excess dirt from the beets (which counted against you when you weighed in the beet truck at the "dump"). And since our beef herd was usually brought up to the farm area from our river bottom property during this time, I frequently had the job of corraling them at night, either on foot or with my horse. Since I worked at home, my dad did an interesting thing for me. When I was ten years old and started 4-H, he gave me a dairy heifer and a Hereford (beef) heifer. All the calves they had over the years belonged to me, which helped pay for my college expenses.

Naturally I also helped with daily chores to care for the livestock and chickens. I learned to love the land and animals. I learned what it meant to work hard to make a living. At harvest time our whole family worked in the field. Mother drove a truck. I did double duty with chores before and after school as well as meal preparation.

An unspoken concept I learned from my parents, especially from my mother, was that there was no clear demarcation of duties into a "woman's job" and a "man's job." If something needed to be done and you could do it, you did it—even if the task might be unpleasant. Mother wore Levi's and helped my dad outside, spreading fertilizer and driving a truck; yet in the house she cared about her personal appearance and our home. My sisters and I were expected to help keep the house neat and clean. It was obvious that my dad appreciated this even though he didn't often mention it.

Since farming doesn't provide a monthly cash income, I was accustomed to discussions of how to manage until the next cash crop was harvested. We lived frugally and carefully. Yet we lived comfortably and I never felt deprived of any major thing. Mother's "egg money" provided our Sunday school tithe and piano lessons. Nothing was thrown away unless it was hopelessly beyond salvaging. Cleaning the attic was always an adventure. Mother had three huge drawers up there, about four feet long and going back as far as the pitch of the roof would allow. The bottom one must also have been about four feet deep, and took two people to pull out. These yielded a seemingly unending supply of fabric or clothes to alter for our needs, and Mother always tried to come up with the outfit we desired. With no bakery or delicatessen for miles around, we learned to plan and prepare meals as well as do all types of baking. We bought flour fifty pounds at a time.

Firm discipline was always exerted on us. As a child I had healthy respect for the stories my two older sisters could tell of the discipline they had received at *my* age. Usually it was Mother who meted out punishment, but she was backed up 100 percent by my dad. If he ever spoke to us, we knew we'd better jump. Sometimes I wish Dad had taken a more active part in speaking to us about our behavior; yet we knew what he thought without his saying much. When she was twenty-one my oldest sister dared him that he couldn't spank her any more—and with a big grin on his face he promptly turned her over his knee. I was only nine at the time and it left quite an impression.

Another facet of our discipline was that we were expected to do any job the best we could. No halfway stuff. Partly this was encouraged through our 4-H club work, but it was a basic tenet of the way we lived. Even laundry was hung on the clothesline so it looked neat.

Christianity was an accepted and important part of our family life. Yet we never had family devotions or prayed together except at mealtime. Sometimes I wished we did, especially when I would hear at camp how meaningful it was to other Christian kids my age. Our home always had Christian magazines available, mainly *Christian Life* and *Moody Monthly*, as well as religious books—though some were of the light, frothy type. We made regular trips to the county library, ten miles away, and checked out ten or fifteen books at a time. Dad had good basic Bible study books: *Halley's Bible Handbook,* a concordance, etc. My father almost always picked up his Bible to read whenever he had a few minutes before or after meals, to prepare for teaching the adult Bible class.

My parents made it possible for me to go to a week of Bible camp every year and to many local Youth For Christ rallies. Though I made a commitment to Christ at a church service, it was at Bible camp that I really began to understand what it meant to be a Christian. Camp Bible studies and being with other Christian kids encouraged me to live the Christian life the rest of the year, when I usually didn't know more than one or two other teens who were Christians.

As an early adolescent I often felt very alone. I remember thinking that I could hardly wait to be grown-up, as it must be easier to witness about your faith then. In high school, however, two other girls from our church and I had a trio. We spent a lot of time practicing with our pastor's wife, who directed us, and as a result we had a Bible study with our pastor for about a year. During that time we prayed for specific people, and it was then I realized the power of prayer. Many requests came true in dynamic ways. But other than these two Christian friends, most of our church's youth activity was sporadic. Attendance varied according to the moods of the kids and the program offered.

As I grew older I realized that my parents had a difficult time living the Christian life before their neighbors. It seemed to them a little nutty that we took our church and Christianity so seriously, and some of them looked down on us. I often felt this at school too. Yet my parents didn't lower their standards, fight back, or be mean in revenge. They figured that time and the Lord would take care of it. And the Lord did. My closest high school girl friend was from one of these families. One of the neighboring men later became a Christian.

Since the little Baptist church we attended was very small, my parents played a major role in its survival and ministry in the community (population, 101). My father was head deacon and Mother was busy with the Sunday school, teaching preschoolers and part of the time serving as superintendent. (I'm sure I acquired my "saving" habit from her saving all sorts of things for their craft projects.) As a teen I at times resented the fact that my parents expected my behavior to measure up to their responsibilities (I suppose the way many "PKs" feel). Yet it was an important lesson to realize that accepting a responsibility as a Christian also demands behavior as an example to others. I remember my parents going to prayer meeting even a little late after my dad had finished his chores. To stay home would certainly have been easier.

At times we considered going to church in a town twenty miles away, where there were more teens, more activities, and perhaps a better pastor. Yet my parents felt that it was important to stay with the church in our town to minister to the community. Because of this decision I learned a lot about leadership before I finished high school. I learned how to be comfortable speaking or teaching in front of a group, something I've discovered not everyone enjoys.

One parental misconception was to assume that I knew more than I did about sex. Mother assumed I had picked up quite a bit as she talked to my older sisters, but I really hadn't paid much attention. Both my parents thought that in caring for animals, seeing them mate, and having calves born, I had learned about sex. While this was true to a certain degree, a few explanatory statements and clarifications would have been helpful. It wasn't until I had a college biology class that I finally "got it together."

Even though we were in an isolated area with a small population, we were exposed to as many outside experiences as possible. A favorite summer excursion was to the Bighorn mountains to go fishing. We took visiting friends and relatives to Yellowstone Park, 150 miles away. Mother frequently drove me and a carload of my friends over 100 miles to concerts that college groups were giving in the area. We went to community concerts and plays in neighboring towns given by touring performers. I don't know where my mother learned to like music, especially all that variety. Though she never had any training, she could play the piano a little and was determined that we would hear anything that was in the area to hear. My aunt gave us piano lessons, so we were exposed to classical music. (But no one knew anything about art. That was a foreign area.)

Since we had a large home we entertained visiting missionaries, guest speakers, and musical groups who came to our church. I'm sure all this helped me realize the scope of Christian ministry and played a part in my decision to major in Christian education in college. We also had the unique experience of having three foreign students stay with us for several weeks, one each from Turkey, Finland, and Pakistan. This was under the International Farm Youth Exchange, a government program under the Department of Agriculture. This exposure helped me understand cultural differences in a way that no geography or world history course could have done.

Both parents, especially my father, enjoyed people. And not just close friends. We frequently had guests at mealtime, especially in the summer because that was when my father was in the house and had time to talk. If we were on a trip or outing, it was common for my dad to strike up a conversation with people he happened to see. One time as we were having breakfast in a restaurant on our way home from a trip, my dad started visiting with tourists. He invited them to stop by our farm to see how irrigation was done. A few days later they pulled into our yard. We spent a couple of hours giving them a farm tour and letting the kids ride the horses. I'm sure my dad couldn't afford the time, but he enjoyed every minute of it. As an adult I've come to realize that friendship evangelism takes a lot of time just being ourselves—spending time with friends and neighbors when we probably could spend it working. Yet it's important if we're to be able to share our Christian faith.

A girl friend and I often joked about being "afterthoughts" in our families. We were both ten years younger than our closest sister or brother. I can remember asking my parents to adopt somebody—and I think they even considered it though they never did it. Yet being younger than my two sisters by so many years had some built-in advantages that weren't planned by my parents. For one thing they weren't so severe in their discipline with me as with my two sisters. When my sisters would point this out later, my mother always reminded them that there were *two* of them to get into trouble.

When I was eight years old, I missed six weeks of school when my parents took me with them on an extended trip. We went to Chicago for a national Farm Bureau convention, on to South Carolina to visit friends, and then home through Mississippi and Kansas. On the way we visited relatives and friends whom I would otherwise never have met. My teacher's only request of my parents was for reports of places we visited. So as a result, my parents made sure we did some sightseeing we might have missed. I'm convinced that travel for children teaches more than sitting in a classroom can ever do. Some of my high school classmates had never even been to Yellowstone, and many never set life goals beyond what they knew from our locality.

By the time I was eight years old my sisters were working away from home or were in college. My parents frequently had meetings to attend or friends they liked to visit. We were part of a large tight-knit family structure, which enjoyed having reunions at the slightest excuse. I disliked baby-sitters and much preferred to go with my parents, even if we might not encounter any other children. Consequently, I learned to enjoy adults and to appreciate what older people had to say. Even now I enjoy being with older people. I have strong convictions that respecting one's elders is not just for children, but is for adults as well.

I enjoyed my parents, and as I grew older we had many long talks and discussions together. I never rebelled at staying home helping, instead of working away from home at a part-time job while in high school.

Love was given freely to us and was demonstrated between our parents as well. I have fond memories of seeing them walk hand in hand, talking about crops or the cattle. They enjoyed working together, relaxing together; and sharing together their aspirations for the ranch and for the three of us as we grew up. They were united in their faith. This was apparent to all of us.

29
Gordon Stromberg

Gordon Stromberg, an artist with experience in educational (Harper and Row) and religious communications (Inter-Varsity Press, HIS magazine, TEAM) has recently begun his own graphic design office in Chicago. Married and a father (Linda, 7), he also teaches design at Wheaton College and directs his church's Sunday Bible school.

Personal faith in God has always been important in our family. But as I've thought about my parents and my relationship to them, it seems hard to decide which aspects of my personality have been influenced by them and which by members or pastors of my church. That may sound strange in a day when church attendance and church matters are so commonly bypassed for weekend trips. Yet I don't regret the difficulty in distinction. Some of my earliest family recollections are of attending or traveling to the Baptist church a little over a mile from our home in Chicago.

My mother was an integral part of women's groups that in retrospect seem quaint and harmless. No doubt they were as effective in sharing new life in Christ with the people of that day as current groups are. Mom's ministry was with a recipe, a few ingredients, and a hot oven. Few cooks surpass her ability in the kitchen and the love she expresses with it.

My father, now retired, has been a truck driver as long as I can remember, though he studied electricity and continues to apply that knowledge. During World War II he purchased his own truck and delivered wooden boxes for a box company. Many photos in the family album show him as the cutup and tease that he continues to be. But his jesting was always in good taste.

Dad didn't make a big thing about getting my brother and me to study the Bible, though we were encouraged to do our Sunday school lessons. But I often saw him reading the Bible himself. He took a consistently active role in church work, showing concern for kids and adults in a variety of ways. He served as deacon, but I remember him best as a Sunday school teacher, faithfully studying the next week's lesson.

Dad tried to keep his lessons moving, and he still has a reputation for having a knack with boys. He usually solved discipline problems in unique ways. One boy who made a disturbance was especially proud of his cowboy boots. Dad challenged him either to "take off those manly cowboy boots and leave them outside the classroom door, or behave like a man!" The boy responded with model behavior. Dad took his teaching as a serious responsibility in lesson preparation, punctuality, parental contact, and involvement during the week with the boys in his class (on birthdays and occasionally on a weekend outing). Mom often cooked meals for a large class of twelve-year-olds, later awesomely described as "bottomless pits." There seemed to be few results at the time, but their love paid dividends. Several boys later went into the ministry.

At the junior age I was a pupil in my father's class when an evangelist visited our Sunday school. I remember Dad's entire class returning to our room, where he went to each child and explained what inviting and accepting Christ as Savior of his life really meant. Then he prayed with each one as we asked God for forgiveness. Several years later, during a boys' camp, I questioned whether I had earlier invited Jesus Christ into my life. So I confirmed that earlier step and chose to follow Christ and His life. That was over twenty-five years ago and I've never regretted the decision. For me it has meant depending on God to resolve the anger, selfishness, and sharp words that come naturally. It has meant having a significant goal in life. During my college years at Illinois Institute of Technology, I responded to our pastor's message about the Lordship of Christ and offered my life's work to God for any use He might have for it.

I'm grateful to my parents for cutting me short when I was young. It's a lot easier than when you're older. I remember being seven or eight when early one morning in church someone asked how I was. My response was a lackluster "okay" or "pretty good" with a certain whine to it, probably to invite further inquiry. I was severely warned by Dad—privately, to save face—that if I was healthy and awake I'd better be positive in my response to anyone's inquiry.

I was about eight when I took Mom's diamond ring from a drawer in the front hall to show my friends. Somehow I lost it in the snow after denying to a playmate's parents that it was a real diamond. I've never gotten over feeling bad about that, though I know Mom has forgiven me.

During my childhood summers, my parents reacquainted me with several sets of relatives in Wisconsin. We usually stayed at my grandparents' farm. Mother's sisters and brother with their families would often visit. Those were days of freedom when I learned about livestock, chores, crops and how to manage without electricity—a good alternate to city life.

One thing I would have liked during childhood and teen years was to travel to various states during the summer. I have no resentment against Mom and Dad for not doing this (it was their sole chance to visit relatives), but stories from classmates at the end of summer made me a little disappointed we hadn't ventured onto some different roads.

Some home magazines were always around our house, and regular use of the library was encouraged. I received a reasonable but seemingly small allowance to spend as I pleased. My parents emphasized taking care of what we owned. Money though adequate wasn't lavished on us; allowances were usually expected to suffice. Comic books were never purchased for us and rather discouraged, though not banned. At the ripe age of nine or ten I remember finally buying a humorous Looney Tunes comic book and being so disappointed with its shallow contents that I returned to the candy store to exchange it—only to learn that this wasn't an accepted practice. Comic books were looked on with a little more favor when my brother Elden, seven years younger, reached the same age. He made a rather lucrative business of buying old comic books from friends and then reselling them at a handsome profit.

In retrospect I wish I'd had a wider exposure to children's classics, but by my midteens I was regularly saving my allowance to buy about thirty classic children's books, some already too young for me. I was attracted to them as much for their fine illustration, design, and binding as for their stories.

Elden and I were very different. He was athletic, outgoing, and mechanically oriented. Books weren't his thing, which isn't to say he wasn't sharp. In contrast I was nonathletic, more withdrawn, more contemplative, and certainly not mechanical. Consequently, discipline problems were different with the two of us. A sound spanking with a switch or board, or a bar of Fels Naptha soap in my mouth, usually solved my problem. But that wasn't necessarily true for Elden. The best-known episode of his discipline involved a severe spanking after which he said, "That feels good, Dad. Do it again." Parental tactics had to differ, so Elden had privileges withdrawn. Some toy or a friend's house were off limits for a certain period. But whether verbal or physical discipline was applied, it was never in front of others.

I don't mean to sound pious in relation to Elden. I'm sure I was just as mouthy and self-centered in my own way. I griped about appearances: neatness of shirts Mother had ironed, having to wear hand-me-downs that weren't in style, or wanting a *House Beautiful* look to our living room.

Another aspect I cherish of my parents' personality and ethic was their hesitance to promise anything they couldn't fulfill. You could clearly hear the lively music from Riverview, a large amusement park just over a half-mile from our house, any summer night. Once or twice a year we spent an afternoon or evening there—a highlight of the summer for us, if not for Dad. Dad would promise to take us to Riverview or to a museum only when he *knew* he could. A promise was a firm commitment. No doubt we could have gone to Riverview much more often if Dad had chosen to let us, but we learned instead the careful use of time and money. And the anticipation was almost as good as the real thing.

I well remember the extremes of reward and punishment received at the hand of my father for good and bad grades in school. Top grades were rewarded with one dollar each. This didn't cost my dad much at first, but later it became a rather regular financial outgo. Of course the enjoyment of having a good report card to bring home was in itself a reward of almost a spiritual nature. But those dollar bills certainly reinforced the situation. I suppose the money phased out during high school, but the impetus remained to please and honor my parents (and myself) by working hard in most classes. Later that paid off in several scholarships. On the other hand, though it was rare, I can still picture myself sitting on the back stairway crying after being spanked for not working hard enough on some subject at school. Obviously Dad knew I could do better, and the report card or perhaps a note from the teacher had alerted him to the problem. I was mad at the time, but also aware that he was right. This, I suppose, has helped me have a better sense of responsibility, accountability, and self-worth than a lot of kids seem to have today.

School supplies and clothing were always provided for me in addition to my allowance, but ways occasionally turned up to earn extra money—like painting the back fence white or shoveling and wheeling the winter's supply of coal into the gangway. These jobs paid on the motivation basis, per board or bushel. I hated the work, but I liked the money. Now I appreciate the early experience of not having everything given to me. Dad's need for money or a greater salary was rarely discussed. No doubt we could have used more, but strength of character and a job well done were stronger goals.

My interest in art probably began because of a good series of teachers during primary grades. In my school, art was considered just as vital as reading or math or music. By fourth or fifth grade I had achieved a certain proficiency in this area, though neither of my parents are artistic. (They'd be the first to tell you that.) They did, however, encourage me, and so did their friends.

Everyone in seventh and eighth grade was expected to take

part in a square-dancing class related to physical education. But Mom and Dad decided that this wasn't consistent with a clear witness as a believer committed to Jesus Christ. I reluctantly concurred, though I hated to be different from the rest of the class. That experience helped me realize the necessity to stand up for my convictions (with graciousness) early in life. As persons committed to Jesus Christ, both Mom and Dad also felt that the use of alcohol and tobacco was a poor way to treat a body, and consequently these were no temptation to me as I entered my teen years. In fact, it always rather baffled me why anybody used them. At that time I didn't realize the tensions adults have.

Knowing my parents' background is helpful to see their involvement in the things of God. Both my grandparents' families emigrated from northern Sweden directly to northern Wisconsin. My paternal grandfather was one of five brothers and sisters, all Christians, who came to the U. S. in the early 1900s, helping each other get started. All came because they couldn't get ahead in Sweden, where the system of land being inherited equally by children caused even large farms quickly to become small ones. Homesteading was over in Wisconsin when they arrived, but they bought virgin land, cleared it by hand, and established farms. Hard work was a "given." Dad, two years old at the time, was from a family of seven. My mother was the oldest of nine and she took on many "assistant to the mother" chores.

The recent films *The Emigrants* and *The New Land* give a glimpse into that heritage of struggle. Visiting Sweden nine years ago, I learned of my grandfather's love for God: he regularly walked seven miles each Sunday to start a fire in the little Baptist church, in days when it was in disfavor with the Lutheran state church. (Baptisms were often held secretly.)

Because Dad's mother died when he was seven, I think he was concerned that my brother and I have Mom around when we needed her, rather than off working somewhere. Consequently we had the security of knowing that Mom would regularly be at home. She always had a snack and a listening ear when school was over. She always had suggestions for making things right. She was the family gardener and during World War

II especially we planted large "victory" gardens. But flowers were always plentiful too.

Mom enjoyed cooking and baking. We regularly invited some friend (often single, and usually from church) home for Sunday dinner. This meant returning them to their home later in the afternoon if they had no car. Regularly Mom would stay home from church to cook those meals, despite the family's protest. But we also (selfishly) expected a hot meal when we arrived home, so it's not hard to see why she chose the stay-home course. Automatic ovens have changed all that.

I honor my parents for their support of my ideas. When I was a freshman or sophomore in high school, a Wisconsin cousin asked my dad if I was going to have to go to college. Dad calmly responded that this was my decision and that he could ask me. Since my Dad was supportive of my decisions, I felt that my future was between myself and God, not a thing predetermined by parents. The same held for my choice of career. It made me grateful, responsible, and aware that I'd better think seriously about what I'd do after the high school graduation gown was returned.

One of the bywords among all of us at home was a verse from a sermon our pastor had preached. "Have no anxiety about anything, but in everything by prayer and supplication with thanksgiving let your requests be made known to God" (Philippians 4:6). At first the whole verse was quoted whenever someone would get overly upset or uptight about something. Later it was abbreviated to "Be anxious for nothing," but we all knew what it meant and it gave perspective on the situation.

As a teenager I got in the habit of making a dash to the back door of the church and into the car as soon as the sermon was over, avoiding as many people as possible. Dad, on the contrary, wanted to greet visitors. He felt that this was the minimal hospitality any deacon should show in his church. Finally he called me on my habit and made me aware that a lot of people needed the honest smile and handshake of a teen, and an inquiry into their health, regardless of how cliché I thought the whole scene was. I tried it and, though painful (especially in relation to my peers), discovered he was right.

Mom put up with a lot from me during my preteen and teen

years. She served more than one breakfast to a crabby Gordon. I marvel at her endurance during those years when nothing seemed "right" to my perfectionist outlook. I wish my personality had paralleled my aesthetic idealism during those years.

As a teenager I was also aware of the intense social power of the new television medium. Sprawled on the floor at the neighbor's house, we enjoyed seeing a variety of shows. It's hard now to believe the fascination they had for Elden and me. Mom and Dad hesitated to buy a TV set, probably because of cost and the lack of significant programs. Too, they resisted aligning with a medium that had the status of being in every tavern in the city.

Probably the major reason for the eventual purchase of the seventeen-incher was to regain us two boys from Hopalong Cassidy episodes at the neighbor's. Long before remote control on TV sets, we talked of getting a "blab-off" unit that would allow us to turn off long-winded phony commercials. Dad realized the power of such advertising on all our lives and made us laugh at the dishonest value system that the harmful and expensive products were pushing. He also to a degree controlled what we watched, limiting the quantity or length of programs for any one evening, and forcing us into more careful choices.

I remember Dad's honesty about something like medicine versus Mom's rosy description. If a medicine had a pain or distaste to it, Mom would tend to overlook that aspect, coaxing us just to "close our eyes and swallow." Of course we calculated for that unintentional dishonesty after a while, but still it was there—something that challenged our trust. In contrast, Dad would describe a medicine or treatment for what it was, and then expect us to rise to the occasion with Stromberg spirit.

In both my parents I saw humility. A Scripture reference my Dad occasionally quoted was "Let another praise you, and not your own mouth" (Proverbs 27:2). It was good to remember this in my teens and early twenties, when I might be burning inside to call attention to myself or my work. And even now I recall it, along with other Scripture I memorized as a boy.

I suppose I'm most grateful for early and regular exposure to the Bible and its precepts. This came through church, Sunday school, prayer meeting, and Bible stories read at home. I later used all I had gained in exposure to biblical symbols—both concrete and abstract—in designing. But the Bible was best seen applied in the lives of my parents and the faithful members of our church, who were following God's concept of living in love. They took sincere, personal interest in my brother and me.

I couldn't begin to count the times my parents have helped Marge and me before and after we were married. It's impossible to go to their home without Mom's slipping one of us a bag of goodies from her kitchen as we leave. Dad fixed our first car continually, regularly bolting the motor onto the frame and holding the whole thing together with baling wire. He still fixes our car. He's a regular visitor to our home with his tools. All Dad's repairs, as well as their baby-sitting fee, if billed, would reach into thousands of dollars. They do it all with a heart of love, and although we've tried reciprocating, it's impossible. God will repay them, I know. We cannot.

30

Beatrice Cairns

Beatrice Cairns, now a Canadian, is the accountant and office manager for a log owner's cooperative association (the only one of its kind in the world). She is interested in snowshoeing, handcrafts, photography, reading, and does IVCF and Pioneer Camp work.

Looking back, it seems that my parents did many things right, even though at the time *right* was the last word I would have used to describe some of their actions. To show how the attitudes and actions of my parents moulded my character, I need to explain my background.

My father's family traces a strong, proud, Protestant heritage back to about 1660, when the family was part of the Cromwellian Scottish transplant to Northern Ireland. They lived through the siege of Londonderry in 1690. A monument still standing on the walls of the old city bears the name of John Cairns, one of the sons of the original family. (The monument was erected to honour the young men known as the "Apprentice Boys of Derry" who closed the city gates against the attackers, King James of England and his allies.)

The male members of the family were Orangemen; it was the "done" thing. The Orange Order may have now degenerated into little more than a social club, but it is intriguing to read the original conditions of entry imposed upon its members. One would have to be an evangelical Christian to maintain these conditions.*

My mother's family also has a strong Protestant background, being Church of Ireland or Anglican, while Father's was Presbyterian.

An important aspect of my childhood was the strong family relationship that existed, with grandparents, uncles, aunts, and cousins all contributing to the moulding of our lives. I was a deprived child, however, with only one set of grandparents. My father's parents both died before he was twelve years old. He was the youngest of seven sons and his father was a seventh son, which in Gaelic or Celtic folklore made him a person with special powers. (The seventh son of a seventh son was said to be gifted with "second sight" or the ability to foresee the future. He was also credited with having a "charm" or "cure" for some diseases. This belief is still firmly held today in parts of Ireland, Scotland, especially the Highlands, and Wales.) I don't know if my father possessed any "special powers," but he was the most special person in my little-girl world.

My father's people were "town-folks" and Mother's were "country-folks." She, however, became "town-folk" when she married and came to live in Belfast, which was the vast distance of six or seven miles from her family home. My father was employed by a steamship company, which operated a cargo and passenger service between Belfast and Hesham, England,

---

*"Disclaiming an intolerant spirit, the Association demands as an indispensable qualification, without which the greatest and wealthiest may seek admission in vain, that the candidate shall be deemed incapable of persecuting or injuring anyone on account of his religious opinions; the duty of every Orangeman being to aid and defend all loyal subjects of every religious persuasion in the enjoyment of their constitutional rights . . . An applicant for admission should have a sincere love and veneration for his Almighty Maker, productive of those lively and happy fruits—righteousness and obedience to His commands; a firm and steadfast faith in the Saviour of the world, convinced that He is the only Mediator between a sinful creature and an offended Creator. His disposition should be humane and compassionate, and his behaviour kind and conciliatory; he should be an enemy to savage brutality and every species of unchristian conduct; a lover of rational and improving society; faithfully regarding the Protestant religion, and sincerely desirous of propagating its precepts, i.e., charity and good-will to all men."—from the Constitution and Laws of the Loyal Orange Association of British America (Toronto: The Sentinel Publishing Company Limited, 1909)

near Liverpool. He was a "goods checker," which, as far as I know, means that he checked the bills of lading as cargo was being loaded and unloaded at the ships' docks.

My parents obviously did not get together and decide on a uniform pattern of "bringing us up." When we were old enough to ask, "Why do I have to?" Father would take time to explain. Mother's answer was usually "Because I said so." As we grew older and asked what we should do in an area of doubt, Father would usually spell out the alternatives and possible results and allow us to make our own decisions. If we made the wrong choice, his shoulder was there to cry on along with his help to start over—usually in the way he had originally suggested. Mother's attitude, while not lacking in love and sympathy, was more "I told you so." Father always said he wasn't rearing children, he was rearing adults. We were increasingly encouraged to make our own decisions.

My parents weren't evangelical Christians as we tend to use that term today. I never remember my father going to church or reading a Bible, though there were Bibles in our home. But my mother would take me with her on her occasional visits to the exquisite shamrock-shaped little Church of St. Matthew. My earliest memory of her is as she lay beside me in the dark, singing me to sleep. She always sang hymns. The only one I remember is, "I stand amazed in the presence of Jesus the Nazarene, and wonder how He could love me, a sinner, condemned, unclean." Remembering the sweetness of her voice on the chorus—"How marvellous, how wonderful, is my Saviour's love for me"—I think it must have been her favourite. Singing children to sleep must have been part of our cultural heritage. (I distinctly remember my grandmother and aunts also doing this.) It was certainly a custom that allayed a child's fear of the dark. My childhood memories are aglow with the flickering of firelight in winter bedrooms and some loved voice singing.

We were always together, the four of us—my father and mother, my younger brother Eddie, and myself. The two of us were "taken" to Sunday school at an early age and "met" coming out by Daddy and Mummy. Then, weather permitting, we all went for a walk before teatime—Sunday school being from 3:00 to 4:00 in the afternoon.

We lived on the outskirts of the city of Belfast on the lower slopes of Divis, the highest "mountain" around—I guess it was all of 1,200 feet—so a few minutes took us into the country. Our route varied, and the walks were never dull. Mother would help us find early violets and primroses in the spring, while in summer Father would use first his walking stick to pull down wild roses and then his penknife to trim off the thorns before he gave me the flowers. In the fall, we looked for acorns and chestnuts. Father would pierce the chestnuts, put each one on a separate string, and teach my brother to play "conkers," which meant that you had to break the other person's chestnut off his string. If you broke ten with one of yours, you had a "conker." It was a game that required skill and good coordination.

In summertime, we spent afternoons at one of the many beaches within a few miles of the city. Father waded in the chilly waters of Belfast Lough with us, and helped us find bright green, scarlet, and wine-red seaweed to decorate our sand castles. Mother helped us build the sand castles and find sea-shells, but drew the line at wading. When we headed for the water, she took out her needlework.

We spent a lot of time with our maternal grandparents. The back of their property was bounded by a backwater of the river Lagan. At that particular place, two long fingers of land divided the water into three widths, the Backwater, the Middlewater, and the Lagan itself. It had a towpath for the magnificent Clydesdale horses drawing the barges of coal and other goods up the river.

The river had a series of locks, the fourth of these opposite Grandmother's back door. To get to the lock, we had to cross a small wooden bridge to the path between the Back- and Middlewaters. The path was called the "Woods," probably because of the giant beeches growing along it. Then we crossed the Middlewater on a narrow bridge (with one handrail) which spanned a shallow waterfall. Finally we were at the locks, where we could scarcely contain our excitement as we watched the lock closing and the water slowly raising a boat to the next level of the river.

When we were old enough to make the expedition alone, we were given strict instructions, and woe betide us if these weren't followed to the letter. Thus we were gradually allowed to assume responsibility for our own safety. We felt a great sense of achievement when we had safely negotiated these "hazards" on our own.

So I grew up in an atmosphere of security and trust, not engendered by abundant material possessions, but by love that provided, protected, and was wise enough and strong enough to correct and punish me when I needed it. I was loved and guided rather than possessed and managed.

Life was not all sunshine and roses, however. I never remember my father giving either of us a strapping, but if we were caught misbehaving, we were warned that if caught a second time, we would be punished. And we were. My bookworm father would seat us on two straight chairs, make us fold our arms, forbid us to look at or speak to each other, and settle down opposite us with a book. We would sit this way for anything up to an hour, according to the seriousness of the misdeed. No plea from Mother or tears from us would gain our release until the appointed time. We would have taken a strapping a dozen times over, we thought, rather than miss an hour's play on a bright summer day, with the laughter of playmates drifting into the house. (My father worked on rotating shifts to fit the arrival and departure times of vessels, so on some afternoons he was home by two o'clock.)

We learned lessons from this that have shaped our lives. Father was quiet, gentle, and loving, and we learned to respect his quiet strength of purpose. He never punished us without giving us a chance to explain our actions or warning us that punishment was forthcoming. If our explanations were found untruthful, our punishment was more severe, and we were always told the reason. We found that it didn't pay to lie to Father.

He shared the hours of punishment with us. I'm sure he didn't enjoy being unable to give his reading his undivided attention or giving up a game of lawn bowling to supervise us, but if he had promised us punishment and we deserved it, we got it. So we unconsciously gained security by knowing that he meant what he said.

Father died when I was eleven and he thirty-nine. Although

he had been ill about three months, his death was sudden and unexpected. Life was never quite the same again. He left me a legacy of appreciation for good books, a wide taste in reading, a trust in people, and an eye for beauty, encouraged by his skill in drawing and painting. Only two of his small paintings have survived, as he used these skills mostly to while away wet winter hours for us. He bought books and borrowed them from our excellent and extensive public library system. (I haven't found anything so good in North America. In fact, our local branch at home was better stocked, then, than the main branch in Vancouver is now!)

My mother was tiny, quick, impulsive, and impatient. She and Father must have had many serious disagreements, but I remember only one. It arose from his refusal to take her to an opera for which she had tickets. She insisted on going anyway, and on taking me with her. I don't remember how old I was, but it was old enough to be torn by feelings of guilt at leaving Father and delight at being allowed to stay up late and be dressed for the opera. We often went to plays and the cinema, but usually in the afternoon so that we could be in bed by the regular time. I don't know why such a shattering argument took place over this opera, but I experienced the agony of a child caught in the middle of a parental quarrel.

On the night of my father's death, I received a gift from my mother which is priceless to me today, although I accepted it at the time without any sense of its value. I wonder if she knew herself. Sometime in that timeless day, someone put my brother and me on top of a large double bed. Somewhere out of the dark, my mother came and lay down between us, putting an arm around each of us and holding us close. "You know," she said, "there are only the three of us now. We have no Daddy, but we have a heavenly Father who has promised to be a father to the fatherless and a husband to the widow, so everything will be all right." And then, "Let's say our prayers." We repeated the Lord's Prayer together as we had done every night since we could talk.

For me, from then on, that was real: we were God's special charge. He was responsible for us. The Bible said that, Mother believed it—and that was enough.

Life changed in many ways after Father's death. New clothes and summer holidays were no longer taken for granted; they were things for which we saved and planned. Although Mother went back to work, I don't know how she managed. We spent more holidays with grandparents, aunts, and uncles, but our friends still came home with us—and Mother fed us all.

One of Mother's younger brothers had made his career in the medical corps of the Royal Air Force. He had met and married a colleague's widow, who was older than he, had two children, and was Roman Catholic. Banned from the family home, my uncle came to my mother, who listened with love and sympathy. To her he also came when his wife lay dying after birth of their third child; it was she who brought about reconciliation with the family. My grandmother and an aunt cared for his children until he placed them in a convent in England when he was transferred. I didn't realize that I was learning tolerance and courage.

Then came the war. In retrospect I realize it taught me how little value there is in material possessions. Crouching with eyes glued to the ceiling, we would listen to the flap of a parachute carrying a landmine, as a vagrant wind carried it blocks away. One morning we discovered that the friend to whom we had said good night a few hours before had been buried for hours in the wreckage of her home. Two of her brothers had been killed. We learned to stand still and take stock.

When the sirens signalled an air raid, we went up the mountain and lay beside other children in the hedgerows, with cherished fur coats covering us. After raids, those whose homes were undamaged gave what they could to those whose possessions had been destroyed. As she went through pantry and linen closet, the phrase most on Mother's lips was, "We can do without that." She taught me to share whatever we had.

They weren't perfect, these dearly loved parents. There were arguments, days when silence lay heavy between them. Ed and I were uncomfortable in that silence. Sometimes my mother's impatience and occasionally undeserved criticism filled me with resentment and led to quarrels. She wasn't always understanding when I needed it. But looking back now, I can see that a lot of the tensions between us in the years after Father's death were caused by our inner struggles to adjust to the changed circumstances.

Eddie initially came to Canada on a leave of absence from his college in Belfast to work on a prototype aircraft being built for the Canadian government. His wife and children followed the next spring and were to be accompanied by Mother, who planned a three-month visit. She died six weeks before they were to sail.

She and I had lived together until her death and were companions and friends. We hadn't planned it this way—it happened because I was "jilted at the atlar," almost literally.

I came to Canada later that year to spend Christmas with the family and stay six months. It has been a long six months.

31
Naomi Baylis

Naomi Baylis—wife of Bob (chapter 32), mother of Jonathan (chapter 3) – is a home-maker, Sunday school teacher, camp coun-selor, and church worker in northern Califor-nia. Trained as a teacher, the mother of three, she is now active with her husband in a Logos Bookstore.

I was born into a family of four girls, two older and one younger. That had its drawbacks, I suppose—especially when we were growing up and had to split everything four ways. Being one of four had the advantage of never needing to seek out a playmate, but the disadvantage of being "one of a multitude." (I'll never forget overhearing someone say, "I can't be bothered learning a name for each one of those girls!") Yet I'm convinced that God-given wisdom allowed my parents to balance out whatever negatives there were in having a "female quartet" with much that was positive and right.

My parents met while singing in a church choir in Santa Rosa, California. My dad came from Pennsylvania and had a farm in Sonoma County with twenty or so cows. My mother was a school teacher from a British family that had come to California after a stay in New England, where my mother was born. The fact that my parents were in their thirties when they were married had a great deal of bearing on our "rearing," and incidentally gave my mother time to complete eleven years of public school teaching. I think they were much surer in their minds what they wanted of their offspring than younger parents generally are. My parents were new Christians when we were little, and we were all given Bible names: Ruth, Mary, Naomi, Priscilla. At different stages of my life I counted these biblical "handles" positive or negative, according to my attitude at the time.

Our family left the farm when I was two and moved to southern California. This move probably had something to do with the economic situation of 1929, but was also in part due to a search for new Christian fellowship. Having been raised in a rather liturgical denomination and finding the Lord in a more informal church, my parents were anxious for a "real Bible-centered evangelical church" with which to fellowship. They chose a Plymouth Brethren group.

Our new community, Hermosa Beach, was quite rural, with many fields of vegetables in our neighborhood which we passed on our long walk to school. This also meant that we had a multiracial set of playmates, and my sisters and I were in and out of our neighbors' homes quite naturally and comfortably.

An outstanding event of the year in that coastal town was the Children's Special Service Mission vacation Bible school held on the beach for four weeks each summer. We were driven down and back each day, even though carting us to activities wasn't typical of my parents. But getting us to a gospel enterprise was always worth it to them, in spite of the time it took. It was fun to be on the beach by the ocean, but added to that was singing and marching in the sand with our lively, personable leaders. Building Bible mottos in the sand was an afternoon class of its own. To build anything using sand, seaweed, driftwood, pebbles, and shells was great fun—but to be in competition for decorating "Christ died for us" or "Love one another" in your own way was almost more excitement than grade-schoolers could stand. And then to see a flag (first prize) waving over your work of art was the greatest success you could possibly achieve. We memorized Scripture and songs, learned Bible stories via chalk talks and other visuals. I remember my glee when all the teachers, students from the Bible Institute of Los Angeles, came to our house for dinner. Perhaps a bit of hero worship was involved, but what an impression their enthusiasm made on me. This was the time when I became aware of God's love particularly for me and my need to respond to Him, which I believe I did.

Some of the happiest times in those years were spent with other Christian families. We drove half an hour or more to attend Goodyear Gospel Hall (we always looked for the Goodyear blimp in its hangar on the way) and it wasn't unusual for us to spend the afternoon with another family in their home. We, too, often had visitors, which made the larger Christian family a loving community to me.

Each night after dinner Daddy would read the Bible and sometimes we each would pray. I remember being thankful for "food and raiment" and years later finding out what raiment really was. We always prayed for certain missionaries, having met them at Sunday school or at least having heard about them there. Sometimes we got to meet them, always a thrill, having become familiar with them through praying for them.

Family Bible reading wasn't always a pleasant time, I must admit. I don't remember being unhappy about it as a child, but when I was older, it seemed that although we missed the Bible reading sometimes, we never missed on a night when I had to hurry to an evening activity. I don't remember anything specifically that I learned at these evening sessions, but the practice certainly conveyed to me the importance of the Bible and my parents' dependence on God.

Somewhere along the line we memorized Bible verses together too, although I don't recall occasions of sitting down and being instructed. My father probably had the idea and my mother no doubt did the teaching—but subtly; I can't recall an ounce of rebellion at having to learn them. (My own children rebelled. I guess their teacher was less well-equipped.) Today I can still repeat the entire "alphabet of verses" we learned:

A. . . All have sinned, and come short of the glory of God (Romans 3:23).
B. . . Be sure your sin will find you out (Numbers 32:23).
C. . . Come unto me, all ye that labor and are heavy laden, and I will give you rest (Matthew 11:28).

I still review these and try to add to them instead of counting sheep on sleepless nights.

I don't know what my father did for a living at this time when the country was in the midst of the Depression, but I'm grateful for the fact that economic crisis was not the tenor of our household. I have no doubt that times were hard, because eventually my dad did work for the WPA and we had cans of food with government markings on them. But our home was not marked by a depressive atmosphere.

One saving feature was my father's great sense of humor. It carried us over and protected us children from some tense situations. After a severe, very frightening earthquake, our family laughed over the fact that some of the dishes had fallen off the shelf into the garbage pail. At another time when we were in a financial bind, we had a large jar of jam that my father referred to as "the jam that tastes more like grapes than grapes do." I realize now that the jam must have been imitation and he was diverting our attention. He was a great tease too, always ready with a quip and a hug for the sad one. I appreciate this gift of humor to us and the resultant protection from dwelling on our meager circumstances.

My dad always wanted to be a missionary, so one fall in the mid-thirties we left southern California in two vehicles and headed east, first of all to tell my dad's relatives of his newfound faith. He drove a "house on wheels," while my mother drove a Dodge sedan. Mother saw that we did our schoolwork, assigning us pages from books our teachers had sent with us. The "bus," as we called it, was painted bright yellow with Scripture verses on all sides in big black letters, with some red ones for emphasis. We girls sometimes stood in the top bunk with our heads out the open skylight and tossed gospel tracts to the people at the side of the road. We spent enjoyable nights at farms along the way, occasionally with friends, generally with strangers, at any convenient stopping place at the close of a long day's driving. The people we stayed with weren't necessarily Christians, but my dad always testified to God's love, and left tracts. The trip took a whole month, but eventually we landed in Pennsylvania, where my dad shared his faith with aunts, uncles, and cousins.

After a year we moved on down the East Coast, my father still anxious to tell God's Good News to others all around the country. This time we landed in Savannah, Georgia, where my next oldest sister spent eight weeks in the hospital. Here we met a small group of Christians and ended up staying there for four years. Dad worked at odd jobs when we stayed in one place for any length of time, though eventually he went to work as a carpenter. Here in Georgia he worked on the docks unloading ships. God's people were always generous with money, clothes, and food for our family wherever we stopped.

These were my upper elementary and junior high years, which meant several school changes as well as adjusting to a very different system. The schools in Georgia, for instance, didn't supply paper and writing materials unless the student paid a small sum. I've never been sure whether we couldn't afford it or if my parents, coming from a state where these things were free, wouldn't pay it. But this isolated us, because our paper and pencils were always "different." The worst trauma for me was going alone to and from school on a bus (my sick sister was closest to me and not able to attend school for a full year). I'd never ridden on a school bus before, for one thing, and had never been alone in any school. I remember being spit on by a child out the bus window as the bus pulled away from my stop. I was painfully shy and took all this very personally. Yet my family was emotionally stable and although I didn't get lots of sympathy, home was a comfortable place to be.

Our parents participated in many Christian activities during the week and therefore so did we. This included Wednesday night prayer meeting, Friday afternoon boys' and girls' class in town (from junior high we just walked to the church), and Friday night KYB class (Know Your Bible), which we loved. Families went to one home in town, and one person made up questions about a given chapter and quizzed the rest of the group. We kids each had our turn, believe it or not. On Sundays we visited prison farms and old peoples' homes, long days because of these services. We three younger ones always went along and were expected to help in small ways: carrying things from the car, distributing hymn books, and giving out any literature we had. Eventually I was allowed to play the piano for the singing. The people probably suffered, but it was great for me.

The compelling factor in all this was that the good news of the gospel needed to be shared. My father was controlled by this and it affected every phase of our lives.

We returned to California in the early '40s, where I finished my schooling. Family rules were strict about what we could and couldn't do: no bowling, dances, skating at rinks. Even parties were out (and so was colorless nail polish). This, of course, was wartime and there were servicemen galore at these places. I graduated from high school, a naive, immature, pigtailed sixteen-year-old. Looking back, I remember chafing under the strict discipline. I wasn't courageous enough to ask why, and seldom daring enough to disobey. But I know that those "rules" were good for me at the time. I personally needed such guidelines.

We traveled twenty miles to attend Sunday school in a friend's home, because our Plymouth Brethren families agreed on ways of worship. After a while, however, our family started attending a church nearer by for Sunday evening service. My parents attended these evening meetings regularly, but they allowed us girls to choose. Eventually we too became involved with activities in this church, where we were consistently challenged to be single-minded in our commitment to the Lord. Although my parents' Plymouth Brethren convictions were in another direction, our affiliation with that Bible-believing church was the right thing for me in my high school years.

My father was always a very hardworking, practical man, and my mother, who died when I was twenty and away at university, was a teacher through and through. They loved the Lord and this permeated our family life. Their values came across to us clearly, sometimes verbally but often subtly. I have often wished my mother were around to coach me, especially when my own children were small.

32
Robert H. Baylis

Robert H. (Bob) Baylis is owner of a Logos Bookstore (near the University of California, Berkeley campus), director of Christian Students Abroad, and one of the founders of Valley Church of Moraga. He is a former Inter-Varsity Christian Fellowship staff member and high school English teacher.

When I was a teenager, I was an eloquent critic of my parents' faults and shortcomings. Now that I've had a few years to reevaluate, I think that God gave me a remarkably secure and happy home, though certainly far from perfect. To analyze what my parents did right in bringing me up probably requires some description of what they were like, so I'll start there.

Both my parents were born in San Francisco in 1892. Both belonged to families who had left denominational connections to identify with the local Plymouth Brethren assembly. My two grandmothers were deeply religious, and extremely proper and strict Victorian ladies. They were friends and baby-sitters for one another. Thus my mother and dad couldn't remember a time when they didn't know each other. They fell in love more or less at puberty, were married at age twenty-four after going together for nine years, and were faithful to each other for over half a century until Dad died in 1968. As an example of conjugal fidelity, that record is hard to beat. It had to have some sort of stabilizing influence on me.

The funny thing about my parents, however, is that despite the similar family circumstances (at least externally), they were totally unalike. My little mother, who is still going strong at eighty-one, has always been cheerfully nonverbal in theological matters. Her faithfulness to the Lord has always been assumed, just like her faithfulness to my father. She has simply looked to Dad or to the assembly to give expression to her faith. At the same time her love toward me, in a finite way like the love of God, was immensely practical and unfailingly optimistic. When I was growing up she was always willing to listen, forgive, and lavish on me any good thing at her disposal. Her good nature was a tonic I could depend on. What she did right was to express Christ in dependable human terms that spelled out love and security despite whatever scrapes I got into, without necessarily approving of the scrapes. As long as Mom was there, I always had some place to come home to.

Dad, on the other hand, was a Victorian in morals and sentiment. He had a strong sense of propriety and couldn't bring himself to talk about personal matters like sex. He had no interest at all in sports and very little in any other forms of entertainment. He often embarrassed me by weeping during sermons or in sentimental situations. He thought and spoke a great deal about death. Yet, though sober and serious, he wasn't morose. He loved a good joke and got much pleasure out of the natural world and human relationships. He was loved by many, and I can quite honestly say had no enemies, even among those who didn't understand him.

Two or three things come to mind when I think of what my dad did right on my behalf. Perhaps the first of these is that he was a faithful witness. As a little kid I remember seeing him in his old-fashioned nightshirt on his knees by the bed, praying for me and my brother. As I got older and conflicts grew between my world and his (in those days there was little in the church to appeal to young people), he consistently tried to face me with the gospel in as positive a way as he knew how. When I quit Sunday school, he would take me to Sunday evening services in larger, more lively churches. Sometimes his steady aim to "get me saved" got under my skin and I would vow never to go to another meeting. I went into the Army at eighteen, and for three years I stayed fairly well away from anything religious. But in the end Dad's strategy won. He got some girl cousins to open communication with me, and just two months before my twenty-second birthday (at a gospel meeting I didn't want to go to), I gave in to the Lord.

Another of my dad's characteristics that made an indelible impression on me was his ethical uprightness. Regardless of how unattractive his brand of Christianity seemed to me as a teenager, I couldn't avoid the fact of his goodness. I remember arguing with a neighbor kid who was trying to cut me down and challenging him to point out any immorality in my father's life. Because of his upbringing and temperament, Dad apparently didn't have too great a difficulty avoiding the usual neighborhood sins of infidelity, profanity, and drunkenness. He was good in positive ways. He was scrupulously honest. He genuinely cared for the people who lived around us and with whom he worked. He went out of his way to do things for them. He would talk by the hour with merchants and business people, some of whom (like Jake the Jewish immigrant from whom he bought secondhand suits) became lifelong friends.

My dad rarely played games with me. He wasn't a "pal" like some fathers. He had a way, however, of getting me to talk (or listen) that worked, right up through my twenties. Every evening almost year 'round we walked a block or two to the local creamery and got ice cream cones. Those ice cream walks were an important part of my upbringing. At times we didn't say anything. Other times we argued the whole way—about whether school was better in Dad's day than in mine, or whether or not the English traditions of our family made any sense, and so on. But communication was taking place, which was the important thing. This rapport probably had a lot to do with the fact that, though I was a rebel, I never quit talking to my dad (even if I was verbally rough on him at times). Once I grew up and had a family of my own, we continued to be friends for the remainder of his life.

Dad further influenced me with his determination to accomplish some measurable goals during his lifetime. The life of the Spirit was the highest reality for him, and he often would amend his talk of the future with a clause like "if the Lord doesn't come" or "if the Lord spares me." Yet he had a tremendous drive to get things done here and now. He was, for example, always busy improving his house and property. In his late sixties and early seventies he completely painted his large stucco house and excavated a basement bucket by bucket. He also had goals for succeeding as a Christian leader. For two decades or more he worked steadily as a church elder and as treasurer of a rescue mission. He always longed to master a deep understanding of the Bible (having had less than a high school education). One of our last conversations was about a commentary he was reading on the book of Isaiah.

Finally, despite the narrowness of their backgrounds and the economic pinch we experienced throughout my growing-up years, both my parents tried hard to make life for my brother and me as joyful as they could. We always went for rides in the country on Sunday afternoon. After church on Sunday evening Dad would often stop to buy candy. Movies were out of the question, of course, but we would have some simple treat on Saturday evening. Later, when Dad got more prosperous, we'd go out for dinner. Christmas and vacation camping times were always delightful, even during the worst years of the Depression. That sort of remembered joy also kept me loyal to my home, even when as a teenager I started getting involved in heavy drinking and other plastic thrills.

There are plenty of things that my folks didn't do right in bringing me up, I suppose, but in the final analysis I think they scored pretty high. I'm probably much like them in their weaknesses, but I hope that some of the best has rubbed off too.

33

Gretchen Weber

Gretchen Weber is involved in her parish as music and liturgy resource person, Sunday organist, and banner lady (making decorative pieces for liturgies), and is available for cartooning, free-lance writing, wedding music, and balloon blowing. She and her physicist husband went to his current post at Iowa State University from Notre Dame, and are the parents of Liz, 13; Katie, 12; Mary, 10; and Madeleine, 7.

I am reluctant to call myself a committed Christian; my commitment has hardly been tested. But having tossed the notion around in my head for weeks, I'll admit that the exercise in reflection has been valuable. Pondering "what my parents did right" has helped me make some personal decisions about my own role as a mother and about our family's present life-style. So I dare to share my reflections.

Into the midst of grasshoppers and dust storms, I was born in mid-North Dakota in the mid-'30s, the first child of four. Then came a sister, Martha, who joined me on Daddy's lap to hear him read Edward Lear and Robert Louis Stevenson verse. We always furnished the rhyming words. We also sang songs with him, our two piccolo voices with his bass viol.

The pungent smell of turpentine and oil paints awakens early memories, too, of Mother painting in a warm, sunny living room. Martha and I must have sat for her. Our portraits still hang in the house in North Dakota. She also sketched us in charcoal—fat cheeks and wispy locks of hair, miniature buttons down the front of our dresses. We liked to look at our pictures in her drawing books.

We were three and four years old when I remember hearing Mother's violin. She practiced Kreutzer and sections from Mendelssohn and Vivaldi and we hated it. We begged her to stop. We weren't impressed that she was really quite good, or even that we might one day play the smaller violin she kept in a black wooden case. We were uncooperative on weekends when the Metropolitan Opera or the New York Philharmonic poured out of the Philco radio.

Ten years later we were begging her to play for us and she did. I learned to accompany her at the piano and to hear what she was trying to hear those afternoons. I always enjoyed piano practice when I finally got to take lessons, and I found the organ even more delightful to play.

We moved to the Twin Cities for a few years when Martha and I were preschoolers. Mother took us out of the apartment every afternoon for a long walk down Summit Avenue and along the river roads with their green yards and beautiful homes. We pretended to be bears in the woods, gathering nuts and berries for our meals. Running back and forth to the bushes, we covered twice as much territory as Mother.

Meal times were occasions for games too. While Daddy worked at the post office over the supper hour, Mother kept us from tangling with each other by having us name things in categories: dogs, trees, flowers, foods. We often ate supper by candlelight. I remember having bread with milk and sugar in thin pale-blue milk-glass bowls.

Martha and I spent part of those summers back in North Dakota where Mother's parents still lived in a big frame house on First Avenue. The front closet had a stained glass window. The backyard was divided in two by a long grape arbor. One side was fragrant with tomato plants and dill weed, the other bright with snapdragons, bleeding hearts, roses, delphiniums. In the very back, baby's breath popped out of a rock garden. Wrens sang from their little house in the box elder tree by the back porch and robins splashed in a stone birdbath.

Dama, our tiny Irish grandmother, took us for picnics in the hills outside of town. We collected sparkling stones and dreamed about living in the Irish castles she told us about. When we were tired, we sat on the scratchy grass and watched fluffy, bright clouds change shape and blow across the sky. We made up stories about the animals we saw in them.

Grandfather, whom we called Dappy, was German-Jewish and had come to America as a stowaway when he was twelve. Now he owned the Dakota meat market where we visited him daily to get a piece of spearmint gum and to sit in the captain's chair next to his high desk piled with ledgers. The shop was fragrant with sausage spices and the smell of smoked meat. After work we sat on his lap and he told us stories about Beanie and Snoopie and about his own wild animals, the hysocrum and hipponostrum.

When my brother Raymond was born, and Martha and I were ready to start school, the family moved back to North Dakota. We lived only two blocks from St. John's Academy, where we were to spend the next twelve years with the sisters of St. Joseph of Carondolet. Mother and Dama had both gone through the Academy. Every year was my favorite year and I was quite sure that this would be the grade I would one day teach.

I did teach singing and phonics after school to an imaginary class in our basement. At Dama's house we put on plays and musical reviews in her attic gowns. She loved our productions, clapped and laughed and fed us cookies. We liked to play maid at her house, dusting and helping her straighten the magazines and doilies.

We helped Mother with dishes sometimes, but not as a regular job. It was fun to work with her and laugh about how things were when she went to school. She was always interested and pleased with what we were doing. She praised our smallest successes at school and made us feel proud. I guess we agreed that the sisters there were very special people—if not infallible, nearly so.

Helping Mother hang clothes out to dry, I discovered that even an orderly clothesline could be beautiful. She made a pattern in hanging up towels and wash cloths, putting colors together, letting the white sheets soak up the sunshine.

Mother peeled potatoes like an artist too. With a sharp paring knife, she removed only the thinnest skin and then carefully cut solid shapes for boiling. For Sunday dinner she made roses on the butter, slicing thin strips of cold butter and curling them into a small flower, sprinkled red with paprika.

Both Mother and Daddy read books, bought books, and collected them. Mother's art books were the delight of hours we spent sick in bed. We followed parental example and spent many hours in the Free Library. Mother recommended titles of some of her favorite books and kept encouraging me to look up Willa Cather.

It shouldn't be surprising then that one of the most significant experiences of my early teens involved setting up a church library. Up to this time our involvement in the life of our parish consisted of confession on Saturday, mass on Sunday, and going to the Catholic school. Then the Christian Family Movement came to North Dakota with the appointment of two newly ordained priests. (The CFM was an American counterpart of the European JOCist, Young Christian Worker Movement. Its members met weekly or biweekly to read the gospel, reflect on its meaning in their lives, and attempt some social change from their study.) The liturgical movement in the U. S. began at this time, with its emphasis on intelligent participation in Sunday mass and reexamination of the gospel's social implications.

The library, one of our early projects along these lines, aimed at setting up some adult education in our parish. It began on our dining room table amid cans of shellac, cards and pockets, and stacks of new and donated books. I was thrilled to be part of the adult activity and took my place as one of the permanent librarians under the Romanesque arches. The job left me with hours for reading and talking about books with the adults who used the library. Thomas Merton's *Seven Storey Mountain* and *Seeds of Contemplation*, Eric Gills's *Autobiography*, Dorothy Day and the *Catholic Worker* (one cent an issue), Catherine de Hueck's *Friendship House* became my friends and models.

At the same time a small group of high school girls and boys were meeting weekly. We prayed together and then studied the social documents of the Church in simple form. We carried out assignments of service in the community, visiting children in the hospital and neighbors who were shut-in, helping with the census. We passed magazines from family to family and took care of a pamphlet rack in the church. I loved to "fix candles"—i.e., replenish the vigil lights that burned day and night at the church.

As a family we weren't particularly pious, though I saw Mother and Daddy pray on their knees every night. We began to experiment with some of the home rites we were learning about: blessing the Christmas tree, the Easter breads, lighting an Advent wreath, eating special foods for special days. Daddy, however, kept a tight reign on "Byzantine liturgies," as he called the lengthy ceremonies. I loved the poetry of it all, the drama, the music.

The priests and sisters became very influential. Besides the library, I worked to set up a small gift shop with cards, imported medals, and art pieces. An exhibit of liturgical art brought on tour to Jamestown gave me many ideas and sources for obtaining beautiful things.

The Academy was comprised of an exceptional group of teachers at that time—recovering, in several cases, from the pace of the Twin Cities' schools. The head of the college art department and the college Shakespeare and journalism teacher encouraged and stimulated my embryonic interests. I was asked to write for the school paper, and then to edit it. They opened opportunities for me to write for national publications about our school and parish. With only twenty-five in my class we got to know our teachers as friends. Many of us shared their interests and enthusiasm for the flowering life of the Church in the early '50s.

My piano lessons became organ lessons with the arrival of a priest who was an accomplished organist. I learned to play Bach on the pipe organ and to accompany the choir in Gregorian masses. We worked on beautiful choral music too, entering spring contests, giving concerts, entertaining for St. Patrick's Day.

It was a unique time to grow up, during that renaissance of social awareness and liturgical life in the Church. I was able to drink it all in, thanks to the trust my parents gave me, the beauty they shared with me, the freedom they gave me to develop in my own way—yet encouraged and praised.

I have reflected on my own four children and our pattern of life as I write this. I have made some changes. I am attempting to be more present to them, sensitive to their interests and feelings, to encourage them—and especially to spend more time with them as my mother did with me. I have had to eliminate some after-school conflicts and even daily mass (a lifelong habit) on some days. I hope I am doing some things right.

34

M. O. Vincent

*M. O. Vincent, M.D., C.M., is medical
superintendent of a large psychiatric hospital
in Ontario. Author of* God, Sex, and You, *he is
the father of four teenage sons.*

Life for me began in the fall of 1930 in the Baptist parsonage of
Charlottetown, the capital city of what was then Canada's
easternmost province, Prince Edward Island.[1]

In a more romantic sense my beginnings can be traced back to
the campus of Mount Allison University in New Brunswick,
where Dad was working toward a B.A. and getting his best
marks in mathematics and Greek. At times he fancied himself
becoming a math professor, but most of the time he was quite
certain he was being led into the Christian ministry. On the
same campus was a farmer's daughter with chestnut curls, "a
quiet winsome personality" (according to a character reference
in her scrapbook), known for her soprano voice. She was working toward a music diploma, majoring in voice. In the end she
obtained her diploma from Acadia University and obtained my
father from Mount Allison.

Dad's enthusiasm for Greek scholar A.T. Robertson took
him to Southern Baptist Theological Seminary in Louisville,
Kentucky, where he obtained his Master of Theology in 1929.

---

[1] Newfoundland (which had been an independent British colony), to the north
and east of Prince Edward Island, became Canada's tenth province after World
War II. The Dominion of Canada had been formed in 1867 after a historic
meeting of the "fathers of Confederation" in Charlottetown.

His master's was followed shortly by his marriage and, in time, by me.

My childhood in many ways was unremarkable, with neither great tragedies nor peaks of euphoria, neither wealth nor poverty. Unlike many ministers' families, we did not move frequently. Dad was pastor of the same church in St. John, New Brunswick, when I graduated from high school as when I began grade one. I believe this gave me a greater sense of "belonging" in one place than many ministers' children develop.

As with many of my generation, my father was overseas (as a chaplain in the Canadian Army) during World War II. During these four years, we lived close to my mother's parents. From age ten to fourteen, Grampa Tingley was the main father-figure in my life. Gramp was a warm, relatively imperturbable farmer, who first let me drive a car around his farm at age twelve, and on the highway (illegally) at age fourteen. Summers, I was a "hired man" on his farm. I was hired primarily for the "haying season" and for the harvesting of grain. I mowed hay with a team of horses, raked hay with a horse and rake, and unloaded and stowed the hay in the mow in the barn, the hottest of all jobs. I milked cows until I had the good fortune to become allergic to cows. Since my grandfather was paying me, we had to work on days that weren't fit for haying, such as cloudy or rainy days. We would do such homely things as load the manure spreader with horse and cow manure, and then drive out to fertilize the fields.

I wasn't overly ambitious, but I don't think I actually resisted work. There was an element of pride in it all, in that I and another boy my own age had been hired as "men" because of the scarcity of males during the war. Even so, that isn't to say we didn't often drive my grandfather to distraction with our clowning around.

During my childhood the pattern of our family life stands out more than specific issues or events.[2] The pattern was one of

---

[2] My life is so busy that I have little time to sit back and meditate on the problems of the past and how they were resolved even ten years ago, let alone thirty years ago. One could look on this as being a terrible repression. But on the optimistic side I am impressed that most of my neurotic patients dwell on all the problems of the past and can describe the minor difficulties of long ago as vividly as if they happened yesterday—with the result that they haven't accomplished much today. How about that for rationalization?

consistency. Mom and Dad were consistent Christians. They practiced what Dad preached. They consistently, as much as was possible, saw that I practiced it too. There was a mixture of demanding that I do certain things (such as various church attendances), demanding that I not do others (such as attend high school dances), somewhat paradoxically coupled with a great deal of freedom—about how much I studied, what time I got in, who my friends were, how often I could have the car when it wasn't in use. These things combined to give me a sense of security and the realization that my parents considered me to be generally reliable and to have good sense.

I believe it is important that while there was never any question in our house about Dad's being "the head of the family," Mom (perhaps the backbone) always supported the head. Further, while I knew it wasn't a democracy, anything and everything was open for discussion, reasoning, and arguing. I was always allowed to state my opinion or to have an argument with my parents, but whether I won or lost the argument, I knew that Dad had the final vote. I suspect that Mom was the family diplomat: she used to uphold Dad's decisions as well as try to explain Dad's position to me. I suspect that sometimes she was explaining my position to Dad when *I* wasn't around. In high school I moved gradually from obedience out of necessity to obedience out of respect for parents whom I loved and admired. Because of this I was prepared to go along with them even when I *knew* they were wrong.

What kind of a dad produced me? One who was very busy, always involved with people, but who had some contact with me almost daily until I left home for university. In childhood he was clearly a father as opposed to a pal. We rarely played together. Though I was always on hockey teams, I believe he saw me play only twice. Dad was a decisive leader among people, known for strong stands and a humorous story for every occasion. Both his leadership and humor were important ingredients in our home life. Only my younger brother could occasionally make Dad blow his cool, but then I had an extremely independent little brother (our family consisted of two boys). Yet sibling squabbles were minor. I was the older by eight years.

My mother was quieter than Dad—more reserved, people would say. A warm person, she exposed more of her sentimentality than Dad. I cannot recall any instance of either of my parents criticizing the other in my presence during my childhood.

Their faith and the way they lived it made faith more possible for me. Their mutual respect for one another made it more likely that I would respect my wife and all women. Mom's admiration for Dad made it easy for me to identify with him and come out with a positive view of myself. Their lives, lived in the service of Christ and others, still encourage me to keep battling the selfishness within, the twinge that keeps saying "me first."

My father could easily have nudged me to enter the ministry. He kept me out. I received my B.A. at nineteen, and was undecided between medical school and seminary. In discussing this with Dad one day, I recall his saying, "If you feel you can do anything else except become a minister, and be satisfied, do it. I became a minister because I couldn't be satisfied with anything else." This statement was a decisive factor in my entering medical school, even though I dreaded it (knowing it would be much tougher than seminary). Also, in retrospect I can see that at age nineteen I knew the role of a clergyman much more than I knew the role of a physician. I was sure I could fill the former. I was very uncertain about the latter.

Enough about me. Is there any general pattern for the Christian family to follow? I believe there is, and I have developed it more fully elsewhere.[3] The pattern is that of the father as "leader-servant." This leadership is patterned after Christ's leadership of the church. It is characterized by humility, lack of selfishness, emptying one's self without concern for status, taking the form of a servant even to the point of death. (Most Christian women could accept obedience to a husband like this. The problem is to find one.)

Christ's method of leadership is by service. His motive in leadership is love. His purpose in leadership is redemption. The result of redemption by Christ is freedom.

---

[3] Vincent, M. O., "Family Leadership," *Proceedings of the 20th Annual Convention, 1973,* Christian Association for Psychological Studies, (6850 Division Avenue S., Grand Rapids, Michigan 49508).

Similarly, a husband is to be the family leader: he leads in serving them and others, motivated by love for God and family, with the goal of their redemption. That is, his goal is that his wife and children will find liberation to attain full emancipation from whatever hinders their personal growth, freedom, and genuine self-authentication. Because the husband in his own imperfection has experienced unconditional love and forgiveness through Christ, he is better able to encourage self-realization, self-acceptance, and personal autonomy, and to demonstrate to his family a forgiveness that costs.

Such family leadership is liberating. It seeks the best for its members. Its purpose is never to enslave or to subjugate.

I have taken this view of family leadership from Scripture. To date, empirical studies do not provide a sound basis for solid conclusions about family leadership.

Sociologist Jetse Sprey makes several interesting observations about the family.

> Family sociologists thus far have failed to explain the causes of family conflict. This is not to say that conflict has been ignored, far from it. It has been, however, primarily treated as a major cause of family disorganization. Actually, the real villain of the piece is not conflict per se but rather unresolved strife.[4]

I would suggest that some system of leadership in the family is essential in coming to grips with the real villain, "unresolved strife."

Sprey goes on to document the lack of consensus about the origin and management of conflict within the family. He notes:

> Successful conflict-management requires the adherence to a set of shared rules, a condition which seems absent in many families. This is as valid for intergenerational conflict as for that between the spouses. Consequently, family members are often set to destroy the opposition rather than coming to terms with it.

[4]Sprey, Jetse, "The Family as a System in Conflict," *Journal of Marriage and the Family,* November 1969, pp. 699-706.

In spite of the lack of empirical certainty, solid empirical studies such as that of Westley & Epstein appear to be compatible with the scriptural view that I have suggested. This multidisciplinary, in-depth study (of the relationship between the mental health of university students and the internal organization of their family of origin) noted the increasing husband-wife equalitarianism in marriage, but stated that this does not eliminate the need for some system of authority. Conflicts still must be resolved, decisions made, and discipline maintained. They note:

> We have found that modern urban families seem to be most successful when they adopt a system of authority that allows for considerable discussion, but in cases of deadlock, allocates the final decision to someone.[5]

The power-system in the Westley-Epstein families was studied by evaluating discipline, conflict-resolution, decision-making, and members' impressions of which parent dominated. They identified four types of families: father-dominant, father-led, equalitarian, mother-dominant. Equalitarian families are completely democratic: all decisions are shared, and husband and wife are considered equal in authority. Father-led families also are basically democratic: decisions are arrived at through discussion and usually by consensus. The husband is considered the leader, however, and has the final word in situations of deadlock.

This empirical study favors a father-led family if it is assumed that the mental health of the children is a value to be sought. Further, the study implies that such an organization has a positive correlation with the mental health of all its members.

> The father-led type had the largest proportion of emotionally-healthy children, followed by the father-dominant, the equalitarian, and the mother-dominant, in that order. In agreement with most other studies, we found that the mother-dominant

---

[5]Westley, William and Epstein, Nathan, *The Silent Majority,* (San Francisco: Jossey-Bass, Inc., 1969), p. 33.

form was extremely destructive of family authority
and that almost none of the children in these families
was emotionally healthy. As far as we could see,
these were families with extremely unhappy mothers
and cold, impersonal family relationships.[6]

Empirical studies come and go, but children keep growing up.
My parents did pretty well by me. As a father of four teenage
sons, I tend to be slightly more democratic than my dad. God
has given me a wife who is highly committed to being a mother.
Children are strange possessions. We raise them so we can lose
them. I hope we have done as well by our children as my parents
did by me.

35

Betty J. M. Bube

Betty J. M. Bube is the wife of a California university professor and the mother of four children, including Sharon (chapter 6). She is active in home, church, and student affairs.

My dad's sense of humor colored much of his thinking. His gentle aphorisms enabled him to get his point across to us children effectively as well as inoffensively:

"If you don't have something *good* to say about someone, don't say anything at all." (Philippians 4:8? ". . . whatever is true . . . honorable . . . just . . . pure . . . lovely . . . gracious . . .")

"You shouldn't always *tell* the truth!" In others words, unkind truth is better left unsaid. (James 4:11? "Do not speak evil against one another.")

Though Dad exhibited virtues befitting a Christian gentleman, his own confession of faith in the Lord Jesus came near the end of his eighty-one years. He never formally joined a church. How, then, could it be said that he contributed favorably toward my own early commitment to Christ? Shortly before Dad died, he credited Mother for her faithfulness in the spiritual training of all six of their children, leading to their salvation and usefulness to society as adults.

Mother came to know the Lord at an early age and enjoyed the benefits of being brought up in a loving Christian home. I don't doubt that her parents' prayers and example played a large role in the salvation of my siblings and myself. These grandparents were concerned about my Dad's lack of commitment to Christ and His church. "I hope those evangelistic meetings continue," Grandma wrote at the time of my older sister's conversion, "until they finally reach H.B.!"

Well, those particular meetings didn't reach my dad, but God did use some fifty years of married life with Mother to bring this about. And in his dealings with us children, I believe that God bestowed "common grace" to enable Dad to support Mother's strong Christian convictions. Even at a very early age, there was no question in my mind that the distinction between right and wrong was clear and was based upon the Word of God. Regular worship at church and training in Sunday school were not options. I never dreamed of not wanting to go.

The Bible was greatly respected in our home and was basic to our training, although it wasn't used as a threat over our heads. We knew that Mother read her Bible faithfully every night before going to bed. In fact, she would be finishing her regular reading schedule (for over thirty years she read through the whole Bible each year) while Dad read the editorial section of the newspaper. Daily devotions weren't a part of our regular family life, although "grace" was said before each meal.

I'm sure it never occurred to me at the time, but in retrospect I can see the fruits of the Spirit in my mother's everyday life. Love. Joy. Peace. Patience. Kindness. Goodness. Faithfulness. Gentleness. Self-control. Perhaps I can illustrate this best by recalling a few incidents in my childhood.

My cousin and I were happily playing "dolls" on our front porch steps. While I went into the house for something, the boy from across the street appeared and decided to join in the fun. Not suprisingly, his idea of fun was to grab my most precious doll (a lovely lady dressed in brown and blue velvet) and throw it to the sidewalk. He then ran off, muttering that "dolls" was such a stupid game to play. I came back outside in time to pick up the pieces and run screaming to Mother for comfort and revenge. Comfort I received. Revenge I did not. She took this opportunity to teach me two basic biblical principles: forgiveness toward our offenders and commitment to the Lord of all our hurts. No, Mother didn't go out and give this boy the spanking of his life (my idea of vengeance), and she didn't take it out on his parents either. They remained friends throughout the years.

I was about six years old when the family moved from our house in town to my Dad's birthplace outside a small village in northeastern Pennsylvania. My paternal grandmother had recently died; and while at that time Grandpa was in reasonably good health, my Mother nursed him throughout his final illness, which lasted for several years. It took some time for the amenities of civilization we had been accustomed to in town to be installed in the homestead. Mother could have spent her time complaining, but she didn't. She was a living example of patience with problems and inconveniences.

A visit from relatives was considered the epitome of pleasure in my family. It surprised me, therefore, to discover as a child that this wasn't the case in all families. Another disturbing factor hit me with great force: the spirit of favoritism among children of some of my friends. "John is his father's favorite, you know," someone would explain. I remember taking this problem to my mother, fearful lest I discover that I wasn't my parents' favorite. Very carefully she explained to me that in our family each one of us held a special place in the hearts of both parents. Not one of us kids could take the place of another. Very honestly she admitted that some traits of personality in one child could be admired over the same traits in another, but that this in no way affected or altered their special love for each one. "You're the only Betty Jane we have. No one can take your place."

After eleven years of being the youngest in the family, I learned from Mother one day that another baby was on the way. I was excited about this news, though torn between hoping for a baby sister (which I thought would be such fun) and wishing that the family pattern of girl, boy, girl, boy, girl (me), and boy (the new baby) not be broken. To say that I never had a pang of jealousy would be dishonest. After all, I would no longer be the youngest in the family with its attendant privileges and duties. Eventually I would even have to give up my own little bedroom. But by being included in the anticipation and preparation, I was more than ready to accept my little brother when he arrived.

What an experience it was for an eleven-year-old girl to have a living "doll" to help care for: to love, scold, play, and suffer with (especially when he was being disciplined by our parents). I remember running to my room in tears when he was receiving a well-deserved spanking. It seemed so unfair to me that such a cute little fellow should be so hurt. Mother used the experience to illustrate the importance of corrective discipline in the proper upbringing of even such a young child. "I want people to *like* my children," she would say. "Nobody likes to be around a spoiled child."

All of us children had a healthy regard for parental chastening. Ideally, the end results were correction of wrongs, clearly defined guidelines for acceptable behavior, and renewed realization of the love and concern Mother and Dad had for us. This prepared us to understand the chastening hand of God, which all His children experience at one time or another (Hebrews 12).

In retrospect it is difficult to place in chronological order the steps leading to my first personal encounter with Jesus Christ as Savior. I'm sure that God used many people (i.e., my maternal grandparents, Mother, my older sisters, Sunday school teachers, ministers, etc.) to bring this about. I do remember being deeply moved by the preaching of a faithful Methodist minister when I was nine or ten years old. I also remember being puzzled and frightened by the thought of death, both my own death and especially that of my parents. The possibility of losing them left me cold with fear and loss. I finally confided this fear of death to Mother. She surprised me by admitting that she, too, had once felt this same anxiety, but that God had enabled her to overcome it.

"You see," she explained, "when Jesus died on the cross for my sins and for yours, He didn't *stay* dead. He rose again and proved He had overcome even death—again, for you and for me. So I'm just trusting Him to take care of me through my own death as well as when those I love die."

"But *how* do you trust?"

"For me, it's something like stretching out on my bed. Jesus had done all that needs to be done for me to be saved, and He wants me simply to take Him at His Word and depend on Him—just as I depend on my bed to hold me up."

"The minister has been talking about being saved. Mother, am I saved? I really want to be."

And so my mother had the joy of leading me to the Lord Jesus Christ. She then encouraged me to begin reading the Bible for myself on a regular basis, suggesting that I start with at least ten verses each night before going to bed. "Saying my prayers" had been my practice from infancy on. Now I was thrilled to expand my prayers beyond "Now I lay me down to sleep." My mother's regular custom of Bible reading and prayer before retiring was thus consistent with her profession of Christian faith and her advice to me. Had she not been so faithful in this respect, I doubt that her "confession of faith" would have been quite so credible to me.

One might feel that a ten-year-old could get little from reading the Scriptures on her own. After all, it could be argued, haven't great minds throughout the centuries spent whole lifetimes struggling to understand the Bible? Why turn a child loose on an impossible task? Let me first assure you that no great mind of the century need worry about my ever surpassing his ability to understand and interpret Scripture! Yet, like Timothy, I now am reaping the benefits of early exposure to the Word of God: ". . . from childhood you have been acquainted with the sacred writings which are able to instruct you for salvation through faith in Christ Jesus . . . and [are] profitable for teaching, for reproof, for correction, and for training in righteousness . . ." (2 Timothy 3:15, 16). And so, even as a child both in years and in Christian faith, it was exciting to discover how sermons in church, which formerly had to be more or less endured, and my own Bible reading could complement each other.

I certainly felt the effects of my acquaintance with the Bible in my growing-up years. I knew I couldn't get away with certain sins "because nobody could see." The fact that "Thou God seest me" (Genesis 16:13, KJV) had a sobering effect on much of my behavior. "Jesus loves me" continued to be a comforting concept. "Blessed are the peacemakers: for they shall be called the children of God" (Matthew 5:9, KJV) was a verse I recited one Children's Day in our Sunday school. (Being a "peacemaker" still has special desirability for me.)

My public profession of faith in Christ was made when I was

about twelve years old, at which time I joined our local Methodist church. The training sessions held by our minister strengthened my personal faith in the Lord Jesus Christ and clarified my understanding of my position and duties as a member of His visible church. First communion was a moving experience for me.

Long before the present energy shortage, my parents practiced economy out of necessity. "Down to my last pint of gas," Dad would say to avoid driving the family car unnecessary miles. (One Christmas, my sister-in-law gave him a glass jar containing one pint of gasoline. "So you'll never run completely out of gas," she teased.)

It was school day at the county fair. My friends and I, freed from tenth-grade high school classes, dutifully took a quick look at the various "educational" exhibits and then spent the rest of the day in the amusement area. Later, instead of taking the school bus for the return twenty-five-mile trip as my parents expected, I was persuaded to ride home in a car with a boyfriend and two or three other couples. "After all," I reasoned to myself, "it's much better to be taken all the way home in a car, rather than to be dumped at the school by the bus and still have to get home from there."

My nagging conscience began bothering me when it was decided that we would take in a movie on the way home. Then, having missed the first show, we naturally waited for the next one, which didn't end until after 11 P.M. By this time, I knew my parents would be really upset, so I urged a speedy trip home.

We all piled into the car. The driver let out a groan. "Oh, no!" he said, "we've got a flat tire!"

"O.K., let's get the spare," my friend helpfully retorted.

"What spare? I don't have a spare!"

The drugstore across the street was about to close as I ran in to phone Dad. I figured I needed his help badly enough to face his wrath. "Stay inside the drugstore until I get there" were his instructions. (The manager kindly kept the store open just for me.) My dad quickly got into his clothes (he'd been in bed) and drove the seven miles to meet me. He offered to take the others home, but they had nearly finished repairing the tire and chose to stay with the car.

I braced myself for a well-deserved "bawling out" as Dad and I drove home that midnight. Like the prodigal son, I had rehearsed what I'd say to him. After all, I had disobeyed fundamental rules of our family, which included my parents' knowledge and approval of where I was at all times and when I should be expected home. I had caused them deep anxiety and concern. I had even dragged Dad out of bed at night to drive fourteen unnecessary miles, etc.

"I'm sorry, Dad," I began.

"I know you are," he interrupted, "and I surely wouldn't want a repeat of tonight's performance! You did the right thing, though, by phoning me. I'm glad you realize that you can always call on me no matter what the circumstances."

That hit me hard. This wasn't the weakness of an over-indulgent parent, nor was it giving me license to repeat such behavior. We both knew this. To me, it was the strong, assuring love of an understanding father dealing with his penitent daughter. It had the desired effect: I never did *that* again. And I also had new appreciation of how much my rather undemonstrative Dad cared for me.

During my late teens, I attended an independent church that stressed intensive Bible study, personal relationship with God through Christ, witnessing, and Christian fellowship. I became deeply involved, and greatly benefited from the sound Bible teaching I received there.

"What they did right," in my opinion, includes not only what directly influenced my personal relationship with Christ in salvation, but my parents' continued positive influence by precept and example toward mature Christian living. Let me illustrate.

When I graduated from high school, I was unable to go immediately to college as planned. Mother was in and out of the hospital for a few years. My little brother was just entering first grade—in fact, I took him for his first day of school in Mother's absence—and needed a lot of care. And since we couldn't swing hospital bills and college bills at the same time, I stayed home, practicing my latent homemaking skills (?) on my longsuffering dad. As Mother recovered her health, she and I shared the housekeeping duties and enjoyed a rather rare mother-daughter relationship. Yet it bothered her that I had somehow "missed out" on further education and training.

So it was Mother who encouraged me some six years after high school to accept a scholarship to a business college about 100 miles from home, where I finally received my college education and prepared for a career as an executive secretary. It would have been easy for my parents to decide that they simply couldn't get along without my help, that I owed a duty to them in their old age and should stay home and care for them until they died (a familiar story in many families). Instead, they encouraged me to go, gently nudging me from what had become a comfortable nest.

During my "career" years, working very happily as an executive secretary in New Jersey, I spent nearly all vacations with my parents. "What a shame you have to go home the few free times you have off, instead of traveling or doing other fun things," a colleague of mine once remarked. She felt I must be doing it out of a sense of duty. Actually I was doing what I most wanted: to be with my family as much as possible. Home was still home to me, even in my early adult years.

The electronics laboratory where I worked as a secretary was located in a small university town. A graduate student friend introduced me to his new roommate: a tall, dark, and handsome giant who was then working on his master's degree in physics at the university. And, wonder of wonders, he was also a Christian. Since we all had common Christian interests, my own roommate and I enjoyed the company of these two students for some months. This ultimately narrowed down to just "him" (6'7") and "me" (5'2"). So, having met that wonderful man whom God was to give to me as a husband, my first impulse was to have him meet and love my family, and I his.

With such close family ties, one might have expected interference in the lives of their married children by our parents. Rather, they displayed the kind of love which God blesses: they were unselfish and outgoing, and desired the best for their adult children. "I want to be a sweet old lady," Mother said. We loved to tease her about this, all the while thanking God that He was working this quality in her as she grew older.

Mother was about seventy-five when Dad died. She continued living alone in the homestead, spending winters with her married children. (Incidentally, all six of us became professing Christians, and each married a Christian.) As Mother became physically more feeble (although her mental and spiritual capacities never dimmed), she realized that if she were to insist on staying alone in her own home, which was very dear to her, it would cause worry and concern to her children. So she agreed to live with my youngest brother and his wife on a regular basis, visiting the others as opportunity arose. Interestingly, each of her six children and their spouses were eager to have her join their families. She was delightful to have around. Her cheerfulness and sense of humor were contagious. She was able to joke even about her infirmities: she suffered for many years from a palsy which caused her hands to shake, much to her embarrassment and dismay.

In whichever home she happened to be, Mother respected the fact that she was a guest. She resisted the temptation to interfere in the internal affairs of that family. "Love means never having to say you're sorry": thus goes the popular saying. Don't you believe it! Love includes being able to acknowledge and apologize for sins and mistakes. On one occasion Mother reprimanded one of our young sons in my presence. (In our absence, she of course corrected the children in her care as was her rightful duty.) She quickly apologized both to my son and me for having overstepped her bounds. It impressed both of us as a lesson in true humility.

"There is great gain in godliness with contentment" (1 Timothy 6:6). Mother had suffered a heart attack. She was in a hospital near Philadelphia, and I flew from our home in California. "Now look here, Mam-mam," I teased her, "I flew 3,000 miles just to see you. Don't you expect me to come back for your funeral!" Her blue eyes brightened, and she retorted, "I couldn't care less if you came to my funeral; you came *now* when I can enjoy you!" Before I left her to go back, she confided to me, "You know, I'm happy to go—and I'm just as happy to stay. Whatever my Lord has for me, I'm content." A few months later, at eighty-one, she entered into ultimate contentment: the presence of her Lord.

God has blessed my husband and me with four wonderful

children. Our successes and blunders in bringing them up make a continuing story of the abundant grace of Jesus. "One generation shall laud thy works to another, and shall declare thy mighty acts" (Psalm 145:4). "From generation to generation we will recount thy praise" (Psalm 79:13).

36

Donald A. Miller

> Donald A. Miller, now pastor of an independent church in Missouri, is ordained by the Christian and Missionary Alliance. He has had extensive conference ministry with youth, adults, and Inter-Varsity Christian Fellowship.

My father was a preacher, and a good preacher. We children were aware of the success of his ministry by the growth and vitality of the churches he served, and by his countless friends. But his greatest fans weren't the folks in the pews but his family in the parsonage. We were sure he was the greatest, an idea that still lingers with us though we are all now middle-aged. This Pennsylvania-born minister had a way of being spiritual yet human and practical at the same time.

As I look back I'm aware of the tremendous influence he had on my life, yet I can think of very few times when he lectured me. Maybe he thought that because the family heard him preach week after week, more sermonizing wasn't necessary. He influenced me by the way he lived: with his family, in the community, in his profession. If teaching is best done by repeating the same thing over and over, then he taught me by demonstrating qualities of life and work so constantly and consistently that they became part of my life.

When I went to college his letters to me majored on the importance of prayer. He advised me to pray about my daily life, my future, my wife (whoever she might be). Those encouragements to pray meant everything to me because he was a man of prayer. And his prayers were answered.

He had a little book (no one saw it often except him) in which at the beginning of each month he would write down his personal and pastoral needs. At the end of each month he would put *ans* after the prayer requests that had been answered. It was amazing and exciting to see how God month by month met the needs of our family. Stories without number could be told about how God supplied.

A time came when because of sickness he was without a church for a number of months. There was no visible support. As was his custom, he brought to the Lord his financial needs. One day he received a letter with a check from a person in Pittsburgh. The letter said, "This morning your name began to go around in my mind. Finally I said to my wife, 'Where is Tracy Miller these days?' She said, 'I don't know.' " So this man had called across the city to the pastor of the church where my father had been some years before. He was told that Dad was disabled and without a church. This man sent a check. Dad went into the kitchen where his wife was. "One might have thought that all the other answers to prayer were coincidental, but when *this* man sends a check it proves God's ability to answer." He was someone who had often been in disagreement with my father, but God nonetheless used him to answer Dad's prayer.

The whole family realized that prayer was important. We got the idea that what Dad asked for, God gave. My brother Vern, who today is a "Y" director in California, went to him and asked if he was praying that he would go into the ministry. "No," Dad said, "I'm praying that you will know the will of God for your life and do it. Why do you ask?" Vern, knowing Dad's prayers, said, "Well, I just thought if you were praying for me to be a minister, I better get with it."

We got the idea that God was interested in every part of our lives. We knew we were constantly being mentioned before the Lord day after day for His direction in our lives. But even in this area we had some surprises. I started going with a girl in my junior year in college, and sometime later we were engaged.

One day Dad said to her, "Doris, I've been praying for you for many years." She was surprised, for Dad had been acquainted with her only a little longer than I. Naturally, she wondered how he could have been praying for her for over twenty years. "When Don was born, I began to pray for God to provide a wife for him, and the right wife for him. And every day I've prayed for that girl who would be his wife."

Seeing God answer prayer had great impact on my life. In his first pastorate in Pennsylvania, just about the time I was born, the newly married pastor and his wife needed a new stove. Having asked God for one, Dad was assured that one would be forthcoming and he announced this fact to his wife. She wasn't so sure. After all, there was no money at hand and further, there was something special about that needed stove. Their kitchen was quite small, so the place where the stove would fit was a little smaller than one for a regular stove. Some time later as Dad walked down the street, a woman stopped him and said, "Pastor, I'm getting a new stove. Would you like to have my old one?" She wanted something fancier, although the one she was getting rid of was nice and not very old. So the stove was taken to the parsonage and—you guessed it—it fitted perfectly into the place it had to go.

Now this didn't mean that Dad wasn't practical. Many times we think that a man who is "heavenly minded" doesn't know how to relate to life's common experiences. Dad was willing to "help God out" at times. My sister Marion got interested in a dashing, handsome young Marine who wasn't a Christian. It looked as if she was going to throw her life away. In fact, feeling under pressure, she decided to leave home one night. Dad had been praying earnestly about the situation for some time. So as Marion packed her suitcase, Dad arrived and unpacked it just as quickly. Realizing she was fighting a losing battle, she wisely planned "to leave another time." A pastor's wife today, she remembers with gratitude how her father helped God to change the course of her life.

Dad had opinions and convictions that he felt should be lived out regardless of the circumstances. He traded with a butcher in one of the large markets in Pittsburgh. They seemed to know each other well, and often talked at great length on various subjects including religion. One day when the butcher used profane language, Dad rebuked him. The butcher then attacked Dad and beat him up. At the time I was doing theological training at Nyack Missionary College, and my brother Vern was at Taylor University. When news reached us in different sections of the country, we determined to march on Pittsburgh and together give that butcher a taste of his own medicine. Dad vetoed this. He firmly believed that if you fought your own battles, God would let you fight them—and from time to time you would get the worst of it. But if you let God fight your battles, He would do a better job. "Vengeance is mine; I will repay, saith the Lord," he would quote.

Near my eighth birthday my mother died, a shattering blow to my father. He reeled through life in following months. She had gone to the hospital to have a baby, and her death was unexpected. That night I stood by his side as he called relatives to let them know. The tears that fell from his face made my heart ache. Often during the next weeks I would think I heard my mother calling me while I was at play or in my room.

Dad never understood why God took Mother. I never saw him bitter about it, but he was perplexed. Years later, after he was married a second time (and very happily), he would talk to me about it from time to time. One afternoon playing golf, when we stopped to rest a bit he said, "I have asked God many times why he took your mother, and He has never given me an answer."

There were three children, and I was the oldest. (The newborn baby had not lived long.) Some decision had to be made about what to do with his family. Relatives suggested that we be divided among them, but Dad decided against this. Within a year he married a younger woman who had been in his first church. She had often been a baby-sitter for me when I was a baby, and she had a love for me that had begun years before. Though she served and loved us children faithfully, and without complaint, she didn't have the visible influence on my life that Dad had. More than ever after Mother died, and in years that followed, I felt closer to him.

Things that I thought catastrophic Dad taught me to take in stride. A vacant lot near our home in Newark, New Jersey, was often the scene of our ball games. One day a moving car ran into a baseball I'd just hit. I couldn't flee the place of my crime (I had always been taught that one's sin would find him out), yet I feared the wrath at home when I brought the bill for a broken windshield. Although those were Depression days, Dad accepted it calmly as one of life's little tragedies. I had to pay for it out of my earnings as a magazine salesman. He encouraged me to get the other fellows to share the cost, which I more readily did because I was responsible otherwise.

Being a preacher's kid has some advantages, but mainly "PKs" grow up in a fish bowl, with more expected of them than of other youngsters in the neighborhood or church. I was aware I was a "PK," and often the reason was that other folks reminded me of it. If I did something that the older generation didn't agree with, they were quick to say, "Now, we would expect that from other children but not from the preacher's children." I didn't get that kind of admonition at home. We were just kids like everyone else. There were standards in our home that other homes didn't have, but that was because ours was a Christian home, not a preacher's home. Rather than being reminded that I was a "PK," I was reminded of the importance of our name. I was urged to live in a way not to bring shame to the name and thus to the family. So at home we were treated like the growing children we were.

Dad believed in discipline, but only after patience had run a long course. He would say, "I am coming to the end of my rope," and we knew then that he'd taken about all he could of our meanness or misbehavior. Yet when we finally were disciplined it seemed to take more out of him than us. Once when he gave Vern a whipping, he had to lie down for a while afterward, it so affected him. By then Vern was already out playing again. We weren't disciplined often, but when we were, we remembered it. I learned something about God's punishment in those sessions. God has to punish. When a person breaks His law, or goes a way that will bring disaster, God may step in. Yet how reluctant He is to do it, and His own heart is affected when one of His children has to be disciplined.

I accepted Christ when I was quite young and so I didn't feel that the standards of our house were imposed on me. Like many young persons there were some erratic periods in my service for Christ as I grew up, but for the most part I was in agreement with the rules that Dad had set up for us in a Christian home. Perhaps his great influence on us kept us from talking over some of these things as we sought to make decisions for ourselves. For if there's a danger in having a father whom you highly respect and nearly worship, it's that you accept his views without always thinking through their validity for yourself.

Our home had some strict Christian standards, though they weren't considered strict then. I didn't grow up feeling that life was a series of no-no's. Some things I couldn't do, some places I couldn't go—to dances or movies, for instance. But in their place were all kinds of sports activities, games to play, books to read. And always we vacationed at the ocean during the summer. Dad never took something away from us without putting something in its place. He never allowed a vacuum to develop.

Early in my life he saw to it that I was introduced to books. When I was in fifth grade, he went away on an evangelistic mission. When he got back, he told me there were some things on the bed for me. I raced upstairs and found a number of books. There were adventure stories, flying stories, Boy Scout stories, and my introduction to Horatio Alger. I have been in love with books ever since. But again, reading wasn't something he told us to do; he was an avid reader himself.

Dad had only an eighth grade formal education. Later he went to business college, and after his conversion he had one year at Bible college. By the time I was in high school I realized he was an educated man. He knew more things about more subjects than any man I've ever known. He simply read and read until he had an outstanding education. Yet his own lack of college education made him sensitive to what a college education might mean and he determined that each of his children would have one.

I knew I was loved. Dad wasn't the hugging type with his male children, but we knew his love. It showed in his eyes and in his actions. After finishing college and wanting further theological training, I was a little hesitant about taking money from him; for two years Dad had had two sons in college. So I decided I'd make it by myself at Bible college. Sitting in a car in front of the same market in Pittsburgh where he'd been assaulted, I told him I'd rather not take any more financial aid from him. He was silent a bit, and then with just a trace of tears in his eyes he said, "But, son, I love to do this for you."

Yet we always knew where his first loyalty was: it was to God. There never was any doubt. There could be no compromise, and even his family must take second place to this. Dad had been quite a gambler before he was converted, and cards weren't allowed in our home. When I became infatuated with Rook at college, I didn't realize that such terms as ace, trump, and kitty were terms he associated with those years before he met Christ. One day sitting in the living room playing Rook, I was aware that Dad wasn't comfortable. Then he came in and pulled down the window shade. He didn't want people to see us playing cards, he said. To us that was rather strange and surely old-fashioned. Now I realize that it was a sign of another loyalty, to his God.

But neither his prayer life nor this unflinching loyalty to God made him less human. He once said, "I am a great sinner, but I am also a great confessor." He admitted his failures and asked for forgiveness from friends and family.

One night we came to the table and there was gloom all around us. Some kind of fracas had taken place in the family earlier, and each one was sure that the other was at fault. It happened so long ago that I can't remember what it was, but it had put a damper on the fun we usually had at the evening meal. Then, just as we were about to pray, Dad said, "I want to apologize and ask for forgiveness for what I said this afternoon. It was not right and it was not Christlike." Then he went around the table and asked each person to forgive him. He could have stood on his rank and authority, but rather he was sensitive and obedient to God's will. You can bet it was as if someone had turned on the lights. Through such experiences I learned the necessity to keep communication lines open with God and with one another.

In one area he was impractical, though I'm not sure it was too serious. You see, he never expected to die. He expected the Lord to come before then. So he didn't buy a cemetery lot, and when he died, that duty fell to Mother and me.

Anyway, in his preaching he was a great user of stories. He developed his sermons by taking his text and then explaining it and then using a story to illustrate it. One day he was asked what he would like to be doing when the Lord came. Quickly he replied, "I would either like to be in the cemetery and see those grave stones go flying—or else in the pulpit preaching. I would want to be preaching on the Second Coming. I would take my text, explain the meaning, and then 'go up' by way of illustration."

I guess you couldn't expect a person like that to waste time buying a cemetery plot. But the day came when the Lord took him, and this heavenly-minded man left me a legacy of the practicality of the Christian life. He left an example of how it should be lived.

37

Jean Sutherland

Jean Sutherland, senior contributor to this book, is the wife of Dr. Brian Sutherland, Vice-Principal of Regent College in Canada. An M.A. graduate of McGill University with honours in Classics, her hobbies are Egyptology, watercolour painting, and gardening.

It is not easy, after an interval of fifty or sixty years, to remember what specific items in one's training come from one's parents. In my childhood, schools, parents, and public opinion all collaborated to set up standards of manners and morals very different from those of today. Laws were generally stricter, and they were generally enforced. Those who fell glaringly short of the standards were liable to find themselves in disgrace. Teachers and other professional folk were appointed on a basis of moral character as well as professional qualifications.

This is not to say that everybody was good and everything in the garden was lovely. There was much shortcoming and much hypocrisy; but this was definitely recognized as wrong. The prophet Isaiah says, "Woe unto them that call evil good, and good evil; that put darkness for light, and light for darkness; that put bitter for sweet, and sweet for bitter!" This, it seems to me, is one great difference between today and the time in which I was brought up. Those who have shaped the thought of more recent generations have done, I feel, just what the prophet deplores. Even in the aesthetic realm they have put discord for harmony and called what is ugly, beautiful.

My ancestors were mostly Presbyterian, but my grandfathers joined the Plymouth Brethren. My mother's family came from the American colonies to Canada in 1776, being Loyalists. My father's great-grandfather went from England to Ireland, and my greatgrandfather came out to Canada in 1847.

The person who most influenced me in my childhood was certainly my father. I was the eldest of four children, all girls; and almost from the time I was first able to think, he treated me as an intelligent person; so that in looking back, in the many years that have followed his death—he did not live to be forty-five—I often feel that in many ways he was more like an older brother than a father. He always upheld his authority, but he showed us great tenderness. I am sure that the dread of disappointing him was a much stronger incentive to good conduct than any fear of punishment—though punishment was by no means left out of the scheme of things.

The lovely Greek word in Philippians 4:5, that is translated "moderation, gentleness, sweet reasonableness"—and to which no translation can really do justice—was very descriptive of him. But cruelty, dishonesty, or meanness roused him to anger, and pornography he loathed with his whole soul. His generosity, kindness, and consideration were known to everyone in our small town, and especially to the very poor (though he was far from rich himself). He was long remembered after his death.

I write this of him, because it was his character and example that were the strongest influence on my life, though he enforced them also with precepts. I believe that if we wish to influence our children for good, we can do so only if our own characters and behaviour are well disciplined by our faith. His faults were the faults of his virtues, as the French say, and though he has now been dead for fifty years, I often find myself thinking how pleased he would be with this or that.

In the first place, we were simply steeped in the Bible. We were brought up in a very small congregation of Plymouth Brethren, which became smaller as time went on, so that most of our spiritual instruction was at home. We had family prayers every morning, and they were not hurried. In this connection I may observe that everyone got up to breakfast.

In our own house my husband and I followed this pattern also. However early he might have to go out, we and our six children were up and dressed for breakfast, and they were taught to read the Scripture even before they could quite make out the words. We instituted a further custom while our own children were at home with us. On Sunday evenings we had prayer all round, everyone taking part in turn. For some years we kept a slotted box on the mantel above the fireplace, where private requests could be written out and inserted, so that the whole family could join in prayer for these. This box of prayers was burned in the fireplace on the last Sunday in the year.

I have mentioned punishment. This is nowadays considered a relic of barbarism; and curiously enough, in a world where everyone is clamouring for a return to nature, most do not recognize the inevitable natural law that whatsoever a man soweth, that shall he also reap. I have found that so long as punishment is fair and just, children do not resent it. Injustice is very hard for them to forget, and should be very carefully guarded against. My father never lost his temper with us that I can remember, and I don't think he ever punished us without getting at the facts first.

Manners and conversation received greater attention fifty or sixty years ago than now. Generally speaking—not just in our family—even slang was discouraged, and profanity or dirty expressions were severely punished. As I have implied before, my father never used such terms himself, and really hated them. We were also frowned upon if we became unkindly critical, or cynical, or grumbling. I have quite vivid memories of my grandmother, whenever she heard anything of the kind, saying, "Whatsoever things are lovely!" and bringing us up short.

Since my father had been brought up in one of the stricter sections of the Plymouth Brethren, he was from time to time assailed by tracts or homilies adjuring him to forbid the reading of any fiction, or any music except hymns, or to refrain from keeping Christmas or other such holidays, or even from voting on any political issue. These things he weighed and discussed, and I am happy to say that reason, grace, and common sense generally prevailed. We did not, however, go to movies, or dance, or play bridge. He thought these things tended to exercise too much fascination if they became a habit, and were seldom free of temptation to wrong.

I do not think this generation really understands the value of restrictions. It is my conviction that every activity has its proper restrictions, and that as these are relaxed, there is a proportional loss of meaning and purpose. Many people will not agree with me, but I feel that art, music, and poetry have lost nearly all their meaning, not to speak of sense and beauty, by spurning limitations. Certainly life itself has lost its meaning for large numbers of people who have theoretically or practically abandoned moral restrictions.

In my youth, history was very much to the fore among our studies. I am sure that the disparagement and neglect of this study accounts largely for the sad lack of perspective nowadays. The Christian should reflect that most of the Bible is in the form of history; and common sense tells us that if we are willing to learn lessons from history, we can be saved much of the misery of learning "the hard way."

In my early years there was of course no television, and indeed no radio. We were not in the habit of being passively entertained—and needless to say this concept had not invaded the schools. We went to school to work and to learn. If we wanted entertainment we were largely obliged to furnish it ourselves. In our home there was much reading aloud, and much pleasure in sharing a good book.

When my own children were young I remembered this, and formed the habit of reading aloud to them, particularly during their lunch hour, their father being absent. This continued for many years, since we had a large family, and introduced them to books they might not otherwise have thought inviting enough to open. Kipling, Stevenson, John Buchan,* and others began the long series, and later many of the more serious writers like Dickens and others, all of whom the children learned to enjoy and appreciate. Since then I have come to see what an excellent way this was of bridging the generation gap, since in this way we

---

*John Buchan was famous in Britain for his spy stories about a character based on Lord Ironsides (World War I commander-in-chief of British forces). He was a Christian, simply steeped in Bunyan's *Pilgrim's Progress*. C. S. Lewis, incidentally, mentions him repeatedly.

shared our own background—the best of it—with the children. The lasting, warm family feeling among us all is, I think, partly due to this.

It was taken for granted among our elders, and emphasized in our schools, that we owed something to God and to our country and to the people among whom we lived. It was not considered decent to act on the principle that the world owed us any kind of a living. "Work" was not a despicable four-letter word, or something to be avoided at all costs. It was regarded as the wholesome blessing it is. We learned what satisfaction can come from working honestly for an object and attaining it.

This age has almost totally lost the concept of justice, so that the proper balance of justice and mercy has been completely upset. Even right and wrong have gone by the board, honesty has been redefined out of recognition, and dishonesty means nothing at all. In my childhood it was wrong to steal, or cheat, or lie. This was recognized by everyone, even by those who indulged in these acts. Those who infringed the moral code did not attempt to say that they were doing right. They knew better. I do not think I have language strong enough to condemn those educators who have abolished principles and blurred the difference between right and wrong for the younger generation. To them must apply the terrible words of the Lord Jesus, "Whosoever shall cause to offend one of these little ones. . .it were better for him that a millstone were hanged about his neck, and that he were drowned in the depth of the sea."

Another dreadful thing these philosophers have done is to do away with laughter. Though we were brought up with some strictness, yet we always found amusement and relaxation in seeing the funny side of life. We learned, by example and sympathy, what should be laughed at and what not, and how close to each other tears and laughter are. Above all, we learned to laugh at ourselves. "I hope," said Miss Elizabeth Bennet in *Pride and Prejudice*, "that I never ridicule what is wise or good. Follies and nonsense, whims and inconsistencies, do divert me, I own, and I laugh at them whenever I can." Of this invaluable means of retaining one's sanity in a world that changes with dismaying rapidity, the psychologists have largely deprived their unhappy pupils—since the follies and whims and what-not are precisely what they insist on taking very seriously indeed; and far from laughing at oneself, one is told to look there for the only god worth serving. Christian parents should long since have strenuously resisted this horrible mould into which their children's thoughts have been squeezed, and fortified them well against it. No wonder the weight of things is too much for them.

I have set down most of these things as they occurred to me, and perhaps they are not in the best order. One more thing I should like to make clear. We were not treated as small children when we were no longer small. As we grew up we were encouraged to choose in accordance with our own judgement and our own conscience. I myself left home to go to college at sixteen, and from then on my father laid no kind of prohibition on me.

Our own children did not leave home quite so early—it takes longer nowadays to get through high school! But we tried to exercise their judgement by degrees, so that they might be fitted to take on their own responsibilities. Perhaps I may be allowed to say here, how thankful I am that my husband took his proper share in bringing up the children. I should have been far too timid and fearful to give up supervising them or to let them take risks which he knew were good for them. I am sure that the sound Christian maturity they have attained is due to his wisdom in this respect. He in his turn, like my father before him, was head of his family.

To sum up, it seems to me that our training, while no doubt falling short here and there, as everything human falls short, did include the best possible features—first of all sound Christianity, then common sense, discipline, humour, and kindness.

"What doth the Lord require of thee, but to do justly, and to love mercy, and to walk humbly with thy God?"

38
Virginia Hearn

Virginia Hearn majored in Spanish at Otter-bein College in Ohio, did graduate work at the University of Wisconsin, and has now worked as an editor for over ten years.[1] She and her husband Walter were seemingly described in a novel by Saul Bellow: "Someone had said. . .that [there] all the loose objects in the country were collected, as if America had been tilted and everything that wasn't tightly screwed down had slid into. . .California."[2]

A few years ago Walt and I were taking my parents to my sister's home for Thanksgiving. To make conversation as we drove across backcountry roads in southern Wisconsin, the cold brown landscape awaiting the first snow, my ever-imaginative husband asked them, "If you could have become anything you wanted in life, if you could have gotten the necessary education, what would you have been?"

To my surprise, my father quickly answered, "A preacher." Then, more predictably, my mother said, "I'd have been society editor for the newspaper."

That vignette hints at three basic currents of my upbringing.

---

[1]Formerly with *HIS* magazine, Inter-Varsity Press, the *Journal* and other publications of the Christian Medical Society, and the *Evangelical Foreign Missions Quarterly;* currently with several religious publishers and a California textbook company.

[2]Saul Bellow, *Seize the Day* (New York: Viking Press, 1956), pp. 14, 15.

First, both my parents were frustrated in what had been their youthful dreams—and consequently shared the desire for their children to "have it better." Second, religion—however nominal—was a regular aspect of life. And third, the printed word, writing, reading, books, libraries (call it education) were the route to the good life.

My father was an extremely laconic man, so what little I know of his background has been largely imparted by my mother. After a fire destroyed their home and possessions at the beginning of this century, his family immigrated from Germany to the United States and settled in an area already populated by earlier Swiss-German arrivals. My father, then nine or ten, along with a younger brother, was put into the first grade of a country school, an obviously scarring experience. Evidently, my father was eager to learn—and soon began to receive the book (the Horatio Alger variety) awarded each year to the best math student. Nonetheless, he and his brother were whipped if heard using English rather than German at home.

Food was scarce and nutrition poor. Milk and eggs were sold to help make payments on the farm. The work was hard, hands were few, and my father—who begged to be allowed to go on to high school—was forced to drop out as soon as he had been "confirmed." (Escape came only with World War I, when he was drafted a few months before Armistice Day.) What his response to the beautiful German of Luther's *Catechism* and music was I don't know, but it must have been in that confirmation experience that his boyish desire to be a "preacher" lay. The pastor of that *Evangelische Kirche,* an almost papal figure among his parishioners, was undoubtedly the best educated person, possibly the only well-educated person, with whom teenage Gottlob had come in contact.

Always a deeply emotional, sensitive, though sometimes violent man, generally withdrawn and protected by his laconic exterior, my father may have responded to the majestic and personal God he learned about as a youth. Over forty years later, while listening to one of the televised Billy Graham crusades, faith again made sense to him. At that point, my father began reading the Bible on his own, both *Das Neues Testament und Psalmen* and J.B. Phillips' modern English version. He was tremendously calmed by what he read.

My mother, too, came from a background of great poverty and deprivation. She was of pioneer stock. One of her grandfathers had driven a stagecoach from Wilmington, Delaware, to Chester, Pennsylvania. Eventually her forebears had left the East for land and new life in the Middle West, settling in northern Illinois. My mother's "way with words" was apparent from my earliest memories. Her colorful speech with its folk idioms, now almost lost to contemporary English, I found to my surprise documented for posterity by Mark Twain (e.g., in *Huckleberry Finn*, showing his genius for recording authentic nineteenth-century dialogue). I still hear such speech occasionally in the words of my sisters.

My mother's father died of a heart attack at thirty-six and left no legacy for his widow and small daughter. There was no Social Security. "He wouldn't work," my mother says, though she now recognizes that he may have had some undiagnosed physical disability that made exercise difficult. The hate that my grandmother felt for her husband, as well as for neighboring males who in years ahead defrauded the widow and orphan in various ways, embittered my mother, hurt her marriage, and in turn, affected her own children. (Apart from the grace of God and my gentle, gentling husband, I sense in myself the potential to be a hardened feminist.[3])

My mother attended country school (one room, eight grades), has vivid recollections of teachers, other students, and books, poems, and stories studied, but insists that she was not a good student. She had a speech impediment (no longer discernible), she says, that made her feel self-conscious and inferior. Just before eighth grade graduation, she simply quit attending: whatever paraphernalia the terminal ceremony required would have been too expensive. Years passed, with the two women struggling to eke out an existence on their small farm.

My mother's way with words found a surprising outlet when she became "correspondent" from their village for the news-

---

[3] I don't mean this observation as a putdown of the important affirmative goals of the "women's movement" of the seventies. I am sensitive to and supportive of most of the issues now being raised.

paper in the county seat. She met people and "got in on" some interesting social events. More years passed and she and her mother moved into town, to a small one-acre property with more limited demands but with land enough for subsistence farming. My mother joined a Sunday school class of young single women, of which she has now been a member for over fifty years. (It was called Philathea, "lover of God," and is affiliated with a national organization still in existence.) At some point she "responded" to an altar call, but her subsequent religious practice seemed to emphasize not drinking, not smoking, and great antipathy toward the "lowdown" individuals who did such things and worse. She attended Sunday school and church undeviatingly and later saw that her daughters did likewise.

Living in town gave opportunity for a town job, and my mother held several. She studied organ and typing and dressmaking, but apparently never to a degree that gave her much sense of accomplishment or satisfaction. In time she took a job ironing in the local laundry, where she met the young man who eventually became her husband. The first two years she didn't know he could speak English, and she of course spoke no German. (It was possible to live in that area in those days without learning English, and neither of my paternal grandparents did.)

My earliest memory—whatever child specialists say—is of the birth at home of my sister, when I was twenty-one months old. Another baby girl arrived less than a year later. My mother, by then well into her forties, had three children in diapers. I mainly recall our squabbles, largely of me swiping my little sisters' toys and running off with them. To the delight of my parents, my older little sister would soon abandon the chase, go behind the door, pretending to telephone, and say firmly, "Jail! Ginny naughty!"

Like so many other children, I was taught to say the Lord's Prayer every night—but recall rattling it off mechanically, as fast as possible, with no thought of what the words meant, or of talking to a Father in heaven who was listening. Prayer was not a part of our family life, other than my mother saying a "grace" before meals at times when we had "religious" company, a strange fragmental practice. My father, once his hopeless religious ideal had dissipated, seemed irreligious, indifferent, though he attended church as regularly as the rest of us. (To settle on my mother's denomination instead of his own—which still held German services—as the faith in which to bring up us children, had caused a traumatic clash between my parents.)

I inherited my mother's way with words. I recall occasionally giving snippy answers to Sunday school teachers and other people (though never to "real" school teachers), and thinking it very funny. Sunday school was a "given," but unrelated to life beyond the church door. Something gave me a sensitivity to divine names, and I would refuse to sing the words *God* or *Jesus* when they came in the songs. My father was profane (this much English my older German relatives learned—at least the men) and my mother made clear to us that it was very wrong to speak like that. In my verbosity I was the prime object of my father's wrath. Where I got such an idea I don't know (certainly not from our "liberal" church), but I settled on a little formula: that if my father didn't use profanity more than *ten* times he wouldn't go to hell. I gradually upped the total and then it became too frightening to think about.

My sisters and I without fail earned Sunday school attendance prizes. One prize was a Catholic girls' book, which I read again and again simply as an accessible book. I recognized it as different from our own religion and wondered why the teacher had chosen it. No doubt the reason was the unavailability in our town of religious books, other than some Catholic ones, for children.

A comrade of my father's from World War I, was "converted" and came to visit us. (I saw such a "conversion" take place firsthand in the movie *Sergeant York,* and knew it meant a changed and good life.) My parents were rather embarrassed at his religious fanaticism, but put up with it. He and his wife gave us strange fundamentalist religious books, which I also read without conviction, and sent us girls a newspaper, very small black type on newsprint with no pictures. I read it but was indifferent to the points it was trying to make.

One of the mystifying experiences of my childhood, which seems totally out of character for both parents, was that we went to some summer tent meetings held by itinerant evangelists. They were loud and strange. Some people cried and "went forward," but not my parents. Why we went was never discussed in my presence. Then too, I think at the encouragement of some customer (my father by then owned the laundry), we went to special meetings at the Assembly of God church. Some people wanted to be healed, but weren't.

Not until his own quiet conversion in the late 1950s did my father get any basic Christian teaching, and then only occasionally when he and my mother (who went reluctantly) attended evening services at the Nazarene church. The minister liked my father, seemed to care about him, and treated him with respect—the last perhaps the most important for one so sensitive about his lack of education and his "blue-collar role" as my father was.

My mother documented those years with a large box camera she called "the Kodak." Most childhood pictures show me as a thickset, scowling, plain child, in contrast to my sylphan younger sisters with their soft smiles and more delicate features. "Oh, you look lovely!" my mother would say, as my younger sister came downstairs dressed for Sunday school. And then, "Oh, you're beautiful!" as my youngest sister with her long blond curls appeared. "What about *me*?" I'd plead. "Don't you think *I* look nice?" "Yes, yes, you look very nice," my mother would answer.

Even as a preteen, I felt the slight, and words became my weapon. I fantasized myself as a child movie star, imagining movie titles, the cast of characters, and opening scenes (with me sometimes Shirley Temple, but more often Diana Lynn or Gloria Jean). That was better than life as it was. I turned to books and identified with those characters too, mostly with those of earlier times. I was too sensitive to let myself read animal stories, which always ended sadly.

"Gin, come help your mother set the table." "Come wipe the dishes. I'll burn those books!" Here, too, I was caught in the conflict between my parents. "Oh, let her read," my mother would say. She started taking us to the town library as soon as we learned to read, and, unlike my best friend's mother, soon freed us to go "on our own" although it was quite a walk. To her

I owe my interest in reading, something apparently furthered by our each reading some book to her (we thought) every morning as she braided our hair into waist-length plaits. She has no recollection of this now, so perhaps she didn't really listen. But we got practice in reading aloud and got caught up in the stories. I remember in particular the Laura Ingalls Wilder books.

Both parents gave my sisters and me immense respect for education. If a teacher said it, we were to accept it as true. I incurred my father's rage by correcting his English grammar, and sometimes my mother thought he would kill me in his violence. I blossomed academically. I was one of those strange ones: I liked school. During the summer there was daily vacation Bible school, held at a "stricter" church, and no one had to force me to go. I learned all the books of the Bible, and there was a long poem giving a "summary" of the contents of the sixty-six books:

> In Genesis the world was made by God's creative
> hand;
> In Exodus the Hebrews marched to gain the Prom-
> ised Land. . .
> The Revelation prophesies of that tremendous day
> When Christ, and Christ alone, shall be the trem-
> bling sinner's stay.

I learned songs and games and maps of Bible lands and probably some "verses"—and excelled in my teachers' eyes—but was personally untouched by it all. On our eighth birthday my mother had given us each a Bible with our name in gold letters, and showed us the Twenty-third Psalm. The type was small and printed in two columns, unlike school and library books. I revered it but I did not read it.

From the time I was quite young, I sensed among certain people in leadership in our church a hypocrisy that was abhorrent to me. One minister's wife in particular was so saccharinely gushy to some little girls with their sausage curls and meticulous dresses, and so superciliously oblivious—or else mean and critical—to less pretty little girls and squirmy little boys, that I was repelled. However ignorant I was of what the gospel meant, I knew it did not mean that. I knew to the depths of my being that true goodness wouldn't act that way.

My personal arrival at the age of accountability had been a clear event to me. We were having a second-grade spelling test and *field* was one of the words. Try as I would, I couldn't remember if it was *ie* or *ei*. So I wrote the word on the desk. Unrelated as Sunday school was to life, unvocal as my parents were about childhood moral issues, I knew that was wrong—yet I did it.

Over the years my knowledge of my own lostness grew, though I wouldn't have described it that way. At age thirteen I was "confirmed." We recited a confirmation covenant that said:

> Lord Jesus, take this heart of mine,
> Make it pure and wholly Thine.
> Thou wast born and died for me;
> I will henceforth live for Thee.

But the long weeks of Saturday morning confirmation classes hadn't explained religious things along those lines at all. I sensed the discrepancy, but wasn't articulate enough to question it. Yet that confirmation morning I meant what I said, and I hoped it would make a difference.

The summer after eighth grade I went to a Methodist church camp with a friend. My family wasn't very enthusiastic about my going, but our church didn't then have such camps. There I heard about Christian "missions" in foreign lands and met some real-life missionaries. One of my roommates, a sophomore, whispered a long account late at night to another of the roommates, also older, of how she'd had an illegitimate child a few months before.

But at the end of that camp there was a final service, followed by a candlelight outing—in which each person wrote herself/himself a letter about what the week had meant, and which would be mailed to each one a few months later. To my surprise, as I wrote I found myself responding to whatever sense for God I had gained that week. I am sure I vowed to live for Him. Then I went back home, and the inspiration ended. When the letter came, shortly before Christmas, I tore it up without reading it. I was ashamed of whatever emotion had been conjured up in the past summer, and knew that nothing had come of it.

In junior high science, we read statements, not stated as conjectures, about the beginnings of things. ("Infinity" was a frightening concept to me; how could anything not end? The end of space would have to mean more space.) Various cosmic events involving flaming balls and tremendous gravitational forces had resulted in our solar system and this planet. Life had developed. And nothing was said about God. One spunky little girl, somewhat of a newcomer to the school and who attended the "stricter" church where I had gone to Bible school some summers before, made a big fuss about God's being left out. The teacher, who was also the junior high principal, tried to explain it somehow, but he was embarrassed and she was unrelenting. I listened with interest, reflecting on the theistic omission, and never forgot it. (Years later, when the same atheistic approach was taken in college science courses, I did the same—but by then had gained confidence that there must be scientifically trained Christians who could "put it together." And many years after that. I married one who has been in the forefront of such discussion for years.)

Because my parents were older when they married and had children, throughout my childhood a large number of relatives died. My grandfather who spoke no English, and for whom I recited a little German poem from time to time, kept starting to cry one evening when my father and I visited him. The next day he committed suicide.

My grandmother, my mother's mother, was forcibly moved to our house one winter (legend has it that my father picked her up and carried her to the car). She lived with us for the next five years, by then a retiring, frail woman in floor-length black or dark-blue dresses with tiny flowers. I felt that she liked me and sometimes we would have a cup of green tea with milk together. One evening she didn't eat much supper, not feeling well, and that night she too died. "She's dying!" my father shouted up the stairs as we were taking our baths. My mother left and went downstairs.

My sisters and I were always taken to the funerals, with the heavy flower smell in the air, the soft organ music, the still corpses, and sad people. Death was like infinity, unimaginable. "Up from the grave He arose," we sang victoriously each

Easter Sunday year after year. But somehow I didn't see the connection. My parents moved into my grandmother's bedroom, my sisters and I got separate rooms (at my mother's insistence), and life went on. I couldn't imagine being old, or even grown-up.

By the time I entered high school, the example of my parents had made me into a certain kind of person. They were frugal, hypersensitive, self-sacrificing and extremely hard-working. "Dog eat dog" was the way life was. Religion (that is, attending church) was not to be neglected. Children were to "honor and obey their parents." To get as good an education as possible was the way to a better life than they'd had. The possibilities for daughters seemed to be teaching or nursing. At about age eight, I had considered the latter and my father purchased me a "nurse kit" that Christmas. (He was generous, almost indulgent, with us girls, and even when we were teenagers it was hard for him to pass up a teddy bear.) By fourth grade I had settled on teaching as my intended vocation. Whenever I liked a particular teacher, I decided upon that field as the college major that would be mine.

Until my senior year, high school was a spiritually barren time. I loved foreign languages and took Latin and Spanish, both pooh-poohed by my father. (German had been dropped from the curriculum during World War II.) My remarkably competent and personable foreign-language teacher became one of my closest friends. One girl in my high school class was a Christian, and I admired her. She was different—quiet and serene, an excellent but noncompetitive student—who attended that "stricter" church. Although I once asked her about religion, she wasn't able to articulate her faith in the high school milieu. (She is now a co-author in this book—chapter 18). I was cautiously interested in boys, but not they in me. I never dated, and my suffering at such rejection was intense.

As a result of my parents' decision to give us years of music lessons on various instruments (costing them thousands of dollars over the years), and our personal motivation to practice hard, my sisters and I received many musical honors in our town and district and state. By the end of my sophomore year in high school, and at the encouragement of my own music teacher, I began giving music lessons after school and on Saturdays to over thirty pupils. I lived a relentless schedule and developed a great deal of self-discipline. Negatively, the terribly competitive attitude that my sisters and I developed toward others, and to some extent toward each other, was the worst part of it. Yet, nonetheless, a teacher who had us all, in a letter to my mother, described us as "the politest, smartest girls" she'd encountered in ten years of teaching. My mother, at least, deserved the encomium. Her life was hard, with few spiritual, personal, or material satisfactions, and the three of us—until we, separately, became Christians—did not honor her or my father as we should have.

In my senior year a perception of transcendence suddenly lit upon me. In a theme which greatly impressed my social studies teacher, I wrote about the need to have faith in some great Power, of man's incompletion and failure, of the need to believe in love, truth, kindness, and God, of the ideal of dedicating one's life to Him. It seems naive and trite now, but at the time it was a spiritual breakthrough—away from the limitation of the material, away from sole interest in *me* and whatever acquisitions I could make. I won both academic and music scholarships and was on my own for the first time.

At the university I lived in a house that was largely Jewish. Most of the girls were rich, sophisticated, vulgar, and profane. I knew that Christianity was "something more" than Judaism (not that these girls were religious), yet I had no idea what it was. I started to read the Gospel of John, but didn't understand it. I went to an IVCF party at which no one spoke to me except the friend who'd invited me. I began dating a fellow who had some kind of Christian faith, but his religion sounded childish to me. After some months I recognized that my goals in life were very different from his more provincial ones, and I cruelly turned him off.

The next year I made a close friend at the beginning of the school year. She cared for me and spent time with me. She wanted my friendship. Further, she invited me to a "study" she and another girl were having in the dorm. I went because of our friendship. And in that study (not at all a model Bible study), the gospel dawned upon me as the "good news" I needed. We were reading from Newell's commentary on Romans, "Some Words About Grace.[4]

> Grace is uncaused in the recipient. . .
> There being no cause in the creature why Grace should be shown, the creature must be brought off from trying to give cause to God for His Grace.
> Man has been accepted in Christ. . . . .
> He is not "on probation."

Through those words I sensed what I hadn't grasped before. That for failure there is forgiveness and cleansing. That in one's weakness His strength can be found. That God is a present help in trouble. I began to read the Bible earnestly for the first time, surprised now to understand what it said (at least generally).

Three weeks later, I went home to Wisconsin for Thanksgiving. My dad met me at the train station twenty miles from where we lived. "Gin," he said, "you've got to help us with Mill. She's gone crazy over religion."

My youngest sister, then a high school senior, had gotten involved in a teenage Bible discussion group. A young Princeton Seminary graduate, along with his wife who'd grown up as a "missionary kid" in Iran, had come to another church in our town. Both had Inter-Varsity backgrounds, and they had vision for the high school kids. My sister, along with others from various churches, had found new life through that study. (The wife of Bob Smith, chapter 15, was one.)

"Listen," I said to my other sister Kathy, then a college freshman, "you've got to start reading the Bible for yourself." In coming months the gospel touched her as well. Sibling tensions diminished, and the three of us found unity in our common Christian faith.

My parents, like the old Testament Law for the Apostle Paul, proved to be the "schoolmasters" who brought me to Christ (Galatians 3:24, 25). They exposed me to standards that I knew were beyond me:

---

[4]William R. Newell, *Romans Verse by Verse* (Chicago: Moody Press, 1938), pp. 245-247.

I would have been shocked in my teens if anyone had told me that what I learned [from them] . . . was goodness. But now that I know, I see there was no deception. The deception is all the other way around—in that prosaic moralism which confines goodness to the region of Law and Duty, which never lets us feel in our face the sweet air blowing from "the land of righteousness" . . .[5]

About ten years before his death, my father seemed to find God again for himself. Yet the last five years of his life brought mounting anguish, as a series of strokes left him increasingly debilitated. He prayed to die. My mother has lived with Walt and me for the past four winters, and it seems clear that God is faithful to her even to "old age and gray hairs" (Psalm 71:18). He does not ignore anyone who turns to Him.

---

[5] C. S. Lewis, quoted in George MacDonald, *Phantastes and Lilith* (Grand Rapids: Wm B. Eerdmans Publishing Company, 1964), p. 12.

Appendix: Negative Replies

> *Beginning in October 1973 the editor of this book began to contact Christian men and women, in most cases known personally to her husband and herself, asking which parental influences they now felt to be significant in their own Christian commitment. Of the approximately ninety contacted, one-fourth did not reply. About one-half agreed to contribute an essay, approximately half of these male and half female. (A few were unable to fulfill their commitment when the deadline actually arrived.) One-fourth replied that for various reasons—lack of time was first—they were unable to do so. Yet the range of negative response was remarkable:*

I can't participate. From about age seven I've hated my mother. It's colored my whole life both positively and negatively—a spur to independence, a lack in love. I used to read 1 John and tremble. Now I no longer feel hate, not necessarily because I've grown spiritually, but certainly because I've grown chronologically out of her clutches.

I became a Christian at age eleven by the grace of God through a school friend and without parental guidance.

Dad always encouraged Mother's efforts to teach us the

Christian way but never took the leadership. I think he may have been overpowered by Mother's superior biblical knowledge and her strong personality . . . Throughout our grade school years Mother read a chapter in the Bible with my sister and me each morning before school—Genesis to Revelation, the entire Bible. I count this the greatest gift she gave me.

Too bad you're not asking what they did wrong! I could write about that.

My older brother has rejected Christianity. So whatever my parents did "worked" for me, but not for him. I'm not sure what I think of it.

My own daughter is in serious trouble spiritually, psychologically, morally—and I find I just can't get involved in the emotional output required to write even briefly on this subjective a level.

I have little or no recollection of happenings before I was six, and after that I went to the mission boarding school in Chefoo, China. I draw a blank on specific things to write about.

After all the analyses of family malaise and the how-to-do-it handbooks, it's time we had a look at what Christian parents have done right. . . .

The night I read your letter I lay awake late thinking of what *my* parents did right. And there was a lot to think about. Though not Christians themselves, my parents practiced Christian principles. They date from a time when general culture was more Christian, even though most people in the community didn't recognize that influence for what it was.

When I was in early grade school we lived five miles out of town. In those days, rural Iowa roads were sometimes closed for weeks in the winter. At those times Dad walked to his hatchery and feed business in town. I remember that we didn't see much of him then because he stopped at a neighboring farm to do chores for a widow. Dad never mentioned these things. It was just something you did for others knowing that they would

do the same for you. I was proud of Dad, and following his steps
in the snow would try to match his stride.

As I grew older I saw Dad more and more as an old fogey
from the Dark Ages. I was in college before I had a renewed
pride in him. It was necessary for me to borrow money to
continue my schooling, and a man in my hometown agreed to
lend me what I needed. He wrote a check and I asked if he
wanted me to sign a note. His reply was, "If you are *X*'s boy, it
isn't necessary." That statement of faith was far more effective
than a promissory note could have been. It was by example that
my parents taught integrity.

Mom was unable to finish high school, but she treasured what
education she had. I spent a lot of time with her because she
listened to my ideas, wonderings, and aspirations. The poetry
she quoted to me from memory during those talks warmed me.
There was beauty in it, and there was in it that which was
meaningful to a mother who did without the nicer things in life,
and didn't miss them.

Mom could make anything out of nothing. She could paint
and carve in plastic. She made flowers from all sorts of things.
She made and remade clothes. One of my treasures is a red
tractor she made for Christmas with the simplest of tools. She
made "cleaning chickens" interesting by explaining the
anatomy as we worked. I learned that we live in a fascinating
world. Our garden was a wonderland, our junk drawer a treasure chest.

Since provoked by your letter, I have done a lot of reminiscing and have shared some of those meaningful incidents with
my wife and others. It's only since I've grown as a Christian
that I've realized how much I owe my parents. I'm not usually
given to misty-eyed nostalgia, but I'm sure you won't mind.